Getting Published in Women's Studies

Getting Published in Women's Studies

An International, Interdisciplinary Professional Development Guide Mainly for Women

by

Helen Rippier Wheeler

McFarland & Company, Inc., Publishers
Jefferson, North Carolina, and London

British Library Cataloguing-in-Publication data available

Library of Congress Cataloguing-in-Publication Data

Wheeler, Helen Rippier.
   Getting published in women's studies : an international,
interdisciplinary professional development guide mainly for women /
by Helen Rippier Wheeler.
     p. cm.
   Bibliography: p.
   Includes index.
   ISBN 0-89950-400-0 (lib. bdg. : 50# alk. paper) ∞
   1. Women's studies—Authorship. 2. Women authors. 3. Authorship.
4. Women in literature. 5. Feminism and literature. I. Title.
PN471.W45 1989
808'.02'088042—dc19

88-43483
CIP

Printed in the United States of America.

McFarland & Company, Inc., Publishers
  Box 611, Jefferson, North Carolina 28640

Table of Contents

Introduction

Another publication about getting published? Why a book for women scholars and women's studies? Like affirmative action in academe, gender studies and women are specialized areas. And there aren't *that* many how-to books on the subject of getting acceptably published in academe. Many focus on fiction, poetry, and popular mass media magazine articles for the "working writer." They would probably provide some adaptable tips, *if* there were time and energy to glean them. Women in academe and personnel teaching nontraditional studies are subject to very special problems associated with their getting published. They need articles and books on their resumes and job applications and in their promotion and tenure dossiers. Regular publication of refereed journal articles and books acceptable to officialdom is expected. Conversion of one's doctoral dissertation or thesis to a trade book may be a venue to this route. Reviews and "in" books may also "count," but knowing what will contribute the most, what is likely to accrue the greatest number of points in this system, and how to deal with it, are factors in professional and career development. Employment, increments, advancement, and tenure are dependent on acceptable publication. For many women graduate students and employees of the academy, who for the most part do not expect special consideration, this is yet another coping situation.

Getting Published in Women's Studies is intended to serve as an international, interdisciplinary professional development guide for women scholars and women's studies personnel. "Women scholars" here encompasses students as well as current and aspiring teaching faculty, administrators, counselors, librarians, researchers, coordinators, and other roles in academe. This book is for persons concerned with education at all levels having relevance for females, gender, and the status of women, including but not restricted to women's studies. It is intended for educators who have not published, academic personnel who have published an article or have a dissertation nearing completion (or on the shelf), underpublished people aspiring to tenure or other security of employment, and long-term graduate students—groups too often constituted by women.

1

While touting minority vita banks (and in the past, minority and women resume banks) to recruit some teaching and administrative faculty, many college and university affirmative action managers have neglected the potential of campus professional and staff development programs which will attract and retain qualified personnel by enabling them to achieve tenure and other forms of security of employment. Training in getting published is a significant and low-cost element with great potential in this process. Affirmative professional development is good management because it can enable participants in their career development as well as enhance their professional concerns and insights.

Underscoring these needs is women's studies faculties' inordinant — as compared with interdisciplinary programs focusing on other "special interest" groups — struggle merely to sustain their presence on campus. Some women's studies coordinators are reluctant to turn to their campus managers for enabling which might appear to acknowledge deficiency or expectation of special consideration. Professional development assistance for qualified women and women's studies has not always been as "equal" or as affirmative as that provided other groups.

Developing productive researching and writing topics which are personally rewarding is also a concern. The potentially synergistic relationship of research methodology, including use of libraries and other resources, to scholarship, authorship, and ultimate publication may not be clear to the professionally young academic. Some women's studies programs appear to neglect research methodology, strategy, and skills in their effort to attract and provide students with an innovative freed-up environment.

Foreign areas, Afro-American, American, women (or women's), and other studies are generally regarded as interdisciplinary fields. Current use of "women's studies" to refer to college and university courses administered through a women's studies unit leads to perceptions of interdisciplinary women's studies variously as a subject, field, or discipline. There are more than 30,000 women's studies courses and five hundred women's programs in United States institutions of higher education, as well as numerous related research centers, libraries, and government agencies.[1] Women's studies is also of concern to public and independent school educators at kindergarten through grade twelve levels; there is a National Women's Studies Association Pre-Kindergarten–12 Caucus. The Association

1. "Women's Studies Winning Acceptance But Losing Financing, Ford Report Says." *Chronicle of Higher Education* **32** (July 23, 1986): 22. Of women college freshmen, 20.3 percent agree that married women's activities should be confined to the home; 0.0 percent of college freshmen in the United States considered women's studies a probable "major" in academic year 1978–88. (**34** [January 20, 1988]:A35–A36.) October 1988 letter to NWSA membership from National Director.

membership includes numerous task forces, caucuses, and regional groups as well as a large international membership. The National Council for Research on Women is a consortium of centers and organizations providing instructional resources for feminist research, policy analysis, and educational programs. The Council also works to strengthen ties with centers of scholarship abroad and to join with national and international groups in pursuit of humanistic goals. It exercises influence when its staff serve as evaluators of the scholarly and commercial merit of proposals received by publishers.

Many college and university women's studies courses, minors, and majors are now derived from cross-listing courses established in traditional disciplines and departments. Conventional College's catalog may list an elective, occasionally offered History Department course called something like History of Women; the Afro-American Studies Department, Sociology of Women; and so forth. Completion of several may fulfill "minor" requirements. Women's studies is not just *for* ladies — it is about females, and for people. Think about "blacks' studies" or "ethnics' studies."

The periodical press has been in the big business of producing quantities of magazines aimed at women and serving as proscriptive models of currently desirable roles and as vehicles for promoting consumerism since the nineteenth century. The term "women's magazines" has long meant traditional housekeeping and fashion periodicals, although currently it is also being used to refer to some of the newer political and literary journals.

Women in academe are subject to "publish or perish" in many nations. As in the United States, women educators in Latin America, Australia, Canada, England and other European nations, Japan and other countries appear to be greatly affected by and concerned with this situation. Some merely want to communicate internationally. The International Interdisciplinary Congress on Women has been held every three years since 1981. English-language journals, reference works, and publishers-distributors co-mingle internationally.

Instruction in writing for publication and getting published is offered at cost and for profit by organizations and individuals — live and in print forms. However, none focuses on problems experienced by women scholars and associated with feminist women studies. I learned in the course of equal opportunity–affirmative action consultations, women's studies and other teaching, service on association committees, legal response to female-sex discrimination, expert witnessing, and counseling that women in academe have not had access to bonding, genuine mentoring, and fraternal and other traditional systems fostering visibility within the professional literature. "Networking" for many has amounted to a variation of the old boys' network or simply an au courant way of referring to organizational membership.

The women and men who participate in my getting published training are based in such traditional disciplines as anthropology, economics, history, linguistics, literature, psychology, religion, science, and sociology, as well as such professional areas as administration, business, education, health, librarianship, and social welfare. They may also associate themselves with the field often referred to as women's studies, occasionally as women studies, and rarely as feminist studies. The questions of a few sometimes evince oppression, divisiveness, stress, and expectation of special consideration. "I don't have enough time to do all I'm expected to do . . ."; "I sent an article to one of your women's studies journals, and she didn't even bother to answer"; "I can't get organized"; and "I heard So-and-So was turned down for promotion [tenure, whatever] because her publications weren't any good." (Sisterhood could be powerful.) These too can be converted into learning experiences for everyone, but neither my getting published training nor this book is intended as a consciousness raiser.

Some women scholars and women's studies personnel are unable to attend professional development training programs. Many have been turned off by programs and publications whose titles or advertisements misled them. A university officer casually referred to an itinerant trainer who sells his publication and seminar in package deals with kickbacks for facilitators of bookings with other institutions in their "network," i.e. system, state, region. Having attended and read many, I concluded that none was competitive in providing the basic skills and the strategies and insights that women scholars need. The books vary, but can be grouped for consideration. There are the collections of annotations of periodicals and of instructions to potential authors of journal articles in a particular field; the titles that sound like how-tos for getting published in specific fields but turn out to be collections of original or reprinted pieces, personal narrative or How I Did It Good; and how-tos for getting a book or article in only a "narrow" field published.

Ultimately *Getting Published in Women's Studies* should help most academic personnel, except researchers at advanced levels of basic science, who want and need that first acceptably published article or book. It may therefore include some information and seem to overlap some basics mentioned in other publications, or appear elementary to some readers. It is, however, a pragmatic, user-friendly book.

Chapter One provides background of the publications status quo as it exists for women in academe. Publication of articles in periodicals, especially refereed journals, is considered in the second chapter, and nonfiction books including textbooks and revision of one's dissertation for publication in the third. (Although poetry and fiction may demonstrate meritorious scholarship related to worthy teaching, they are not within this book's scope.) Chapter Four considers some other modes of frequently acceptable publication, including "in" books, thematic journal issues, book reviewing, translations, anthologies and collections, and audiovisuals.

Following each chapter is a list of resources for reference and for further reading relating to its coverage. These publications have been selected with emphasis on availability and, generally speaking, their having been published since approximately 1980. Here's the first tip: recommend that the college library and bookstore stock them, and ask the professional development person also to make this request.

Appendices include a glossary of some terms related to the reader's getting published and tools with which to locate independently publications useful in one's work.

Over the years I have chanced upon numerous employment experiences related to publication—abstracting, indexing, typing, proofreading. These were the things available in the 1950s and 1960s to a woman who needed to earn money while enrolled in college and graduate school. Postdoctoral, I discovered it was still necessary to be involved with others' getting published—punch-up, even ghostwriting—as well as with my own publications.

I have published five books, or rather, five books by me have been published by two publishers. I have also written parts of books. Some of my periodical articles have been reprinted within books; usually these have been contributions to colleagues' publications, but occasionally I have been honored by the request for permission. Scripting and storyboarding audiovisual instructional materials and writing related guides and handbooks are real challenges; I find they can be subject to the greatest need to defend one's brood until they can fend for themselves.

While a graduate student I worked on the National Society for the Study of Education yearbook and as assistant to a professor who was a journal editor. Later he served on my doctoral dissertation committee. He commended the dissertation to a publisher (whose wife pointed out ways I could go about converting, revising, and expanding it). During a dinner interview for a faculty appointment, the dean kept referring to the publishing house he had on the side (while his wife cooked, served, and talked to the dog). During cocktails with another dean, known as The Pincher, there were casual but pointed references to his "successful series." Years later, as a graduate school faculty member, I was instructed to create a "publications committee." The assignment included an inheritance of three hundred student papers from which I was to generate "publications for the School." I have served on the *Women Studies Abstracts* board, edited newsletters for NOW chapters and the International House Association. They have all been learning experiences. Circa 1977 I formalized my consulting. Womanhood Media—from the title of one of my books—provides support for affirmative management of education and employment as concomitants. One of its provisions is professional and staff development training, which includes getting published in education, aging and gerontology, management, and other fields. *Getting Published — A Workshop [Mainly] for Women in Academe* grew out of EO/AA (equal opportunity/affirmative action) consultations, women's studies and other teaching, service on associations' committees, and counseling. It is offered throughout the United States and abroad, and has enabled participants in developing their careers as well as sharing their professional concerns and insights.

Chapter One

To What Studies Have You Devoted All Your Hours?

"...how have you spent your time; and to what Studies have you devoted all of your Hours...?" Charlotte Lennox (1720–1804). American novelist. *Arabella; or, The Female Quixote.* Volume 1. London: A. Millar, 1752. Available from Pandora Press, 1986, in Mothers of the Novel Series.

Why publish in academe? For many scholars, publishing involves researching and writing, and then *getting it* published. Publishing usually also means service to one's institution, field, and discipline. Getting, keeping, and advancing in one's job and communicating one's research are important results. Visibility and ego-building, which can be closely related, come to mind. Why should women concern themselves with getting published? Professional visibility, career building, income, tenure, and survival as well as communication among colleagues out there in the field and throughout the world are as important for them as for men. That women need to concern themselves *more* than men with getting published is a feminist issue. There is disparity between the facility female authors and male authors experience in getting published, in the images of females and males communicated in mass media, and in their employment status in the industry.

Discrimination, feminism, and sexism have in fact become unacceptable terms in the 1980s. The many women failing to gain serious consideration of their theses, monographs, periodical literature, research, and writing continue to belie the contention that women are underrepresented on publishers' lists and payrolls because they have not produced publishable manuscripts. Numerous women are employed in publishing, but as in academe, their roles are inferior to men's in policy-making and management, status, and remuneration.

• • •

"...these women ... wrote in a world which was controlled by men, a world in which women's revelations, if they were anything but conventional, might not be welcomed, might not be recognized, and they wrote nevertheless.... But, over all, it was the men who were the critics, the publishers, the professors, the sources of support. It was the men who had the power to praise women's works, to bring them to public attention, or to ridicule them, to doom them ... to obscurity." Joan Rodman Goulianos (1939–   ). American writer and educator. *By A Woman Writt.* Introduction. Indianapolis, Indiana: Bobbs-Merrill, 1973.

Many of the publishing houses and serials run by and for women which came into existence in the 1970s have changed their style or disappeared.[1] Publishers have their "women's books" because they recognize a "women's reading" market. Together with campus bookstores, they have fostered creation of a euphemism known as the Women's Studies Section. Women in academe have the problem of getting published in order to survive and advance; feminist academics work within traditional disciplines and must adjust to the standard concerns and methodologies which are respected while literally re-searching scholarship. In 1982 a national chronicle devoted a full page to a professor's point of view that women scholars differ from the dominant group more profoundly than any minority, and that their scholarly and professional work, related to their values as women, is "not only novel but even faddish and perhaps irrelevant." Their "interests are strikingly novel and perhaps even bizarre when compared with current acceptable work in a given field."[2]

Feminist action research is difficult everywhere because of the lack of publications and information as well as tools which access their contents and communicate their existence. By feminist research, I mean any research accomplished by feminists for school and college papers, theses, speeches, articles and books for publication, reports, management, or documentation. By *action research* is meant adoption of a methodology designed to yield practical results that are immediately applicable to a specific situation or problem.[3] It is particularly relevant as a tool of objective social science, in order to increase the relevance of social and behavioral sciences research to the improvement of human society. Some scholars now acknowledge the distorted and unrecorded history of females — the *herstory* concept. Some publishing, distributing, and accessing have also been accomplished. By access is meant indexes, bibliographic support, thesauri, on-line and other retrieval capabilities which are standard supports for many academic fields, disciplines, businesses and professions.

Although there are selective bibliographies of women's studies basics, feminist collections of titles in various fields, and library handbooks, there is no publication for feminist scholars about a research methodology that exploits both standard tools and innovative resources and techniques. Searing's *Introduction to Library Research in Women's Studies* is so well done that it can function as more than a guide to library use, and I therefore communicate it as a handbook, but one wishes that there were more than ten and a half (of two hundred fifty-seven) pages devoted to research strategy. Works that seem initially to do this are either very theoretical (e.g. Stanley and Wise's *Breaking Out: Feminist Consciousness and Feminist Research*) or collections of articles oriented fo field and survey research (e.g. Roberts' *Doing Feminist Research*).[4,5,6]

Female-sex discrimination does not make news, but the mere filing of a charge against an academic institution effectively blacklists a woman. Some tenured women have lost their professional lives.[7] The research of sociologist Athena Theodore was seemingly unpublishable for years despite commercial success of her earlier work, in particular *The Professional Woman*.[8] As only one example of numerous, on the grounds that her work was not scholarly, University of California, Santa Cruz Chancellor Robert Sinsheimer refused to accept two University committees' unanimous tenure recommendations for sociologist Nancy Stoller Shaw, and she was dismissed from the University. Shaw filed suit against the University, charging sex discrimination, breach of contract, and wrongful discharge; *six years later* she won a promotion, tenure and financial settlement which will pay only part of the related monetary costs.[9a]

The statistical portrait of women in academe remains bleak: women are only 10 percent of all full professors in the United States. During academic year 1983–1984 women faculty earned an average of 19 percent less than male faculty. Seventy percent of men faculty have tenure, whereas only 50 percent of women faculty members are tenured.[9b] Since 1984 the pace of growth of the number of female college presidents, which had been increasing since 1975, has slowed considerably.[10] The numbers of women graduate students enrolled in nontraditional, male-role fields such as business have begun to decline. Women are rethinking MBA's because they see that they can go only so far—it's still more of a man's world, according to Wharton School admissions director Steven Christakos.[11] In 1982, women were 11 percent of engineering students in the United States.

In 1978 the *Guide To Women's Publishing* listed many presses, periodicals, and organizations which are now defunct or have moved in more acceptable or "mainstream" directions. Among the titles marketed in the 1980s which can serve as background reading is *Words in Our Pockets: The Feminist Writer's Guild Handbook on How to Get Published and Get Paid*, an anthology which confronted the established publishing industry by describing alternative networks and exploring writing genres. Discipline-related publications sometimes indirectly support getting published in academe. *Women in Print [Part] II: Opportunities for Women's Studies Publication in Language and Literature in the Profession* surveyed ways to further publication of women's studies in language and literature in establishment and alternative publishing.[12,13,14]

Compelling analyses of the distortion, misattribution, trivialization, and dismissal that afflict women's research and writing were provided in three 1983 works: Russ' *How to Suppress Women's Writing*, L. Spender's *Intruders on the Rights of Men: Women's Unpublished Heritage*, and a special issue of *Women's Studies International Forum* on *gatekeeping* in publishing and academe.[15,16,17] The first International Feminist Book Fair was held in 1984. Routledge & Kegan Paul have created the Pandora imprint to publish feminist books. The Women's Institute for Freedom of the Press survives. A nonprofit organization founded in 1972 for research and educational purposes and for publishing both theoretical and practical works on the communication of information, it has stood for three principles of feminist journalism: no attacks on people, more factual information, and people speaking for themselves. It sponsored conferences on planning a national and international communications system for women, and until 1988 it published the *Media Report to Women* and its annual *Index/Directory*, major sources for news, documentation, and information on all aspects of women and the communications media.[18]

Because the mass media fail to disseminate news of women's status in academe and the related publishing gatekeeping fully and accurately, one would have to search out and read such periodicals as *Media Report to Women* to become aware that fifty male-controlled book-magazine-broadcasting conglomerates, newspaper chains, and film and record studios dominate United States communications; that of thirty book publishers controlling 70 percent of the market, two—both owned by the Newhouse newspaper chain and Gulf Western—are headed by women; and that six of the top ten best-selling magazines are aimed at women, yet none is edited and published by a woman.[19] Even highly educated women have been socialized in a way which results in most "over the transom" proposals coming to book publishers from men, suggesting that they recognize and do not hesitate to take this initiative.

Lack of equitable access to existing information can limit any scholar. One of the reasons publications on issues and problems concerning them do not reach as many women scholars and women's studies personnel as they should relates to the subject-headings, or descriptors, assigned to them by information scientists. For example, while the four subject-headings assigned by the United States Library of Congress—SCHOLARLY PUBLISHING, RESEARCH METHODOLOGY, LEARNING AND SCHOLARSHIP, and AUTHORSHIP—describe in a general way *Scholarly Writing & Publishing: Issues, Problems and Solutions*, a compilation which was a major project of the Research and Publications Committee of Sociologists for Women in Society, they fail to access the subject matter pertinent to women scholars' research, writing, and publishing.[20] Although cataloging and classification solely on the basis of a book's title cannot be justified, the major restrictions which controlled vocabularies can impose on all disciplines and people continue to be sociolinguistic problems of sexism and societal problems of exclusion.

Women authors have found it necessary to return to the use of euphemisms in writing for publication. Feminist messages, findings, and scholarship often must be contained within a mixture of academic and disciplinary jargon in order to get published. "Rigid," "narrow-minded," "inflexible," "immature," "not creative enough," and variations continue to be the responses to women, who are subjected to higher standards of evaluation than are applied to their male counterparts.[21]

Another communications problem impinging upon women is the sociolinguistic one. Some authorities have recognized the logic of using masculine pronouns to refer to masculine concepts. As a result, they toss in an occasional "he or she" (one wonders why not an affirmative "she or he"?). Their tack is to claim that immediate language change is impossible (like comparable worth) or that it would be too awkward. Stainton assigns all this to "feminist pressures," devoting two pages of her *Author and Editor at Work* to the women's movement's responsibility for a problem that the English language is not capable of solving. "Feminism then has buried Fowler, Strunk and White, and other arbiters of good taste in writing prose . . . let us stick most of the time with *he* as the pronoun for human being until the language develops an acceptable alternative." She refers to some publishers having issued guidelines, and agrees that writers should be aware of the problem and avoid such stereotyped assumptions as expecting secretaries to be women, executives men. In the 1970s several publishers sponsored in-house brochures which are no longer available or current staff cannot identify. The "sticky problem" occurs in traditional use of the masculine for human beings. Good-bye to euphonic style and crisp sentences, Stainton says, if every writer starts expressing a conviction or a philosophy of life through the medium of grammar. . . .[22] What better time and place, *if* one believes that people say only what they mean, and mean what they say, and if one understands and agrees with the hypothesis that language both shapes and reflects society?

• • •

"Gatekeeping: The systematic use of processes of selection and censorship to ensure perpetuation of male views of the world. For example, publishers have an effective gatekeeping system which has helped to ensure that women's understandings of the world do not receive wide circulation in print." Cheris Kramarae and Paula Treichler. *Feminist Dictionary.* New York: Pandora Press, 1986. Page 173.

Smith referred in 1978 to *gatekeepers* in the academic community who set the standards, produce the social knowledge, monitor what is admitted to the systems of distribution, and decree the innovations in thought, or knowledge, or values.[23] D. Spender points out that many of these same people are editors of journals, referees (reviewers), and advisors to publishers, in a position to determine what gets published and what does not, and that most are men. In her important feminist critique of academic publishing, she argues that those who make decisions on what does and does not get published have an active role in shaping a discipline or area, and thus raises legitimate cause for concern for those in attempting to work in ways which challenge mainstream orthodoxies.[24] L. Spender's synopsis of the special *Women's Studies International Forum* issue focusing on gatekeeping declared that

> The commercial publishing industry is controlled by men and under the guise of rational and objective decisionmaking, it manages to produce and disseminate material that it claims to be "universal" and representative of humanity. In fact, through *gatekeeping*, the publishing industry selects and promotes the ideas and knowledge that effectively maintain and support the dominant male view of the world. This contributes a rarely acknowledged "political" dimension in the production of knowledge and in the publishing industry. Alternative views, such as those presented by feminists, are contained at a level where they inevitably remain marginal and without legitimacy that the sheer volume of production and expensive promotion accord to masculist ideals and practices . . . [25]

Little else has been published about publishing gatekeepers and women in academe. Tuttle's *Encyclopedia of Feminism* includes *gatekeepers, gatekeeping theory,* and *publishing* entries.[26] Papenek has referred to "false specialization and the purdah of scholarship."[27]

The training, access to resources, career pressures, and research and publishing opportunities females receive are all strongly influenced by their socialization. The research, education, degree of career equity, and publications which women are able to achieve are to a great degree the result of that socialization. The same could be said of males, *if* one recognizes and acknowledges the regulatory and self-perpetuating nature of patriarchy. What women receive differs from that which men receive, and the results are disparate. Groups consisting predominantly of feminists, or females, or males, differ greatly in what they are willing and able to achieve.

Gatekeeping and gatekeepers of academic women's publishing show interesting variations. One of the new publishing companies of the 1970s campaigned for manuscripts at a professional association conference and circulated an announcement which declared they were "especially interested in books by women writers or books with strong female protagonists!" The company president's response to a woman scholar's gender-related book proposal was "Although we are woman run and staffed, we are not a feminist organization. And although we are interested in manuscripts dealing with sex discrimination, your approach is much too hard in comparison to ours." They published nonfiction titled *The Cookbook for Swinging Singles, Or How To Make It In the Kitchen* and *Treadmill to Heaven,* by male writers.

Large professional associations operate internationally, and they are often publishers. The stance of one such publisher (the American Library Association) is that "research and discovery in women's studies are a matter of inventive thought with no clear relation to subject classification or documents indexing." This response to submission of a book proposal arrived after more than a year. The Association for the Study of Higher Education and the ERIC Clearinghouse on Higher Education have published a study partially funded by the United States Department of Education concerning faculty evaluation and tenure in which the author adopts the definition of productivity as the number of articles appearing in a refereed journal over a one-year period.[28] She accepts without criticism and shares a study which concluded that no significant differences exist between productivity levels of published articles of tenured and untenured faculty, based on their having been matched according to age, seniority, discipline, and highest degree. Gender was not deemed a relevant factor to take into consideration.[29] (Indeed, it *should* not be.)

The bias in research, reporting, decision-making, and publication evident in the sex imbalance of research populations was noted by scholars before the contemporary women's movement. The use of research populations in which gender is not considered exert a potentially discriminatory influence on subsequent decision-making, funding, research, and publication based on it. Today its effect is being noted in the formulation of survival "benefits" old women receive and will not receive based on research populations consisting entirely or largely of old men. An imbalance of sex in subjects used in psychological research was noted in 1961; ten years later, following a period of considerable growth in the field, little change in this practice had taken place.[30] Prescott reviewed the situation in psychology in 1978, declaring that "Awareness of biases in behavior science reporting may lead gatekeepers to request that researchers identify the sex of subject used, and note sex differences in the review of literature section."[31] Her paper was published in *Sex Roles* and cited but not abstracted by *Women Studies Abstracts.* The need still exists for recognition of bias in research methodology and beyond . . . into publishing, publication, and access.

• • •

"Women who do not rebel against the status of object had declared themselves defeated as persons in their own right." Charlotte Wolff (1897–   ). German-born English psychiatrist. *Love Between Women.* London: Duckworth, and New York: St. Martin's, 1971.

Pressure experienced by women to compete in a male-dominated education-employment system inevitably leads to their having to achieve at higher levels and to accomplish more, including getting acceptable articles and books published. *Getting Published* workshop participants' questions and comments reflect these unique needs. They range widely from naive queries of the professionally young (although conscientious and capable) to pragmatic challenges by the more experienced who have recognized dubious situations. While many are interested in knowing "about refereed journals," others ask specifically about how referees are selected and whether they are paid. Whether one can do anything about referees' reports which are illegible, illiterate, inconsistent, defensive, even sexist is frequently asked; whether one *should* is asked only occasionally. The connection with so-called peer review is often sensed. Whether one must be a member of the association which sponsors a journal in order to get an article published is one of the unanswerables.

The attitudes and experiences conveyed by their questions demonstrate need for the basic skills relevant to any academic's getting published, and some might acquire these with experience in the system. But many continue to evince the deprivational needs of women in academe and of some women's studies scholars. For example, "Should I grab the contract I've been offered by A B C Press?" "Is it all right to ask for money in advance?" Can't I just go to the D E F Association convention and talk to the publishers in their booths?" "Would you believe I received a sarcastic letter from a man at *Ms.* magazine [when I submitted an article]?" "I've had an offer to publish my dissertation. Won't it be worth the fee to get a book publication? He advertises in women's magazines...." "What's the difference between a magazine and a journal? a serial and a periodical? "Do I *have* to use that style manual?" "Is a bibliography a real publication?" "Is a word processor OK?" "Which is better—a journal article or a book? a women's studies journal or a sociology journal? the *G H I Association Journal* or the *Journal of the J K L Association?*" "There is nothing else on my subject, so I'm sure to get published" is really a request for confirmation. "What I'm interested in isn't publishable" seeks disagreement in the sense that her topic or idea *is* scholarly and will be acceptable. "I'm thinking about filing a charge [of some aspect of some type of discrimination]. Should I hold off until I get more publications?" Why there aren't "any women's studies journals in the field of education" is asked. (There are some, e.g. the *Feminist Teacher.*) Why, indeed, are there so few gender-related courses within the field of professional education? Does it relate to the insistence on the Ph.D. in an academic discipline for teachers and coordinators of women's studies?

The university itself employs all types of workers in substantial numbers — civil service, clerical, counseling, food service, instructional, technical — and including many male-role job-fields such as administration, agriculture, law, medicine, publishing, security. National, regional, and professional associations are involved via such things as their accreditation of programs, continuing education, publishing activities, and recruitment. Certification and licensing procedures are closely related in many jurisdictions. Future professionals — editors, lawyers, librarians, physicians, publishers, social workers, teachers — are indoctrinated during their college and university years.

Sexism in academe as a possible subject is taboo. There are basics which, until publication of Abramson's *The Invisible Woman,* had hardly been touched upon in the literary market place. Historically there has been a strong tendency to perceive female-sex discrimination as distinct among the several classes included in the laws of the land and, when abundantly demonstrated, to excuse it because it was not intentional! The university is not a more "professional" employer merely because it is perceived as more respectable, pointing up the handicap of assumptions and stereotypes. University presses are associated with many of the institutions which advertise nationally their affirmative action talent and resume banks that do not encompass women, e.g. the universities of Nevada, New Mexico, North Dakota, and Tennessee, and Duke, Harvard, Indiana, Louisiana State, Rutgers, Southern Methodist, and Syracuse universities. Because women must tread dangerous paths to reach even limited goals, they tend to remain where they are, not realizing that they have retreated. Abramson demonstrated how the academic power structure's discrimination against women is different, although her experiences with a university press are typical. Most women academics are still unaware of the dynamics of discrimination and therefore unable to cope emotionally or strategically.[32]

The misuse of part-time and temporary teachers, many of whom are women, leads to inequities. The need, desire, or requirement to research, write, report, and publish typically impacts upon the part-time or temporary woman employee. She represents relatively inexpensive labor utilized to fill in when money is sporadic or to stretch a full-time faculty allocation to cover more than one person. The status and insecurity of the job communicate to her that she and her work are inferior. Whether or not she is satisfied with this type of employment arrangement, she may be expected to publish, or she may be subject to unclear policy applied as needed. Perhaps she recognizes need for publications on her resume if she is to compete when a "regular job" becomes vacant in her program or elsewhere in another institution. Twenty percent of part-time faculty are said to be "hopeful full-timers."[33a] Close to 40 percent of part-time faculty members are female, compared with 27 percent of full-time faculty members.[33b]

The administration is likely to excuse the lower salary and related lack of benefits afforded the part-time temporary lecturer on the basis that regular faculty have other responsibilities including publishing. But in some institutions, full-time and even some part-time temporary lecturers are clearly expected to publish, advise, etc. Of course publishing is important for all faculty who are conscious of career development, and the possibility exists that they have something important to contribute. It might even be argued that research and publication are more important for temporary academic personnel in order to become "regularized." However, their opportunity to publish is diminished by their status because research grants, assistants, typings, duplicating, even supplies may not be available to them. Few grants are available to the unaffiliated or to individual applicants.

• • •

"Independence is happiness." Susan B. Anthony (1820–1906). American social reformer and humanitarian. In Ida Husted Harper's *Life and Work of Susan B. Anthony* Volume II. Indianapolis, Indiana: Bowen-Merrill, 1898.

A syndrome of excuses spans the years of the woman who contends she cannot act now because she must get a degree, get a job, get a man, keep a man, have children, raise children, keep a job, retain the children's attention, ad infinitum into the ultimate rationalization of old age. An intelligent, well-educated woman can identify impressive reasons through all the stages of life for not being free to reject a system which imposes disparate levels of responsibility on a woman scholar.

A "successful" career woman reads periodicals and books that instruct in the maintenance of power rather than its redistribution. When individual women realized that affirmative action and existing legislation would not take them far, they concluded that they needed contact with the powerful, and began to attempt to replicate the "old boy networks" through which men have traditionally passed on their power to select. Use of the term "working woman" to refer to a homemaker when she is employed for wages outside the home is obscene. The person who attempts to lead such a double, even triple, life within the status quo is usually attempting the impossible. She or he typically complains of getting-published problems such as finding time and getting organized and evinces tension and enervation.

The reasons many qualified women do not expect special consideration are that they do not need it or they have not been getting it. They have rejected the academic version of the learned feminine role: woman at home *and* place of employment as well-adjusted assistant, endless graduate student, helper, junior, assistant, nurturer, reader, supporter "balancing family responsibilities." They expect other family members to participate equitably in such responsibilities, inasmuch as women generally work and prepare to work outside the home in order to earn money to support themselves and others. Thus there is a difference between many women in academe and those whose employment takes them to the office, factory, or store. Although they are almost all expected to earn, bring home, and cook the bacon, women in academe are frequently subjected to the rhetoric of selectively liberal males who don't do diapers (spouse) and who have traditional wives (employers, supervisors, colleagues).

• • •

"I felt that blank incapability of invention which is the greatest misery of authorship, when dull Nothing replies to our anxious invocations." Mary Wollstonecraft Godwin Shelley (1797–1851). English author. *Frankenstein; or, The Modern Prometheus.* Introduction to the 1818 edition. London: Colburn and Bentley, 1831.

In studies of sex differentials in the academic reward structure, *publications* have been found to account in very important ways for the varied distribution of these rewards. What facilitates and what inhibits research productivity, which leads to publications, become crucial concerns. General facilitators and barriers to women's research productivity were identified in a 1980 survey. Facilitators were found to include being young and located at a selective university; having been promoted to full professor and opportunities to do consulting; expressing a strong need for advancement (being "driven"); spending more time on research and writing than the typical academic; and subscribing to more journals than the average academic. Inhibitors were found to be having come from student status directly to one's present position, and being single. Women were likely to attribute their research productivity to such *personal* factors as hard work, being motivated and interested in their research topics, and possessing the necessary skills. Men attributed their achievement to having *institutional* resources—time, student assistants, and funds.[34]

Finding time and getting organized are two problems frequently reported by women doing research and writing. Whether men have them to the same degree, and if so, the reason they do not acknowledge them is worthy of research. The point of keeping women barefoot and pregnant is obscured when this aphorism is assumed to be passé, pre-pill. Commitments should be fulfilled or renegotiated.

Make a weekly or monthly *schedule* of what you regularly do when. Get
an appointment book which is large enough to include hourly blocks of time
but convenient to carry with you at all times. Pencil into the next twelve
months regular activities—classes, staff meetings, office hours, regular
publications-related work time, your library research time, etc. Allow for
adequate sleep. Make a long-term *goals calendar* of where you want to be
and reasonably can be during the next year and five years. These too include
publishing.

There is no easy short-cut to changing the years of "bringing up" (in-
doctrination) to which everyone is subject and which may include acceptance of other people's definitions of what are actually burdensome or ineq-
uitable roles. Dabbling in support groups and "networking," even attending
too many writing conferences and workshops can deteriorate into respectable substitutes for productivity of which you are capable. Ultimately you
must make an honest beginning—curtail all vitiating, time-filling, and enervating habits which sustain procrastination and rationalization. Lower your
voice and speak up. Don't re-act . . . act. You are responsible for you. A
woman's own personal psychology can be as great a problem as external circumstances. Valian stresses the importance of knowing one's true self,
which she achieved with professional assistance. She distinguishes between
her *work* and her *job*. Work problems manifest themselves in inability to
work as productively, effectively, and unambivalently as one wants. She
faced two problems: difficulty sitting down and doing work, and, having
done so, difficulty progressing on the problem. Earlier, she had been able
to deal with her doctoral thesis by requiring of herself a certain amount of
daily work time and because she was able to set aside concern for the
possibility of rewriting and publication and to concentrate on the intrinsic
satisfaction of the work itself. Success was seemingly guaranteed in the
sense that she would receive the Ph.D. degree if she completed the thesis.[35]

Whatever works for you is fine, provided that *more* time and energy
are not expended while you are hunting for, talking about, and then ex-
perimenting with it. I doubt there exists an academic who would not profit
from psychoanalysis, but few women are able to pay for it, and not surprisingly, some tend to view it as self-indulgence. Early feminist career and
educational counseling as part of Title IX–mandated equal education opportunity in schools may someday help alleviate this. Psychotherapy can be
a significant part of alleviating both time and organization problems.
Psychoanalysis, therapy, counseling, psychology, and psychiatry are various
terms one hears. (Avoid "seeing my shrink," please.) There are significant
differences among them. For convenience, I will use the term therapy. A
woman does not have to be neurotic, lacking in self-esteem, menopausal,
self-indulgent, passive, nonassertive, stressed out, subject to **PMS**, or
psychotic in order to consider exploring therapy and to profit from the

acquisition of self-knowledge. The yellow pages approach to locating qualified professional service personnel is fraught with danger. Phoning a medical society typically accesses names of three, possibly new members who seek business. Mental and emotional weal deserves recognition of the fact that many jurisdictions define the therapist's domain in terms of a prescriptive "marriage, family, and child" counseling licensure. One approach to this social welfare, information access, and control-related problem is to seek out professionals included in the current edition of the Feminist Therapist Roster. Also contact the local feminist health collective or center and request from their files clients' comments about therapists you are considering.[36]

In academe, work support groups tend to be referred to as writing or research groups, brown bag discussions, colloquia, etc., rather than support groups. They vary widely along the challenge-security continuum. In a *research* workshop a participant presents her research, and discussion and critique follow. The *writing* support group may appear less safe because her productivity and independence are most exposed when she rejects the lone scholar myth. This group focuses on the common solution of writing problems, meeting productivity goals, and providing social support. Hood provides guidelines for such a group.[37]

The ally system can be adapted to the process of writing for publication. I recommend pairs. Try to recruit from among your literate friends a woman who is willing to read ongoingly portions of your drafts and to react on the typed page. You will provide the same support for her work, or barter for something of similar value. This arrangement is at its best when two published colleagues in the same field or discipline who live or work nearby agree to go over portions of each other's work as it progresses. Batches of fifty typed pages work well. Commit yourself to doing this review and returning it within forty-eight hours. (I usually need three hours in the middle of the night, my abridged dictionary, and a pencil and eraser.) Is this editing? Not really. It takes place earlier in the process and is more of a response which provides a different perspective. It should not be applied to checking page-proof, which the author should do personally. Writing and setting it aside for a *few* days is also conducive to seeing material and ideas anew.

Women's tendency to be involved in policy and action-oriented research activities may be a critical factor in lowering their own production rates. When tenure denial of a woman associated with the critical legal studies movement was upheld by Harvard President Bok in 1988, Clare Dalton charged that the Law School faculty discriminated against her because of her gender as well as her left-wing political views.[38] And awards for excellent teaching may be the "kiss of death" rather than contribute to tenure. A University of Pennsylvania teacher of English who won a teaching prize in 1983 was denied tenure four years later. Vicki Mahaffey now considers that ". . . for many people, calling someone a good teacher is not a compliment — it's name-calling." The University's position is that "teaching gets a lot of weight in the tenure process, but it's not as important as research publication. We do not tenure on good teaching."[39]

Single woman (about half of all academic women) who wish to succeed within the academic establishment may need to change the timing and nature of their choices of types of research and thus publication. The survey results fostering this conclusion also led the researchers to ponder the possibility that "women academics should be advised to spend less time with students, less time on teaching preparation, less time working with minority and women's centers, and less time on committee work, or even to change their research focus or methodology, merely because these factors are related to lower (or higher) productivity rates." They concluded that it might be wise to publish articles which provide greater visiblity of one's name, rather than books, at the beginning of one's career, and that publication and work in "outside centers" are often considered to be marginal and "soft-core" by male-dominated academe. "Outside centers" appears to be used euphemistically here to refer to activities related to improvement of opportunities for women and minority persons within academe. The practicability of this counsel is reminiscent of that experienced by most of the midcareer academic women who have responded to discrimination in employment based on sex and then not become tenured: "You should have waited until you got tenure." They acknowledge "the content of the numerous structural barriers within academe, barriers that fall beyond the control of or choice of women and should thus be exposed and ultimately eliminated."[40] How, if not by women themselves? When, if not now?

•   •   •

Here are some questions for self-inventorying at this point. They are not intended to test anyone's ability, but should be useful in determining goals and where in the various aspects of this getting-published process you are now. The questions have been grouped to focus on you and where you are, introduce or review some publishing nitty-gritty, and alert or remind everyone of some of the related facts of academic life and the media industry. Some elicit responses related to your personal situation; information about the others appears throughout this book. Questions involving a relatively specific answer (e.g. number 40) are followed by at least one page number where related information can be found. Where there are choices (e.g. number 16), think in terms of the "best" answer.

1. What is your field? Within that discipline, what are your particular concerns? What is or will be your area of expertise? What are your research interests?
2. Think of a topic you are currently researching or involved with. Express it in a sentence and then as a title. Don't be vague; be specific. Include all keywords, terms, and concepts.
3. What are the titles of three periodicals which can be referred to as scholarly journals that would be good candidates to receive your manuscript of an article or paper on an aspect of your field? (Good in the sense that they specialize in this concern, and that you would be happy to see your work published therein.)
4. What is the title of the appropriate style manual for your preparation of that manuscript (question 3) or for publications in your field?
5. What is the title of the unabridged dictionary you usually consult and on which you rely? How does it differ significantly from other standard unabridged dictionaries? What abridged dictionary do you own? How does it differ significantly from other abridged dictionaries? When was it published?
6. How might membership in a professional association be conducive to one's getting published? What is the title of the journal sponsored by one of the professional associations of which you are or will be a member? Does it also publish a newsletter? Does that association publish books . . . is it a publisher? (pp. 51, 167)
7. In what way might regular scanning of a periodical such as the *Chronicle of Higher Education* newspaper be conducive to getting published? (pp. 52, 166)
8. You want to identify the titles, publishers, addresses, editors, etc., of three journals in your field which would be good candidates to receive a manuscript on an aspect of your field or research. How would you proceed? (pp. 54–59)
9. Does the institution on whose faculty you are or hope to be employed publish books? Is there a "university press" associated with it?
10. What is the name of the faculty person responsible for professional development?
11. An abstract is always evaluative. TRUE?   FALSE?   (pp. 62, 63, 202)
12. Commercial "mass media" magazines published by large companies generally pay writers of the articles they publish, whereas scholarly journals published by professional associations generally do not pay the writers of the articles they publish. TRUE?   FALSE?   (p. 00)
13. Why is it wise to select for your submission of articles journals which are indexed in standard periodical indexes, e.g. *Social Sciences Index, Psychological Abstracts, Science Citation Index,* RILA? (p. 55)

14. Two ways to identify the titles of the periodical indexes which regularly index the contents of a given journal as well as other periodicals in the same field are to consult _____. (pp. 40, 54–57)

15. Serials is an umbrella term for magazines, journals, periodicals, and _____. (pp. 207, 208, 210, 211)

16. In preparing the manuscript of an article for submission to the journal editorial office, unless there are other specific instructions, be sure that your name _____.

    appears once, on a separate cover-page

    does not appear anywhere on the manuscript and only in a cover-letter

    is on every page, in the upper left corner (p. 64)

17. There are approximately ___(#)___ words per double-spaced, typed manuscript page. (p. 111)

18. In preparing the manuscript of a journal article, it is usually well to organize it using _____.

    a table of contents

    an index

    frequent sub-headings

    all of these (p. 64)

19. Many journals which publish "thematic" issues appoint an Issue Editor who solicits specialist-authors. TRUE?   FALSE? (p. 52)

20. Multiple submissions of the same manuscript to several journals is a good way to alienate journal editors. However, if you decide to try it because you have published nothing and you judge that your biological or tenure clock is ticking away, it is doubtful that anyone will ever be the wiser. TRUE?   FALSE?   Why? (pp. 47, 111)

21. You have an abundance of riches: interest in possible publication of an article which you've written has been expressed by the editors of two prestigious journals! What factors will you take into consideration in selecting one of these journals to make you formal submission? (pp. 47, 52–55)

22. _____ scholarly journals utilize their own salaried staff-writers.

    Few

    Some

    Many

    Most (p. 207)

23. _____ scholarly journals solicit articles and select persons with whom they make arrangements to write some of the articles.

    Few

    Some

    Many

    Most (p. 207)

24. The title of a journal which pays authors for their articles is _____.
25. When a journal does not pay an author for her/his article, compensation will probably consist of _____. (pp. 48, 149)
26. How do reprints, preprints, and offprints differ? (pp. 209, 210)
27. Books published by *vanity presses* and *self-published* differ in that _____. (pp. 130–134)
28. In addition to those basics of scholarly and professional publication — journal articles and monographic books — several other forms can take on the character of potential contribution to the promotion tenure dossier, scholarship, and one's profession. Some of these other modes of publication are _____. (p. 148)
29. Currently the manuscript for a book generally consists of at least _____ double-spaced typed pages. (p. 189)
30. Academicians review books (check any applicable).
     to get a free copy of the book
     as a professional contribution to their field
     for the fee from the publisher of the periodical in which the review appears
     for a fee from the publisher of the book (p. 149)
31. "Signed" [book] reviews are the norm today. TRUE?   FALSE? (p. 149)
32. A. You've been awarded your doctorate. Your dissertation is probably indexed in *Comprehensive Dissertation Index* and abstracted in *Dissertation Abstracts International* in both print and online forms; it's available on microfilm and perhaps in print from University Microfilms. After all that work, how might you go about revising it justifiably in order to generate a publishable journal article manuscript? (pp. 61, 62, 65)
    B. How would you go about utilizing it in order to generate a publishable and marketable book manuscript? How would you proceed? (pp. 125, 128–129)
33. The term "_____" on your resume refers to books and articles which you have completed and which have been accepted for publication, but which have not yet been printed and distributed. (pp. 66, 121, 207)
34. A profile of 1986 recipients of doctoral degrees shows approximately _____.
     one female to two males
     the same number of females and males
     two females to one male (p. 191)
35. Title IX forbids education programs receiving financial assistance from the United States federal government to discriminate against women and men in employment and education. TRUE   FALSE? (pp. 212, 213)

36. Nations with students enrolled in United States institutions of higher education are located mainly in _____.
    Africa
    Asia
    Latin America (p. 193)
37. A survey of attitudes and characteristics of fall 1987 United States college freshmen revealed that 26 percent believed that married women's activities should be confined to the home. What percent of women freshmen agreed? (p. 2)
38. Women's studies was identified as a major field within the social sciences in this survey (question 37). The other major fields included within the social sciences were anthropology, economics, ethnic studies, geography, political science, psychology, social work, and sociology. _____ percent of freshmen indicated women's studies was their probable major field of study.
39. Single women constitute _____ percent of all academic women; single men _____ percent. (pp. 19, 28)
40. According to *Ulrich's International Periodicals Directory*, there are approximately _____ periodicals (including journals, not including newspapers) worldwide. (p. 33)
41. There are _____ book publishers in the United States and Canada. (pp. 75, 80)
42. In 1986 United States book sales increased over the previous year. Publishers paid more than one billion dollars in royalties to authors and copyright owners. Manufacturing costs accounted for about _____ percent of book sales. (p. 76)
43. The best return in 1985 in book publishing sales was garnered by textbook publishers in the _____ market.
    college
    elementary and high school
    TV, motion picture, and video "how to" scripting (pp. 141, 145)
44. In 1986 Bertelsmann, a German publisher, became a giant of world publishing when it acquired Doubleday for a reported $475 million. _____ remained the biggest United States book publisher, with revenues of more than $920 million for the year ending July 31, 1986. Its parent company is _____.
    Bantam/Bertelsmann
    Biomedial, Inc./McGraw Hill
    Simon & Schuster/Gulf + Western (p. 76)
45. Most of the thousands of United States book publishers are very small. TRUE? FALSE? (p. 74)
46. During 1986, _____ was formally established in Canada to pay authors for library use of their books.

46. During 1986, _____ was formally established in Canada to pay authors for library use of their books.

    the Canadian Government's imposition of a 10 percent tariff on United States trade and reference books

    copyright revision

    Payment for Public Use (p. 196)

47. The American Association of Publishers' International Copyright Protection Group estimates that pirates located in _____ and other countries bilk United States authors and publishers of at least $400 million a year.

    Canada

    the Dominican Republic

    England

    South Africa (p. 196)

48. The annual subscription price to an average magazine in 1987 was _____.

    less than $25.

    between $26. and $50.

    between $51. and $75.

    over $75.00 (p. 51)

49. Surveys indicate that leading scholars in the humanities and social sciences are dissatisfied with their journals. About one third say they rarely find articles of interest in their discipline's primary journal. A significant minority think the peer review system for determining what gets published in scholarly journals is biased in favor of _____. (p. 41)

50. What are some of the advantages of a small publishing house (A) in general and (B) for a women's studies book? (p. 87)

Notes

1. For example, "Persephone Press Folds," *WLW Journal* **8** (1983):26–27. To acquire 25 percent of the ownership of *Ms.* magazine, Warner Communications conglomerate invested $1 million; founded in 1972 as a monthly for women who wanted to break down the "sexual caste system," by 1982 *Ms.* was "committed to exploring new lifestyles and changes in roles and society."

2. Degler, Carl L. [Stanford University Professor of American History and author of *At Odds: Women and the Family in America from the Revolution to the Present*, Oxford University Press, 1980]. "The Legitimacy of Scholarship By and About Women." Point of View feature. *Chronicle of Higher Education* **25** (September 15, 1982): 56.

3. *Thesaurus of ERIC Descriptors, 11th edition*. Phoenix, Arizona: Oryx, 1987.

4. Searing, Susan E. *Introduction to Library Research in Women's Studies*. Boulder, Colorado: Westview, 1985.

5. Stanley, Liz, and Sue Wise. *Breaking Out: Feminist Consciousness and Feminist Research.* New York: Routledge & Kegan Paul, 1983.

6. Roberts, Helen. *Doing Feminist Research.* New York: Routledge & Kegan Paul, 1981.

7. Wheeler, Helen R. "Delay, Divide, Discredit; How Uppity Women Are Kept Down, Apart and Out of Academe." *WLW Journal* **8** (July-September 1983): 1–5. Reprinted with corrections in *Alternative Library Literature 1982–1983: A Biennial Anthology.* Edited by Sanford Berman and James Danky. Phoenix, Arizona: Oryx, 1984.

8. Theodore, Athena. *The Professional Woman.* Cambridge, Massachusetts: Schenkman, 1971.

9a, 9b. September 1987 letter from the American Association of University Women Legal Advocacy Fund, Sharon Schuster, president. The Fund is the AAUW legal arm, 2401 Virginia Avenue, N.W., Washington, D.C. 20037. Stoller's publications include *Forced Labor: Maternity Care in the United States* (New York: Pergamon Press, 1974). A few other such persons include: Clare Dalton, Law, Harvard University; Sharon Leder, Literature, SUNY Buffalo; Sondra O'Neale, English, Emory University; Diana Mary Paul, Religion, Stanford University. ". . . I made the mistake of including these two papers [about status of younger women and plight of the older woman] in my vitae and thus took an extra year to be awarded faculty tenure. My male faculty associates said, 'Look, she's not really a serious psychologist; she writes about trivial, unscholarly subjects like women.'" Troll, Lillian E. "The Psychosocial Problems of Older Women." In *The World of the Older Woman: Conflicts and Resolutions,* pp. 21–35. Edited by Gari Lesnoff-Caravaglia. New York: Human Sciences 1984. p. 22.

10. "The College President: A New Survey by the American Council on Education Finds That the Typical Chief Executive is White, Male, and 53 Years Old." Personal and Professional Section, *Chronicle of Higher Education* **29** (March 30, 1988): A1, A14–A15. A collection of articles about and related to the American Council on Education (Washington, D.C.) survey issued in 1988.

11. Baum, Laurie. "For Women, the Bloom Might Be Off the MBA." *Business Week* #3042 (March 14, 1988): 39. Quoted and relied on variously including "Fewer Women Seeking MBAs," *California Business Weekly* [School of Business Administration, University of California, Berkeley] **8** (March 14, 1988): 10.

12. Joan, Polly, and Andrea Chesman. *Guide to Women's Publishing.* Paradise, California: Dustbooks, 1978.

13. West, Celeste. *Words in Our Pockets: The Feminist Writer's Guild Handbook on How to Get Published and Get Paid.* Paradise, California: Dustbooks, 1985.

14. Hartman, Joan E., and Ellen Messer-Davidow. *Women in Print. Volume II: Opportunities for Women's Studies Publication in Language and Literature in the Profession.* For the Commission on the Status of Women in the Profession. New York: Modern Language Association of America, 1982.

15. Russ, Joanna, *How to Suppress Women's Writing.* Austin, Texas: University of Texas Press, 1983.

16. Spender, Lynne. *Intruders on the Rights of Men: Women's Unpublished Heritage.* New York: Routledge & Kegan Paul, 1983.

17. Spender, Dale, and Lynne Spender. "Gatekeeping: The Denial, Dismissal, and Distortion of Women." *Women's Studies International Forum* **6** (1983).

18. Women's Institute for Freedom of the Press is located at 3306 Ross Place, N.W., Washington, D.C. 20008; Dr. Donna Allen, founder and president.

Beginning in 1988 *Media Report to Women* newsletter has been published by Communication Research Associates, Inc., 10606 Mantz Road, Silver Spring, Maryland 20903-1228. The annual *Directory of Women's Media* ["to aid networking and increase communication among women nationally and internationally"], edited by Martha Leslie Allen, can be obtained from the Institute and women's bookstores.

19. *Media Report to Women* 14 (March–April 1986): 6; Celeste West's *Words in Our Pockets.*

20. Fox, Mary Frank. *Scholarly Writing & Publishing: Issues, Problems, and Solutions.* Boulder, Colorado: Westview, 1985.

21. "Plaintiff held that her promotion had been unfairly delayed while less qualified males were promoted. Keene State College said officially that her work was not mature or creative enough, but the president told Sweeney that she was rigid, narrow-minded, and inflexible. The judge ruled for Sweeney, saying that 'one familiar aspect of sex discrimination is the practice, whether conscious or unconscious, of subjecting women to higher standards of evaluation than are applied to their male counterparts.' The judge also reprimanded officials at Keene State for not pursuing their affirmative action program vigorously enough. Christine M. Sweeney was awarded back pay and attorneys' fees in this often-cited case" [filed four years earlier]. Sweeney v. Keene [New Hampshire] State College 569 F.2d 169, 176 (1st Cir. 1978), 439 U.S. 24 (1978), 48 U.S.L.W. 3465 (January 31, 1981). For a review of this (pp. 15–16) and other cases up to 1980 regarding *Academic Women and Employment Discrimination,* see Jennie Farley's critical annotated bibliography, No. 16 in Cornell Industrial and Labor Relations Bibliography Series, published in 1982 by the New York State School of Industrial and Labor Relations, Cornell University.

22. Stainton, Elsie Myers. *Author and Editor at Work.* Toronto: University of Toronto Press, 1982. pp. 37–38.

23. Smith, Dorothy. "A Peculiar Eclipsing: Women's Exclusion From Man's Culture." *Women's Studies International Quarterly* 1 (1978): 281–96. (p. 287).

24. Spender, Dale. "The Gatekeepers: A Feminist Critique of Academic Publishing." In *Doing Feminist Research,* pp. 186–202. Edited by Helen Roberts. New York: Routledge & Kegan Paul, 1981. p. 187.

25. Spender, Lynne. "The Politics of Publishing: Selection and Rejection of Women's Words in Print." *Women's Studies International Forum* 6 (1983):469–73. Synopsis, p. 69.

26. Tuttle, Lisa. *Encyclopedia of Feminism.* New York: Facts on File, 1986.

27. Papanek, Hanna. "False Specialization and the Purdah of Scholarship." *Journal of Asian Studies* 44 (November 1984): 127–48.

28. Orpen, Christopher. "Tenure and Academic Productivity: Another Look." *Improving College and University Teaching* 30 (Spring 1982): 60–62.

29. Licata, Christine M. *Post-Tenure Faculty Evaluation: Threat or Opportunity?* ASHE-ERIC Higher Education Report No. 1. Washington, D.C.: Association for the Study of Higher Education, 1986.

30. Carlson, Earl R., and Rae Carlson. "Male and Female Subjects in Personality Research." *Journal of Abnormal and Social Psychology* 61 (1960): 482–83.

31. Prescott, Suzanne. "Why Researchers Don't Study Women: The Responses of 62 Researchers." *Sex Roles* 4 (1978): 899–905.

32. Abramson, Joan. *The Invisible Woman: Discrimination in the Academic Profession.* San Francisco, California: Jossey-Bass, 1975. Abramson's 1979 *Old Boys, New Women: The Politics of Sex Discrimination* was published by Praeger.

33a. Nielsen, Robert. "Consensus; Part-time Faculty: A Full-Time Problem."

On Campus [official publication of the American Federation of Teachers/AFL-CIO] **6** (November 1986):16. Women are better represented in the academic underclass than they are in the traditional tenure-track group. Data in a 1984 American Association of University Professors survey showed 40 to 50 percent of nontenure track posts held by women — striking in view of the fact that women held only 25 percent of the full-time positions covered. The role of temporary teachers on their campuses "in some respects does not differ from that of teaching assistants . . . Ultimately the two-tier system brings with it a class consciousness that affects the faculty's perception of themselves, the students' perception of the faculty, and the outside world's perception of academe." *Chronicle of Higher Education* **32** (July 30, 1986): 23, 26. Campbell, Patricia B. "Racism and Sexism in Research," Volume 3:1515–1520. *Encyclopedia of Educational Research, 5th edition.* New York: Macmillan, 1982. Many clerical workers at Ohio State University responded to a questionnaire surveying their concerns that they were not encouraged to advance professionally, would support a merit-pay system, and are not given fair consideration for promotions (*Chronicle of Higher Education* **34** [February 10, 1988]: A12).

33b. Aisenberg, Nadya, and Mona Harrington. "2-Tier Faculty System Reflects Old Social Rules That Restrict Women's Professional Development." *Chronicle of Higher Education* **35** (October 26, 1988): A56.

34. Astin, Helen S., and Diane E. Davis. "Research Productivity Across the Life and Career Cycles: Facilitators and Barriers for Women." In *Scholarly Writing & Publishing: Issues, Problems, and Solutions,* pp. 147–160. Edited by Mary Frank Fox. Boulder, Colorado: Westview, 1985. pp. 147, 149.

35. Valian, Virginia. "Solving a Work Problem." In *Scholarly Writing & Publishing: Issues, Problems, and Solutions,* pp. 99–110. Edited by Mary Frank Fox. Boulder, Colorado: Westview, 1985. p. 102.

36. Contact Dr. Gwen Keita, Officer of Women's Programs, American Psychological Association, 1200 17th Street, N.W., Washington, D.C. 20036, for the name of your state's coordinator.

37. Hood, Jane C. "The Lone Scholar Myth." In *Scholarly Writing & Publishing: Issues, Problems, and Solutions,* pp. 111–125. Edited by Mary Frank Fox. Boulder, Colorado: Westview, 1985.

38. "Tenure Denial at Harvard Upheld by President Bok." *Chronicle of Higher Education* **34** (March 16, 1988): A2.

39. Heller, Scott. "Teaching Awards: Aid to Tenure or Kiss of Death?" *Chronicle of Higher Education* **34** (March 16, 1988): A14.

40. Astin, Helen S., and Diane E. Davis. "Research Productivity Across the Life and Career Cycles: Facilitators and Barriers for Women." In *Scholarly Writing & Publishing: Issues, Problems, and Solutions,* pp. 147–60. Edited by Mary Frank Fox. Boulder, Colorado: Westview, 1985. p. 159. Single men constitute 3.6 percent of all academic men.

Bibliography

In addition to many of the titles cited in the Notes, the following publications should be consulted:

Aiken, Susan Hardy, et al. *Changing Our Minds: Feminist Transformations of Knowledge.* Albany, New York: SUNY Press, 1988.
Apter, Terri. *Why Women Don't Have Wives: Professional Success and Motherhood.* New York: Schocken, 1985.

Bakos, Susan Crain. *This Wasn't Supposed to Happen: Single Women Over 30 Talk Frankly About Their Lives.* New York: Continuum, 1985.

Baruch, Grace, et al. *Lifeprints: New Patterns of Love and Work for Today's Women.* New York: McGraw, 1983.

Bernard, Jessie. "Reflections on Style, Structure, and Subject." In *Scholarly Writing & Publishing: Issues, Problems, and Solutions,* pp. 139–146. Edited by Mary Frank Fox. Boulder, Colorado: Westview, 1985.

Blum, Debra E. "Black Woman Scholar [Sondra A. O'Neal] at Emory University Loses 3-Year Battle to Overturn Tenure Denial, But Vows to Fight On." *Chronicle of Higher Education* 34 (June 22, 1988): A15–A16.

Bombardieri, Merle. *The Baby Decision: How to Make the Most Important Choice of Your Life.* New York: Rawson, Wade, 1981.

Burgwyn, Diana. *Marriage Without Children.* New York: Harper, 1981.

Crowdes, Margaret Stephanie. *"I Am a Woman and a Human Being": The Routinization of Gender Presuppositions in Ordinary Language.* Ph.D. Thesis. La Jolla: University of California, San Diego, 1983.

Daniels, Pamela, and Kathy Weingarten. *Sooner or Later: The Timing of Parenthood in Adult Lives.* New York: Norton, 1982.

Denmark, Florence. "Women's World: Ghetto, Refuge, Or Power Base?" In *Women's Worlds: The New Scholarship.* Edited by Martha Mednick, et al. New York: Praeger, 1985.

Eichenbaum, Luise, and Susie Orbach. *What Do Women Want: Exploding the Myth of Dependency.* New York: Coward, 1983.

Eichler, Margrit, and Jeanne Lapointe. *On the Treatment of the Sexes in Research/La Traitement Objectif des Sexes dans la Récherche.* Ottawa: Social Sciences and Humanities Research Council of Canada, 1985.

Farnham, Christie. *The Impact of Feminist Research in the Academy.* Bloomington, Indiana: Indiana University Press, 1987.

Fischer, Margaret B. and Margaret Ruth Smith. *Writing as a Professional Activity.* Washington, D.C: National Association for Women Deans, Administrators, and Counselors, 1980.

Forrest, Linda, et al. *The Elimination of Sexism in University Environments.* Paper presented at the Annual Campus Ecology Symposium, June 1984. Available from ERIC: ED 267–348, 1984, 37pp.

Fox, Mary Frank. "Publication, Performance, and Reward in Science and Scholarship." *In Higher Education: Handbook of Theory and Research.* Edited by John C. Smart. New York: Agaton, 1985.

————. "Women and Higher Education: Sex Differentials in the Status of Students and Scholars." In *Women: A Feminist Perspective,* 3rd edition. Edited by Jo Freeman. Mountain View, California; Mayfield, 1984.

————, and Catherine A. Faver. "Achievement and Aspiration: Patterns Among Male and Female Academic-Career Aspirants." *Sociology of Work and Occupations* 5 (November 1981): 439–463.

————, and ————. "Independence and Cooperation in Research: The Advantages and Costs of Collaboration." *Journal of Higher Education* 55 (1984): 347–359.

————, and ————. "Men, Women, and Publication Productivity." *Sociological Quarterly* 26 (Winter 1985): 537–549.

————, and ————. "The Process of Collaboration in Scholarly Research" *In Scholarly Writing & Publishing: Issues, Problems, and Solutions,* pp. 126–148. Edited by Mary Frank Fox. Boulder, Colorado: Westview, 1985.

Freeman, Jo. "How to Discriminate Against Women Without Really Trying." In *Women: A Feminist Perspective*, 2nd ed., pp. 217–232. Edited by Freeman. Mountain View, California: Mayfield, 1979.

Germano, William P. "Helping the Local Faculty With Publication Support." *Scholarly Publishing* 15 (October 1983): 11–16.

Gilbert, Sandra M., and Susan Gubar. *The Madwoman in the Attic: The Woman Writer and the Nineteenth-Century Literary Imagination*. New Haven, Connecticut: Yale University Press, 1979.

————., and ————. *No Man's Land: The Place of the Woman Writer in the Twentieth Century*. Volume I: *The War of the Words*. New Haven, Connecticut: Yale University Press, 1988.

Hall, Roberta and Bernice Sandler. *The Classroom Climate: A Chilly One for Women?* Washington, D.C.: Project on the Status and Education of Women, 1983.

Hartman, Joan E., and Ellen Messer-Davidow. *Women in Print. Volume I: Opportunities for Women's Studies Research in Language and Literature. Volume II: Opportunities for Women's Studies Publication in Language and Literature*. New York: Modern Language Association of America, 1982.

Kaufman, Debra Renee. "Associational Ties in Academe: Some Male and Female Differences." *Sex Roles* 4 (1978): 9–21.

Kimball, Gayle. *The 50–50 Marriage*. Boston, Massachusetts: Beacon, 1983.

Kolodny, Annette. "Respectability Is Eroding the Revolutionary Potential of Feminist Criticism." *Chronicle of Higher Education* 34 (May 4, 1988): A52.

Kramarae, Cheris, and Paula Treichler. *A Feminist Dictionary*. New York: Pandora, 1986.

McMillen, Liz. "Legal Experts Eye 2 Sex-Bias Lawsuits Brought by Women's Studies Scholars: Plaintiffs Hit Tenure Evaluation Process, Raise Questions About Status of Feminist Scholarship." *Chronicle of Higher Education* 32 (April 9, 1986): 23–26.

Media Report to Women, 1975–1988, Women's Institute for Freedom of the Press, 1988–   . Newsletter published by Communications Research Associates, Inc.

Menges, Robert J., and William H. Exum. "Barriers to the Progress of Women and Minority Faculty." *Journal of Higher Education* 54 (1983): 123–144.

National Education Association. *Report and Recommendations on Part-time, Temporary and Nontenure Track Faculty Appointments* [brochure]. Washington, D.C.: NEA Office of Higher Education, 1988.

O'Rourke, James S. "Publish or Perish! In the Scholarly Press These Days, the Latter Seems to Be Getting Easier." *Educational Technology* 21 (May 1981): 40–42.

Richardson, Barbara L., and Jeana Wirtenberg. *Sex Role Research: Measuring Social Change*. New York: Praeger, 1983.

Ruddick, Sara, and Pamela Daniels. *Working It Out: 23 Women Writers, Scientists and Scholars Talk About Their Lives and Work*. New York: Pantheon, 1977.

Schenkel, Susan. *Giving Away Success: Why Women "Get Stuck" and What to Do About It*. New York: McGraw, 1984.

Seldin, Peter. *Changing Practices in Faculty Evaluation*. San Francisco, California: Jossey-Bass, 1984.

Sharp, Nancy W., Judy VanSlyke Turk, Edna F. Einsiedel, Linda Schamber, and Sharon Hollenback. *Faculty Women in Journalism and Mass Communications: Problems and Progress*. Syracuse, New York: Gannett Foundation, 1985. (From Association of Education in Journalism and Mass Communications, College of Journalism, 1621 College Street, University of South Carolina, Columbia, South Carolina 29208-0251.)

Spender, Lynne. *Intruders on the Rights of Men: Women's Unpublished Heritage.* New York: Pandora Press, 1983.

Stanley, Liz, and Sue Wise. *Breaking Out: Feminist Consciousness and Feminist Research.* New York: Routledge & Kegan Paul, 1983.

Stimpson, Catharine, with Nina Kressner Cobb. *Women's Studies in the United States.* Naugatuck, Connecticut: Ford Foundation, 1986.

Strainchamps, Ethel. *Rooms with No View: A Woman's Guide to the Man's World of the Media.* New York: Harper, 1974.

Sturdivant, Susan. *Therapy with Women: A Feminist Philosophy of Treatment.* New York: Springer, 1980.

"Tenure Denial at Harvard [of Clare Dalton] Upheld by President Bok." *Chronicle of Higher Education* 34 (March 16, 1988): A2.

Thorne, Barrie, and Marilyn Yalom. *Rethinking the Family: Some Feminist Questions.* New York: Longman, 1982.

Wheeler, Helen R. "Mass Media and Communications." In *The Women's Annual: 1983–1984.* No. 4, pp. 124–144. Edited by Sarah Pritchard. Boston, Massachusetts: Hall, 1984.

White, Arden, and Nelda Hernandez. *Perceptions of Women and Men in Counselor Education About Writing for Publication.* Available from ERIC : ED 265–445, 1985, 15 pp.

Wiley, Mary Glenn. "Becoming an Academic: Early Vs. Later Professional Socialization Experiences." *Sociological Focus* 14 (April 1981): 139–145.

Woodward, Diana, and Lynne Chisholm. "The Expert's View: The Sociological Analysis of Graduates' Occupational and Domestic Roles." In *Doing Feminist Research,* pp. 158–85. Edited by Helen Roberts. New York: Routledge & Kegan Paul, 1981.

Zikmund, Barbara Brown. "The Well-Being of Academic Women Is Still Being Sabotaged — By Colleagues, By Students, and By Themselves." *Chronicle of Higher Education* 35 (September 1, 1988): A44.

Chapter Two
Truth for Authority: Journal Articles

"Truth for authority, not authority for truth." Lucretia Coffin Mott (1793–1880). American feminist, social reformer. Her motto. Quoted in *The Peerless Leader* [who apparently was William Jennings Bryan] by Paxton Hibben. New York: Farrar and Rinehart, 1929.

Periodical literature can be divided into two main groups: general and professional. Exmaples of general or popular magazines are *Good Housekeeping, Ms., Nation, Reader's Digest, Time,* and *Working Woman.* They are likely to be among the hundreds of magazines indexed in *Readers' Guide to Periodical Literature.* Magazines like *Psychology Today* and *Scientific American* can serve as source material to document work and developments and to provide insights to the social and behavioral sciences. They are usually indexed in *Readers' Guide . . . and* one or more semispecialized periodical indexes. *Psychology Today* is indexed in *Readers' Guide . . .* and *Social Sciences Index, Social Sciences Citation Index, Excerpta Medica,* and other indexes; *Scientific American* is indexed in *Readers' Guide . . .* and *Biological Abstracts, Chemical Abstracts,* and other indexes. These magazines are written largely by salaried staff members, although some, for example *Mother Jones,* also pay authors for commissioned and noncommissioned articles. It is with this market that "working writers" and users of Writers Market, Inc., publications are concerned.

Examples of scholarly or professional journals are *Gerontology: International Journal of Experimental and Clinical Gerontology* (Switzerland), *Manushi: A Journal About Women and Society* (India), *Nuova D W F (Donna/Woman/Femme): Rivista Internazionale di Studi Antropologici Storici* (Italy), *Resources for Feminist Research/Documentation sur la Récherche Feministe* (Canada), *SAGE: A Scholarly Journal on Black Women* (United States of America), and *Psychology of Women Quarterly* (United Kingdom). Journals generally do not routinely pay authors for unsolicited submissions with direct cash payment. Major scholarly journals are likely to be indexed by an abstracting service, a citation index, and other standard commercial and professional serials indexes.

There are approximately 70,800 periodicals of all types including scholarly and professional journals, general interest magazines, trade "journals," and vocational and recreational periodicals from all over the world in more than 542 subject-areas. Additionally, there are 35,900 serials, annuals, continuations, conference proceedings, and other serial publications issued irregularly or less than twice a year.[1,2] Examples of irregular serials are *Goteborg Women's Studies* (Sweden), *Harvard Women's Law Journal* (United States), *Papers in Australian Linguistics* (Australia), *Women & Literature: Scholarly Journal of Women Writers and the Literary Treatment of Women* (formerly *Mary Wollstonecraft Journal*) (United States), and *Working Papers on Women in International Development* (United States). These figures do not include newspapers, of which there were 11,077 in the United States and Canada in 1988.[3]

The significance of serial publications for the users as well as writers cannot be overemphasized. The most recent material on a subject, especially in science, technology, statistics, economics, and politics, as well as on new, obscure, or transient topics is not covered by books. Interest and opinion trends of a given period can be traced easily, with recent issues providing current information and back issues a record of past ideas, problems, and accomplishments. Parts of books are sometimes first published in periodicals. Professional literature is updated and new developments or ideas are introduced by journal articles on subjects of concern to particular branches and sub-branches of knowledge. Usually written by members of the professions, they keep educators, scientists, physicians, economists, lawyers, and members of other professions up-to-date. About 100,000 scientific and technical periodicals publish over two million articles each year.[4] Journals are the place where scientists report the progress and discoveries of their research — where it is subjected to a form of peer review before it is accepted as fact or shared with the general public. Johnson, Kolodny, and Masters were severely and publicly criticized when they published their conclusions about Acquired Immune Deficiency Syndrome (AIDS) in book form with a popular news magazine excerpt without first sharing them with colleagues.[5]

The word *journal* in the title of a periodical does not always indicate a scholarly journal. Many commercial periodicals which focus on a field or discipline's activities and concerns incorporate journal in their titles, e.g. the *Library Journal*, published by the Bowker Magazine Group, a subsidiary of the Cahners Publishing Company, which is a division of Reed Publishing. Some serial titles without journal in their titles may be considered major scholarly journals; these sometimes include *review* in the title. The *1988 Directory of Women's Media* listed 616 periodicals in the United States and abroad.[6] The first edition, in 1975, listed 131. Not enough of these periodicals are valued as acceptable scholarly journals by the gatekeeping authorities, although some titles include the word journal and some are indeed making significant scholarly contributions in and outside of academe, e.g. *Nuova D W F (Donna/Woman/Femme); Rivista Internazionale di Studi Antropologici Storici* (Italy), *Manushi: A Journal About Women and Sociology* (India), *Resources for Feminist Research/Documentation sur la Récherche Feministe* (Canada), and *Women's Studies International Forum* (Britain).

In some fields and institutions, regular publication of articles in specialized scholarly journals is valued more than publication of a book. Research is valued more than teaching at some institutions of higher education with graduate programs. The emphasis in academic employment on journal publishing, especially in the sciences, over other forms and other activities is usually justified by its being the main way relatively rapid dissemination of findings are subjected to peers' scrutiny, communicated, and acknowledged. This work phase may involve the graduate student or young doctorate as secondary or tertiary author. (The mentor relationship within this context is potent.) Publication of journal articles is also emphasized in the social sciences. Only in the humanities might a professionally young scholar-educator take a career risk by not assigning publication of journal articles a high priority over other types of professional publication and activities such as teaching.

The personal essay may be publishable in a journal when written by a well-established woman scholar. Euphemisms are often employed in their titles and contents, but no amount of doublespeak or saving interface can deem an article acceptable if it implies criticism of the academy.

A journal in the social sciences if often a theoretical qualitative analysis, or a quantitative research study. In professional fields (e.g. education, medicine) three types of articles are sought by editors: research reports, discussions of current issues—sometimes called trends—and descriptions of practices and procedures. The large and increasing number of journals in the fields of education and quasiprofessions (e.g. social welfare, librarianship) publish research findings as well as newsworthy descriptions of effective programs and stimulating, some of which have been referred to as "How we do it good" articles garnering visibility for author, program, and institution. The overall situation, combined with the large number of scholars competing to get published in journals (one in ten *New England Journal of Medicine* manuscripts is published) makes a judicious selection of journals for their submissions important to all professionally young scholars and especially to women in academe.[7]

Journal consumers' needs should also be recognized. The ability to learn as rapidly as possible about developments in the field in which they are researchers and practitioners is vital to the reinforcement, validation, and progress of their own research as well as to the refutation of fallacies and inefficient practices. Sharing of research, theory, and practice is a cycle in which everyone should be able to participate responsibly and equitably as reader and contributor.

• • •

"...if those only wrote, who were sure of being read, we should have fewer authors; and the shelves of libraries would not groan beneath the weight of dusty tomes more voluminous than luminous." Lady Marguerite Blessington (1789–1849). Irish novelist, poet. *The Confessions of an Elderly Lady*. London: Longman, Orne, Brown, Green and Longmans, 1838.

Academic library holdings have increased over 10 percent in the past decade or so.[8] To aid the researcher in efficient use of periodicals, there are separately published indexes to periodical literature which regularly analyze a group of periodicals in a field such as art, psychology, chemistry, or education by grouping articles from hundreds of different journals under detailed subject-headings. This breakdown, together with innumerable cross references *from* one subject-heading *to* another, can also aid in generating topical ideas and focusing *or* developing a subject. Because each index regularly covers a group of similar periodicals, it is wise to identify and consult several appropriate indexes in order to located the varied periodicals and information needed for interdisciplinary research.

There are numerous standard research tools with potential utility for all, but the user must have mastered periodical indexing and must recognize the need to proceed cautiously. Often the young instructor does not integrate teaching, research methodology, and library use. The holder of an advanced academic degree may have been exposed to relatively few standard references in her or his field, and possibly some basic biblio-graphic tools for getting around in it. Mere awareness, however, rarely leads to commitment and intimacy.

Indexes are as important for retrieving information from serials as the on-line or card catalog is for finding books. Journals, magazines, and newspapers emphasize subject matter, rather than featuring specific authors and titles. Because indexes sometimes access periodical articles' contents under authors' names, there is more than one approach to an arti-cle when using a periodical index: one or more subject-headings plus the author entry. Whether searching a thesaurus such as the Library of Con-gress' *Subject Headings* (which is the basis for subject-headings accessing books in most catalogs) for wordings, or a periodical index such as the *Social Sciences Index* under subjects it uses, some good ground rules are: be specific, check under the specific words you are thinking, and then get creative. Lists of some Library of Congress subject-headings and some

ERIC descriptors related to professional development by publication are provided in the Resources section.

Some of the techniques of organization of a card or on-line catalog are apparent in periodical indexes. Both use subject-heading systems with subdivisions and cross-references; they list journal articles under more than one subject-heading; and they point out such useful things as bibliographies, maps, illustrations and portraits, charts, reviews, etc., provided with the articles. Although there are similarities between a periodical index and a card or online catalog, a subject-heading system that organizes subject matter contained in books cannot organize the type of information contained in current issues of periodicals. In using specialized periodical indexes to find articles on subjects within specific fields, do not expect that subject-headings noted in catalogs will always work, but you can start with them. Then reword, combine, keyword.

In a catalog the cards or online entries for new books are interfiled right in among those already filed. To keep up-to-date systematically with new periodical articles, a periodical index usually *cumulates*. This means it is first published in the form of temporary paper supplements. Every few months this indexing is interfiled into temporary-but-larger issues or interim cumulations. At the end of the indexing period, generally a year, all of the entries appearing in all of the cumulations are interfiled into one "big," permanently bound volume replacing all interim coverage.

For current topics and up-to-date information on any subject, begin a periodical index search in the latest, small, paperback supplementary issue, and work systematically backwards into combined cumulated issues. But for the information on a subject connected with a specific date or for specific issues of a journal, first check the indexing cumulation covering that date or period. In using periodical indexes to identify specific articles of which you are already aware, first try checking within the applicable time span (volume) under the author's name. The permanent old volumes of periodical indexes provide retrospective indexing: articles written about and at the time of Edith Cavell's execution as a World War I spy, Amelia Earhart's disappearance, Gertrude Ederle's English Channel crossing, "new woman of Japan" Raichō Hiratsuka's interview during her 1924 travels abroad, and the disbanding of the Women's Air Force Service Pilot Training (WASP) *before* World War II had ended.

Abstracting services perform the same basic function in organizing knowledge as the alphabetically arranged periodical indexes just described, but they differ in the amount of information provided and their arrangement. The entries are first arranged in broad subject-areas, rather than under specific subject-headings, and a separate subject index may be provided for each issue and cumulation. Abstracting services provide summaries of indexed journal articles (and some other types of documents, notably dissertations) called *abstracts*. Usually the abstract is also published at the beginning of the journal article in the periodical issue itself. Keep in mind as you prepare the abstract for each journal article you author that locating and reading an abstract of any publication can be helpful in doing research and in using libraries. Think of tools such as *Women Studies Abstracts* and *Studies on Women Abstracts* as periodical indexes with some abstracts as a bonus.

When using abstracting services, it is often necessary to build in a second searching step. First, locate a reference to a publication on a subject of interest, using the alphabetical subject index to get the *abstract number*. Typically, it is then necessary to move to the volume where citations to the indexed publications are arranged in the order of their abstract numbers, together with full information including their abstracts. When tracking down a journal article for which the exact date of publication or the author is unknown, it is especially important to keep in mind that there can be considerable time lag in getting some of these highly specialized serials abstracted and indexed.

Citation indexes are a unique concept and tool. They often index the total contents of periodicals, whereas indexes and abstracts may omit references to such potentially useful things as short articles, letters, and book reviews. A citation index can be used to find references to articles directly related to an article which you have already read and found very useful. Uniquely, it can identify articles published *after* your one great article was published, and which refer to your author's article. The traditional search begins with a relevant document in hand and pursuit of the references cited at the end of the paper in order to identify additional information on or considering the same subject. This technique leads to *older information*. And, if this process is continued, by locating the older works cited and looking at the works they cite, one is led to still older information. Citation indexing can lead one *forward in time* to the authors whose published articles are based on the same information and concerns. Citation indexing is based on the concept that authors' citations to previously published material indicate a subject-relationship between their current articles and older publications; in addition to these relationships with earlier publications, articles that refer to or cite the same publications usually have a subject relationship with each other.

The Permuterm Index portion of a citation index provides a different approach to subject access. Because permuted indexing (something permuted is rearranged) is based on keywords, material that is obscured by the subject-heading structures used by many indexes or by the lack of any subject indexing in some cases can be found. But its value is not so much in finding an article of which you are already aware, as in finding articles you were unaware existed.

How do you decide whether to use a conventional periodical index such as the *Social Sciences Index, Art Index,* or *Applied Science and Technology Index* instead of a citation index such as the *Social Sciences Citation Index, Arts and Humanities Citation Index,* or *Science Citation Index?* Since citation indexes are a relatively new concept, to find articles published in the early 1930s, for example, you would *have* to use the *Art Index.* Citation indexes are essential when you are aware of an article but unable to track it down bibliographically by use of conventional periodical indexes mainly because you are unable to verbalize the subject-headings. Or perhaps the subject matter is so new, radical, or innovative that subject-headings have not yet been introduced by the index or thesaurus. There was a period when AIDS was somewhere in this information science limbo.

Citation indexing relies on keywords in titles. Keywords are "automatic." The Permuterm Subject Index portion of a citation index is based on the keyword concept, not rigid subject-headings derived from a thesaurus. Any word in the title is combined with any other word in the title of the same document. In the printed version of the 1976–1980 *Social Sciences Citation Index* cumulation Permuterm Subject Index portion (volume 20, column 17590), for example, GATEKEEPERS combines with several other keywords including FEMALE and WOMEN. In each case, an author's name is also provided, with full information about the publication in the Source portion of the *Social Sciences Citation Index* for the same time period. One of these word pairs must appear in a publication's title in order to locate it using permuted indexing. But if your goal is a list of articles published during this period and about FEMALE GATEKEEPERS, or GATEKEEPERS and the FEMALE, for example, it will be helpful. Because the process is literal, you should also check GATEKEEPER, GATEKEEPING, etc., and WOMEN, WOMAN, etc. And, as an author, you must make certain to title your journal articles fully and accurately and to include all keywords. In this case, we are led to the 1976 – 1980 *Social Sciences Citation Index* cumulation Source portion (volume 18, column 52195) to an article by S S Whitlow, "How male and FEMALE GATEKEEPERS respond to news stories of women" published in the *Journalism Quarterly.* [Journ Q 54 (3): 573 '77 22R U of KY Sch of J refers to *JQ: Journalism Quarterly* volume 54, issue 3 in volume 54, published in 1977, and beginning on page 573, which included 22 references by the author, who is based at the University of Kentucky School of Journalism]. All twenty-two of Whitlow's references are also identified here. Another bonus is the synergistic discovery of another, seemingly related, article by Whitlow.

Not surprisingly, the 1981–1985 *Social Sciences Citation Index's* permuted index (volume 20, column 18047) provides an increased harvest of potential title-keyword pairs: GATEKEEPERS and GATEKEEPING combine with, for example, BLACK-OWNED, ELITE, JOURNALS, PUBLISHING, and SEX DISCRIMINATION. By consulting the author entry (which also appears with each keyword pair) in the Source volumes, we are led to the following:

- an article titled "Unions as GATEKEEPERS of occupational SEX DISCRIMINATION — Canadian experience"
- a review of a book titled *GATEKEEPERS of black culture: BLACK-OWNED book publishing in the United States, 1817–81*
- an article titled "Editorial GATEKEEPING patterns in science journals — a new scientific indicator" (which also leads to another article by the same author titled "Citation patterns of editorial gatekeepers in international chemical journals").

In the printed version of the 1980–1984 *Science Citation Index* Permuterm Subject Index portion (volume 64, column 330297), WOMEN combines with several other keywords including OSTEOPOROSIS, for example, leading to publications which have both these keywords in their titles.

It is also possible to use citation indexes to track down specific publications and information about them. You understand that sometime in 1982 Rosalyn S. Yalow (who, in 1977, became the second woman to win the Nobel Prize in medicine) published a journal article about competency testing for reviewers and editors. Enter the Source indexing portion of *Science Citation Index* 1980–1984 cumulation (volume 45) and look directly under Yalow R S (column 102717), where such a publication is cited: Behav Brain 5 (2) 244 '82 1R.

This refers to page 244 of issue number two in volume five of *Behavioral and Brain Sciences* journal, published in 1982; it was published with one reference. It may also be possible to locate references made subsequently to Yalow's article by checking the citation indexing portion of the same and subsequent *Science Citation Index* cumulations. The 1986 *Science Citation Index* Citation indexing portion (volume 9, column 81276), under Yalow R S, refers to Garfield E., who has cited this Yalow work on page three of the 1986 *Current Contents*.

There is a special relationship between citation indexing and evaluation of scholarly publications and their authors. The more times an author's name and publications are reviewed or even cited, the greater their visibility. Citation indexes' listing of reviews, authors with their affiliations, inclusion of all of a journal article's own bibliographic references, and their online retrievability make them especially conducive to rapid and widespread awareness of a scholar's presence. And all citation indexes involve simple keyword and name searches rather than thesauri, although it is not necessary for a committee to have access to or to examine either the printed citation index *or* the indexed publication in order to draw conclusions from the results of an online search relating to a candidate's name and publications. Lists of the thousands of international source and citing journals involved in every citation index can be found within each cumulation.

A growing number of English-language journals list, usually somewhere inside the front portion of each issue, the title(s) of any periodical indexes, abstracting, and citation indexes that analyze their contents. Some journals publish annual indexes to their own contents, but these individual self-indexes provided by periodicals may be inconsistent, late, and in event, create multiple searching steps. (Women, feminists, and editors of gender-related periodicals should endeavor to get their serials indexed by standard periodical indexes, abstracting services, and citation indexes and included in such standard directories as *Ulrich's*, etc.).

Manual searching of some printed volumes (time-spans) of some periodical indexes can now be replaced by computer-assisted, on-line searching of database counterparts, available in many libraries. And there are also some database index files which have no printed equivalents, e.g. *ABI/Inform, National Newspaper Index, NCJRS* (National Institute of Justice/National Criminal Justice Reference Service), parts of *Embase*, and *Mental Health Abstracts.* The information generated by an on-line search may be more up-to-date than that available in the printed format, if any. A computer search can save time because the equivalent of many volumes of printed indexes can be efficiently and rapidly searched. With the computer's assistance and the searcher's skills, it is possible to search "on" title words, keywords within an abstract, authors' names, dates, and combinations of keywords, as well as to employ structured descriptors (subject-headings) derived from thesauri. The computer can combine subjects to generate a bibliography which represents only the titles present in the "overlap" created by multiple concepts, e.g. MATERNITY PLANS PRO-VIDED BY EMPLOYERS in INDUSTRY, BLACK WOMEN as portrayed in CONTEMPORARY LITERATURE, AGEISM in CHILDREN'S BOOKS, or the role of WOMEN in the URBANIZATION OF DEVELOP-ING NATIONS.

The Politics of Journal Publishing

"There is nothing more inately human than the tendency to transmute what has become customary into what has been divinely ordained..."
Suzanne Lafollette (1889–1983). United States. *Concerning Women*, 1926.
Arno 1972 reprint.

Studies have shown that the number of published journal articles is a primary factor in determining such rewards in academe and related institutions as rank, salary, and promotion. Even after controlling for effects of age, Astin found publication of journal articles carrying the single greatest weight in determining rank and accounting for the largest proportion of variance in salary.[9] Studies which control for age *and* sex are needed in many areas.

Surveys show that leading scholars in the humanities and social sciences are dissatisfied with their journals. About one third report that they rarely find articles of interest in their discipline's primary journal. The majority think the peer review system for deciding what and who get published in scholarly journals is biased in favor of established researchers, scholars from prestigious institutions, and those who use currently fashionable approaches.[10]

The progress and problems experienced by faculty women in journalism and mass media provide significant insights because of the great influence of these areas on communication. A recent study of leading communications journals documented the extent of participation of women as authors of published research articles. In short, there has been only a small increase in their number, and the pattern of the 1970s continues. Not surprisingly, women were found to have "their smallest impact in those areas in which they would contribute by virtue of invitation."[11] Women, who were 17 percent of communications faculties in 1983, appear to have been as productive as or even more productive than their male colleagues in research activities that were self-initiated and depended on blind judging, in which the judge is said to be completely unaware of the writer's identity. However, they lag in the amount of participation dependent on *invited participation.* In examining leading journals in their fields, researchers found the greater percent of primary authors of journals was consistently male. In fact, *Public Relations Review* and the *Journal of Advertising* percentages of male primary authors were 91.7 percent and 90 percent.[12] Furthermore, male secondary authors as percentages were frequently much greater than female.[13] A directly-related situation, which Sharp's investigation also considered and confirmed, is the imbalance between the numbers of women studying mass communications and teaching mass communications courses at American colleges and universities. Fifty nine percent of the undergraduate and 52 percent of the master's level students who graduated during academic year 1982–1983 were women. After more than a decade of nondiscriminatory affirmative action in the United States, only 36 percent of communication Ph.D.'s were awarded to women, and women made up only about 17 percent of communications faculties.[14] The opportunity to examine their academic ranks, relative salaries, and types of assigned responsibilities might compound the grievous nature of these data.

Publications and scholarly research have often been included among qualifications for recruiting faculty and awarding increments and promotion. Contemporary advertisements and other postings allude to them. For example, from a 1988 national advertisement, "To receive serious consideration, candidates must provide strong evidence of scholarship through significant research and refereed publication to meet requirements for appointment to the Graduate Faculty." (Presumably all applicants receive serious consideration.) A woman's response requesting further information including clarification of this portion of the very brief advertisement was dealt with by nonresponse. What constitutes "strong evidence," "significant research" and even "publication" have varied for individuals. . . . In another region of the United States at about the same time, a university's advertising stipulated ". . . recent publication in refereed journals and ongoing research to qualify for directing doctoral dissertations within a year after appointment." A tenured associate professor who responded to my requests for contributions to this book emphasized that women with relatively advanced ranks and tenure can also expect to be stalled "because of a dearth of publications in refereed journals." Although her publications list filled four single-spaced pages, she does not expect to be promoted to full professor. *Quality, prestigious, reputable, mainstream, of the first tier, recognized,* and *appropriate* are some of the vague and flexible words often heard in connection with the journals in which publication is valued.

In 1985, after Sondra A. O'Neal had taught in Emory University's English Department (Atlanta, Georgia) for six years, it was recommended that she not be awarded tenure, a decision that was upheld by university officials at every level. She was warned by the Faculty Council that, to be seriously considered for tenure, she would have to publish her work in what members considered to be recognized journals and have a book accepted by a reputable press. The Council suggested she submit work to such journals as the *American Quarterly* and the *Sewanee Review.* O'Neal contends that her work published in *Obsidian: Black Literature Review* and *Melus,* a Modern Language Association journal specializing in minority scholarship, was discounted and disregarded.[15]

The peer review process in at least one science area's publications has been questioned to the extent that a congress on editorial peer review has been organized with an agenda that questions its cost and the qualifications, selection, and evaluation of both editors and reviewers. A few of the topics being discussed are:

- how the peer review process is circumvented (e.g. "sponsored" publications)
- how quality of a manuscript can be determined by other than the peer review process

- how faculty appointment committees assess publications for promotion and tenure
- how peer-reviewed literature is used by regulatory agencies
- how the techniques of formal decision analysis are used in selection of papers for publication
- the number of journals using peer review, and in what way
- the place of consensus as a standard of validity
- the costs of the peer review process
- implicit or explicit standards used to judge manuscripts
- similarities and differences of merit review of grant applications and editorial peer reviews
- what citation analysis shows
- by what implicit or explicit standards manuscripts are judged.[16]

In the course of consulting in academe, I have become aware of dossiers of applicants rejected for employment, promotion, and tenure in which evaluators' comments about the candidates' publications communicated that only those published in what the evaluators perceived as refereed journals were regarded. On the other hand, credentials of faculty, as compiled by the same department for accreditation purposes, for example, might organize citations of articles which have appeared in refereed journals with those "in press" interfiled, followed by "articles in nonrefereed or general journals." At a third, descending level was a category of "chapters in books or monographs," with "other publications" at the lowest level. The least regard might be for books, film reviews, proceedings, and brochures. A mixed bag category of "papers, abstracts, and lectures" by faculty unrepresented in any of the other categories may also be provided as needed.

A well-known 1981 study asked professors to comment on the peer review of their most recent published article:

- 76 percent encountered pressure to conform to the strictly subjective preferences of the reviewers;
- 73 percent encountered false criticisms (and 8 percent made changes in the article to conform to reviewers' comments they knew to be wrong);
- 67 percent encountered concentration upon trivia;
- 43 percent encountered treatment by referees as inferiors;
- 40 percent encountered careless reading by referees.

At some time in their general experience with the peer review system,
- 65 percent of the professors believed referees' comments were contrived to impress the editor;

- 53 percent believed that the journal editor regarded their knowledge and opinion about reported research as less important than that of referees;
- 44 percent believed that they were being treated like a supplicant;
- 47 percent accepted a referee's suggestion against their judgment.[17]

Peters and Ceci's 1984 study of peer review journals' practices involved submission of articles with fictitious names and institutions to journals that had originally refereed and published them. Only three (8 percent) of the twenty-eight editors and reviewers detected the resubmissions, which allowed nine of the twelve articles to continue through the review process to receive actual evaluation, which rejected eight of the nine. Sixteen of the eighteen referees (89 percent) recommended against publication, and their journal editors concurred. Peters and Ceci were courageous because editors and publishers loathe this type of action research (researcher) and consider it a deception (deceiver) to be condemned.[18]

It is generally recognized that evaluation of faculty involves a spectrum of approaches including student feedback of teaching (sometimes titled Course Evaluation), self-assessment, evaluations by colleagues (sometimes called peer evaluation), measurements of student learning, and assessment of research, advising, and public service. Instructors should recognize the potential for improvement of their teaching as well as the course by means of eliciting feedback in a structured situation. Over-reliance on the peer review reflects need for built-in assurance of security on the part of administrators, pseudo-peers, editors, and referees. Lloyd has referred to ". . . subtle and powerful constraints and pressures that promote silent submission to the system."[19] "Anonymous peer reviews may be more costly than beneficial. A system that could allow a reviewer to say unreasonable, insulting, irrelevant, and misinformed things about you and your work without being accountable hardly seems equitable. To some degree the reviewer is indeed accountable — to the editor — but the potential for abuse is still too great to be ignored."[20] According to a 1982 article in *Behavioral and Brain Sciences,* the rules for manuscript acceptance require that authors should *not* pick an important problem, *not* challenge existing beliefs, *not* obtain surprising results, *not* use simple methods, *not* provide full disclosure, and *not* write clearly.[21] Lloyd sums up, ". . . our review system can sometimes amount to nothing more than an adversarial confrontation where the defendant is presumed guilty, has no counsel or friend in court by arrangement, and cannot face his accusers, and there are no qualifications for judges. At other times, it can be the reverse, a conspiracy of peers in a field to promote the field (and one another)."[22]

It behooves women in academe to eschew the assumptions which support many aspects of such a system and to recognize that it affects them in disparate fashion and with far greater impact. Stieg has declared that

"Refereeing has become an integral part of the knowledge industry . . . [But] too many academics have a rather fuzzy conviction that refereeing equals scholarship."[23] From a recent doctorate, I received the following naive comment about her experiences:

> I have never been paid for reviewing journal articles. That is, I believe, standard in professional circles. One reviews for the experience and for the lines that can be added to one's own curriculum vita. That may explain the paucity of constructive criticism some authors receive. [sic]

Many journal article referees are not paid, but some journals certainly pay them, e.g. the *American Economic Review.* It can also be argued that for many referees there is remuneration in other forms. No amount of payment justifies the ill treatment an author (peer) may receive from referees (peers), however. Journal publishers and editors have the responsibility to impress upon referees their responsibility to return comments on manuscripts within two weeks of receipt, at which point considerable time is still involved in the process.[24] Some editors have problems with the management role as well as obtaining qualified referees. One woman scholar's letter is representative:

> Since my graduation date I have submitted two articles to refereed journals; both were rejected . . . returned to me in packages much heavier than those I mailed—the additional bulk the result of reviewers comments. One reviewer went through one article, page by page, with extensive suggestions and then added a critical overview. The other article received very helpful suggestions—including additional sources I might investigate to strengthen the piece. While rejections are never pleasant I feel I learned a great deal about my own work as well as the process of publishing. . . [sic]

She appears to acknowledge and accept passively an overall situation which is uniquely significant for all women scholars and would be writers when she concludes,

> sometimes the luck of the reviewer draw is bad, I guess . . .

(She had not applied these suggestions and resubmitted her article). Most women studies periodicals, whether or not they declare themselves feminist or refereed journals, utilize a methodology involving reviewers, who may be out in the field or subfields on call, or whose names may be identified as constituting a review board. These periodicals and these people tend to provide the type of feedback which this writer's "luck" brought her.

The peer refereed journal process is presumed to be characterized by:

- provision of anonymity of author to reviewers
- provision of copies of all reviewers' reports, as well as provision of anonymity of reviewers to author
- a conclusive summary response from the editor which encourages, rejects, or suggests modifications, possibly with encouragement of resubmission
- promptness
- systematic organization and management as evidenced by such things as prompt acknowledgment of receipt of submissions, assigned manuscript number, dates of manuscript receipt by the journal and response to the author recorded, known, and reasonably timed

Usually an editor of a refereed journal reads or scans an article and routes it to two referees (who are, however, referred to as reviewers), who are specialists in the aspects of the journal's field with which the article is concerned. If the editor assumes that something about the manuscript or author will present a problem in reaching a consensus or publication of it, the manuscript may be sent to three or even four referees initially, or after much delay. More usual is the routing to two reviewers initially, and then to a third if there is disagreement between the perceptions of the first two. It is conceivable that the first two will recommend that it be published "as is." It is more likely that they will suggest modifications which imply the likelihood of publication when resubmitted. Or they might both reject it. If your article appears to take much longer than a colleague's to receive a decision from the same journal, the reason may relate to its having presented a problem for the referees, editor, or publisher, which may be a professional association, conglomerate, or university press. Even more time is involved in gathering referees' reactions which will serve to document a "consensus."

Horror stories abound. Stanton has amassed evidence that suggests how a female author's name, apart from the feminist content of her article, is the repository of sexual stereotypes that depreciate the value of her words.[25] (It is not unknown for a scholar whose first name is androgynous and whose biographical material accompanying her submission lists only the institution where she earned the doctorate, to be asked the identity of her undergraduate institution, which might be a women's college. More common is the phone call to the department and the less-but-still devious reference to "her" or "she".) When the author of a rejected article on the subject of women, affirmative action, and education found it necessary to request legible copies of the anonymous (to her) reviewers' reactions, she took the opportunity to ask the editor about representativeness of the journal's reviewers generally. His response was assumptive and defensive:

> . . . although we are unable to provide actual reviewers' names [which she
> did not request], we want to assure you that they are of diverse gender and
> from varied backgrounds both ethnically, culturally, and racially. [sic]

At least one referee knew or assumed the author's gender; another appeared to know or know of the author. Apparently the lengthy delay had been caused mainly by the fact that one had not rejected the article, which became apparent when the legible copy was provided. The editor had simply deemed the article not "relevant."

Decisions of a nonrefereed journal editor or editorial board prevail in selecting and rejecting articles for publication. Information about a periodical, which appears in the preliminary pages of each issue usually, may refer to both an editorial board and an advisory board. Some journals consider that editorial board members are their referees. The names of current editorial board members, perhaps with their institutional affiliations, are likely to be identified. This is a resume, dossier, or directory item for them. Periodicals which boast that they are refereed journals point to anonymous referees who are occasional reviewers, out in the field, currently on the faculties of colleges and universities—the more prestigious the better—and experts in their disciplines and the subfield specialization of the journal.

While colleges and universities value articles in journals which are considered refereed over those in journals which are not, they make far fewer value judgments among *which* refereed journals. I recall working on an article for an administrator who wanted the information disseminated. Ultimately it appeared that two journal editors were interested—one expressed interest in the material as I had described it in a letter. The other was an overseas journal to which the administrator had submitted a rough draft of the paper, which he was using for speech-making during his sabbatical abroad. I sought the counsel of the acting administrator. To which of the two journals should I submit the article? Without acknowledging that he was seemingly unfamiliar with both journals and the paper itself, he responded with alacrity, "The refereed one." Postmortem: Apparently both editors learned in any of several ways possible of these machinations, concluded that *I* had committed one of the two ultimate journal sins—simultaneous submission of an article—and terminated all further discussion. (The other sin is action research such as reported by Peters and Ceci.) Journals often stipulate that you agree not to submit to another journal *and* to see to it the information is not shared; on the other hand, journal editors clearly have their own network. *Frontiers* journal's [1988] form acknowledgement of receipt is representative: "By your submission . . . we understand that this piece is your original work; that it has not been previously published in whole or in part; and that this article, or *any* version of it, is not currently under consideration for publication by another publisher in either article or book form."

Respectability is likely to mean publication in the refereed journal. This relationship to peer review is usually assumed to provide the author with the written, expert feedback of several "peer reviewers." In practice, there may be no copies provided by the journal editor, or one or two, or a copy of the manuscript on which comments have been scribbled. There is no way of knowing whether copies of all of the reviews are provided, even if the author requests them. There may be contradiction between the editor's cover letter of rejection of the article and seemingly one or even more of the anonymous referees' reviews which appear to endorse publication or at least encourage revision and resubmission.

The Economics of Journal Publishing

"The labor of women in the house, certainly enables men to produce more wealth than they otherwise could; and in this way women are economic factors in society. But so are horses." Charlotte Perkins Gilman (1860–1935). American author, lecturer, social reformer. Chapter 1, *Women and Economics*. Boston, Massachusetts: Small, Maynard, 1898.

Getting published in scholarly journals can pay, and association with scholarly journals can pay off. Although most journals do not pay authors for their voluntary submissions or noncommissioned articles, the gain associated with acceptable publications relates to professional advancement — raises, promotion, and tenure as well as sabbatical, consulting, invitations, travel, and the general visibility which impresses some gatekeepers. Compensation provided by a journal may consist of some offprints, tearsheets, or copies of the journal issue in which the article is published. The scholar-author is often faced with a fact of academic life for many: the need to pay — invest, they say — to get some journal articles published. The nomenclature usually involves subscription, submission, or processing fees, or (usually in science) page charges, justified in various ways by the journal and the academy. Journal publishers cite mailing and clerical costs associated with the referee system, and the need to discourage frivolous submissions. An excellent research contribution would consider the possibility that certain scholar groups make frivolous submissions less frequently than others. Page charges appear to be levied in disparate fashion by means of waiving them for *some* authors and articles,[26] although this practice continues to be defended as standard and on the altruistic basis of having some free articles in each issue. Feminist action research might be productive here if only to clarify what is actually general practice.

Advertising is one way of paying for some of the costs of a periodical's operations, but writers of getting-published books, journal editors, and publishers stress two other ways: (1) readers' (and authors' and librarians') subscriptions, and (2) authors' paying in some form or guise. These additional costs impinge on women more than on men because women are paid dollar-for-dollar less than men,[27] regardless of the amount of education they have acquired. (The more education a woman has, the greater the likelihood that she will seek paid employment.[28]) Women are clustered in the lower nontenured ranks, and the sex differential for male-role and administration and management jobs' salaries is also visible in academe.[29]

A few demonstrations may underscore an author's need to ascertain in advance the compensation policies of all journals to which she or he submits articles, and the significance for women scholars of knowledge of standard operating procedures, as well as collective attention to improving aspects of them. A $10.00 submission fee was required *to submit* an article for a "special feminist approaches to gender and education issue" of *Sociology of Education* journal, published by the American Sociological Association. The *Journal of Professional Studies'* call for papers stresses that it is a refereed journal with a $5.00 processing fee. The review process for *Gender & Society*, official journal of Sociologists for Women in Society, "expected [in 1987] to become one of the most prestigious journals in its field," publishing "carefully refereed scholarly materials," requires five copies and a $10.00 submission fee for each manuscript. Since March 1987, authors who submit articles to the *American Economic Review* have paid a $50.00 fee; previously it was "the usual $25.00." The managing editor stresses that the purpose is not to raise money but "to speed up the referees and to get a few authors whose papers aren't ready for submission to think twice." A referee receives $35.00 if the article is returned within four weeks.[30] The American Psychological Association division 35's official journal publication, *Psychology of Women Quarterly*, instituted a submission-processing fee of $10.00 in 1986 "to help cover rising costs of xeroxing, postage, and handling . . . [which] will be waived upon request for those who cannot afford to pay it."[31] The Haworth Press publishes numerous journals, including *Women & Politics*. Its standard instructions for authors include a subscription order form and state that articles are published "at no charge to the authors," and that an "editor's acceptance letter may indicate an 'early publication option' is available. Authors may choose to 'move up' their publication date, if either they, their research grant, or institution can pay a charge for adding extra pages to the very next journal issue in production."[32]

Women tend to accept the standard reasons provided to justify the system rather than to question it or suggest alternatives. One woman wrote:

As for fees—for two years I served on the editorial board of a graduate student run journal and have some knowledge of the problems of submission fees. Journals are generally not money makers. The cost of printing, postage, etc. is enormous. Membership and subscription fees just don't cover the costs involved (example, the X Y Z Association includes journals in the membership fee for students, yet loses about $38. for every student member.) The choice usually becomes one between raising membership dues and subscription fees or trying to give organization members a break. This generally results in choosing to charge authors for the cost of processing their manuscripts (a great deal of time, as you know, goes into finding reviewers, contacting them, using secretarial time to mail manuscripts, keeping a log to determine which reviewers are overdue on their reviews, notifying authors of the decision, and returning manuscripts). The cost of submitting may also discourage some writers from sending in manuscripts that are not nearly ready for submission. [sic]

There are other cost requirements of the author beyond forthright submission fees. Journals frequently require the author to pay the cost of color reproductions and printing, e.g. *Spina Bifida Therapy,* one of Eterna press' periodicals. When journals stipulate that a self-addressed stamped envelope of specified size accompany a submission, they imply that comments will accompany the returned manuscript, for the manuscript copies themselves are rarely reusable. Two cost requirements rarely acknowledged are personal membership in the association which sponsors the journal and personal subscription to journals which are not part of association membership. Although association membership is rarely stipulated as a requirement for publication in a journal sponsored by or affiliated with a professional or scientific association, it appears that journals publish articles by members. You must determine the situation for yourself. It is difficult to document in writing examples of the requirement that an author be a subscriber to the journal. However, "Subscription to the *Journal of American Culture* is required of those who are published in it." Alas, this news came from a woman, who conveyed it in behalf of the editorial board which had just informed her of some after-the-fact changes in the call for manuscripts for a "feature on women's issues." My personal experience has been that, with one exception, I have never submitted an article to a periodical to which I was not then a subscriber or sponsoring association member without shortly receiving a subscription membership form. Notice that authors' instructions sheets are likely to include a subscription panel or be accompanied by subscription information. The *Journal of Thought,* for example, follows its information for prospective contributors with a list of subscription rates.

The problem of book publishers merging and being absorbed by Big Business with conglomerate control and profit-making motives and commitments has received some press. Many, but not all, scholarly journals are sponsored by professional membership associations. Corporation conglomerates and universities also publish journals and books. This trend has also influenced the economics of journal publishing. Although the number of journals throughout the world is growing, when several companies and groups own or control multiple periodical titles (and, some say, their editors), they are able to influence what and who are not published. Periodicals are now subject to the Big Business effects of incorporation and takeover by umbrella groups and consortia much like conglomerate ownership of book publishing houses. Editors of scholarly journals which are owned and operated by profit-making groups are subject to and may pay allegiance to this Big Business marketplace influence. A few of the groups based in the United States (with overseas offices usually) and elsewhere which publish multiple English-language journals include Elsevier, Eterna, Haworth, Heldref, Pergamon Press' Pergamon Journals, Inc. (a member of the Maxwell Communication Corp. Group of Companies), Plenum Publishing Corp.'s Plenum Press, and Sage. Responding to complaints that publishers of scholarly journals engage in "profiteering" and "price gouging," an Association of Research Libraries' study found a median rise of 18.2 percent in journal prices in 1986–1987, with the greatest increases coming from a small number of publishers throughout the world which have a kind of monopoly. The average yearly price of a magazine in 1987 was $71.41; prices increased more than five times the rate of inflation. "Part of the problem is academe itself, which often rewards faculty members for the number of articles they have published, rather than for the quality of the articles."[33] More than four hundred United States publishers regularly publish four or more periodicals of at least sixteen pages and with a frequency from weekly to quarterly, e.g. Aspen Systems Corp. (25 titles), Transaction Periodicals Consortium at Rutgers University (30), Warren, Gorham & Lamont, Inc., subsidiary of the International Thomson Organisation, Ltd. (30), Technical Publishing, a Dun & Bradstreet Corp. company (22), J.B. Lippincott Company, subsidiary of Harper & Row, Publishers, Inc. (38), and Mouton De Gruyter of Berlin, New York, and Amsterdam.[34]

Journals which are sponsored and subsidized by professional association or academic institutions appear to be not quite as concerned with profit-making. A lot is made of the picture of an editor without a professional staff, struggling to keep the journal going in addition to her/his responsibilities as a faculty member or university administrator. Most appear to reap considerable, career-related benefits from such appointments and particularly from involvement with the establishment of yet another such journal.

It is important to belong to the professional association which represents your discipline or profession to support its work and the work of a caucus or subgroup in which you share commitment to principles as well as subject matter. The association publishes a journal or journals, which you support by your membership, and your submissions probably receive more consideration than they would otherwise. Here again action research might show that, despite claims otherwise, many of these association journals are unlikely to consider seriously for publication any article submitted by a former or nonassociation member. When a department or university underwrites association membership fees, which are closely associated with journal publication, and costs related to such publishing, the dole should be on the basis of clear, equitable, and accessible policies. Association membership can often provide new contacts whose interests are compatible with yours and who might by helpful in the work of getting published. Your department or college may have a "publishing committee" of volunteers on which you might make a contribution.

Robert Markley, editor of *The Eighteenth Century: Theory and Interpretation* journal, favors a restructuring of "the politics of publishing," which might render the current system of tenure obsolete. He argues that "the publishing world does not simply further the spread of knowledge. The process whereby journals and presses choose what articles and books to print also maintains a system that elevates a relatively few individuals to positions within academe." He suggests that scholars who publish "should be rewarded with travel money, research grants, occasional leave time, and possibly reduced course loads, but publishing itself should not be a criterion for tenure or vast discrepancies in salaries."[35]

Unlike book publication, where an author might aim to get a contract and *then* complete the book, journal articles are usually written and then submitted and revised. Some journal editors approach people for articles. An issue editor of a special or thematic journal issue is likely to select authors and develop topics in a more or less group process. *Proteus* and *Library Trends* are examples of periodicals which devote each issue to a theme or topic. Some journals occasionally have thematic issues, e.g. the *Journal of Medieval and Renaissance Studies, Women's Studies Quarterly,* and *Journal of Modern History.* Each *Southern Review* thematic issue focuses on an author. Some have occasional special issues focusing on a timely topic such as the ever-euphemistic "women's issues," e.g. *Journal of American Culture.* A journal usually has a plan for future issues, but it is difficult to learn of what it consists if one does not know someone associated with the journal. A request on your letterhead might nevertheless receive a response. "Calls" for articles related to special issues may appear as advertisements in the *Chronicle of Higher Education,* or be announced in your discipline's journals and professional newsletters associated with status of women caucuses. Women's studies–related journals and conferences share this type of information somewhat more openly. Presentation of a conference paper is an excellent way to phase in a journal article because you get feedback, it gets comments, and both you and your article get visibility.

Conference presentations may be published, excerpted, or abstracted in proceedings.

There are several facts about a journal which you need to know in order to select the most appropriate one for your submission as well as to structure the most judicious submission. You can patch together much of this information from directories, recent issues of the journal, colleagues, and the journal's instructions to prospective authors, which you may have to request separately. Confirm as many as possible of the following by checking the current issue of the journal to which you plan to submit an article:

- whether instructions to author-contributors are printed in each issue, or available on request from the journal office
- whether manuscripts are by invitation only, or unsolicited submissions are accepted and if so, policy regarding articles, bibliographies, personal and review essays, and book reviews
- the language (and nation) in which it is published
- the function of the periodical, e.g. newsletter for an association, report, scholarly journal
- its declared subject-specialization and *sub*specialities within that discipline, field, profession, or subject matter
- its audience, e.g. specialized, academic, professional
- regard for it as prestigious, respectable, well known, acceptable, "the" journal in its field — generally *and* on your campus
- whether it is published by a professional organization, an academic institution, university press, university, consortium, collective, etc.
- status as a refereed journal; whether written feedback is provided the author by at least three expert reviewers
- in addition to an acceptable manuscript, whether anything else is required of the author, e.g. association membership, periodical subscription, submission fee, publication charges, etc.
- title of a standard periodical index, major abstracting tool, or citation index in which its contents are analyzed
- length of time it currently takes for acknowledgment, decision, and publication
- the number of articles published in a typical issue
- characteristics of published titles, subjects, and authors during the last three years
- frequency of publication
- whether the journal pays authors, provides offprints or reprints
- possibility of publication of thematic or special issues, what are now planned, and who the issue editors are

- circulation
- when founded
- preparation of the manuscript:
  - maximum/minimum manuscript length
  - use of a particular style manual specified
  - number of copies of the manuscript required
  - whether enclosure of a self-addressed post card for acknowledgment of receipt is recommended, required, not mentioned
  - routines regarding illustrations and other special formats
  - if an abstract is required, any particulars, e.g. length in number of words
  - if an author biography is required at this stage, its particulars, e.g. length
  - whether the journal welcomes or ignores inquiries before submission of a manuscript by a prospective author.

Identification of appropriate journals for your submission and the correct preparation of your article are the keys to getting it published. Compilation of a fine-tuned list of such journals involves efficient use of reference tools and examination of recent issues of the journals. The model methodology for identifying relevant journals for your submission which follows should be adjusted to your professional needs and the requirements of your discipline.

Let's say you have a paper which you are converting into a journal article or have written with the goal of publication in a journal. It is ready to be tailored to one journal's requirements and submitted to it. Do not delay because, whatever the field or subject matter, it is becoming staler with each passing minute. In short, you need to be able to identify journals in your field which publish articles, essays, bibliographies, review essays, book reviews, etc., in the language in which your scholarship and writing flourish and are subject-specialized. And you may prefer that they do not require association membership or subscription or charge a fee to submit! Initially, attempt to locate an up-to-date, selective, annotated bibliography of journals in your *sub*field by checking the library card or on-line catalog using appropriate subject-headings. For example, someone working in the United States in the field of gerontology and concerned with aging and ageism, focusing currently on home care and hospices, might search under the Library of Congress subject-heading GERONTOLOGY—PERIODICALS—BIBLIOGRAPHY, which should lead to Hesslein's *Serials on Aging: An Analytical Guide*. By checking Hesslein's subject index under HOME CARE, HOSPICES, and other subject-wordings she uses, several journal titles are generated. Each is annotated, and periodical indexes in which it is indexed, abstracted, or cited, as well as any data bases in which it is included, are identified. Other useful information which the compiler of such a tool provides includes how materials are selected for publication, whether special issues are published, target audience, and subject and geographical indexing. Comparable subject-specialized compilations related to other disciplines and in library collections can often be identified in the same manner, using appropriate LC subject-headings, e.g.:

AGRICULTURE – PERIODICALS – BIBLIOGRAPHY
ANTHROPOLOGY – PERIODICALS – BIBLIOGRAPHY
HISTORY – PERIODICALS – BIBLIOGRAPHY
INFORMATION SCIENCE – PERIODICALS – BIBLIOGRAPHY
LIBRARY SCIENCE – PERIODICALS – BIBLIOGRAPHY
LIVESTOCK – PERIODICALS – BIBLIOGRAPHY
MARINE BIOLOGY – PERIODICALS – BIBLIOGRAPHY
PHILOSOPHY – PERIODICALS – BIBLIOGRAPHY
OCEANOGRAPHY – PERIODICALS – BIBLIOGRAPHY

Notice that, while it would be possible to search under PERIODICALS – DIRECTORIES or even SCHOLARLY PERIODICALS – DIRECTORIES, bibliographies of periodicals at a subject-specialized level have been specified. Also consult the university libraries' subject specialist in your subject area. Roaming the library stacks even in a subject-specialized or branch library is haphazard for most purposes. A handbook or guide to the literature of your field may list many of its journals. Directories of periodicals in individual disciplines exist, but the information they contain is only briefly current because usually at least a year is involved in publication of a book. Some periodical directories are included in the Resources section at the back of this book. The ideal, however, is an up-to-date, annotated bibliography of journals in your subfield.

For our purposes – a search for specialized scholarly journals – first attempt to locate such a bibliography. Next, use *Ulrich's International Periodicals Directory* current edition because it provides information about circulation, frequency, and book reviews; indicates in which periodical indexes, abstracting services, and citation indexes, if any, a journal is analyzed; and has a subject index (in the front of the first volume) listing many detailed categories, within which there are hundreds of subdivisions. The excerpt from the Women's Interests section (Figure 2:1) describes five periodicals and also provides one helpful cross-reference. If you are interested in knowing more about a periodical titled *Simply You,* consult (see) the subject section CLOTHING TRADE – FASHIONS elsewhere in this edition of *Ulrich's International Periodicals Directory.* The five fully displayed periodicals consist of: one from the United Kingdom (UK centered at the heading of the first line of the display), an Albanian

305.412   UK   ISSN 0037-3370
SHE. 1955. m. £17. National Magazine Co. Ltd., 72
    Broadwick St., London W1V 2BP, England. Ed. Eric
    Bailey. adv. bk. rev. illus. circ. 227,631.
305.415   AA
SHQIPTARJA E RE. m. $7.40. Union des Femmes
    d'Albanie, Tirana, Albania.
323 700   US   ISSN 0161-715X
SIBYL-CHILD. 1974. 3/yr. (in 1 vol.) $9. Sibyl-Child
    Press, Inc., Box 1773, Hyattsville, MD 20788. TEL 202-
    723-5468. Eds. Saundra Maley, Nancy Prothro. adv. bk.
    rev. bibl. illus. circ. 1,000. Indexed: Wom.Stud.Abstr.
305.412   US   ISSN 0097-9740
SIGNS: JOURNAL OF WOMEN IN CULTURE AND
    SOCIETY. 1975. q. $29 to individuals; institutions $58;
    students $21. University of Chicago Press, 5801 S. Ellis
    Ave., Chicago, IL 60637 TEL 312-962-7600. (Orders to:
    Box 37005, Chicago, IL 60637) Ed. Jean F. O'Barr. adv.
    bk. rev. circ. 6,100. (also avail. in microform from UMI;
    reprint service avail. from UMI,ISI) Indexed: Curr.Cont.
    Hist.Abstr. M.L.A. Psychol.Abstr. SSCI. Soc.Sci.Ind.
    Sociol.Abstr. A.B.C.Pol.Sci. Adol.Ment.Hlth.Abstr.
    Amer.Hum.Ind. Amer.Hist.& Life. Amer.Bibl.Slavic &
    E.Eur.Stud. ASCA. Bk.Rev.Ind. C.I.J.E. CERDIC.
    Commun.Abstr. Lang.& Lang.Behav.Abstr.
    Wom.Stud.Abstr.

SIMPLY YOU. see CLOTHING TRADE — Fashions

305.412   FI   ISSN 0359-0267
SINAMINA. m. Kolmio-Kirja, Box 246, 90101 Helsinki,
    Finland. adv. circ. 21,200.
        Formerly: Tarina.

Figure 2:1 Ulrich's International Periodicals Directory.

periodical (AA), two published in the United States (US), and one based in
Finland (FI). Also on the first line of the *Signs* entry are a decimal classification (305.412) for this periodical's subject matter and an International
Standard Serial Number (ISSN), an internationally-used number that
uniquely identifies a serial publication. Note that *Signs* had a circulation of
6,100 at the time this *Ulrich's* edition was published, that it carries book
reviews and advertisements, and is indexed in nineteen periodical indexes
including *Sociological Abstracts, America: History & Life,* and *Social
Sciences Citation Index.* It is unlikely that a journal will be indexed (and in
this case, by so many standards of academe and scholarship) and fail to be

acknowledged and acceptable. From another perspective, commercial and professional indexing tools and their companies and associations begin indexing a periodical *after* it is established and in demand.

Browse through the subject index breakdowns in the front of the current edition of *Ulrich's International Periodicals Directory,* and make a list of the *sub*divisions which apply to your specialization and to the article you want to get published. Then examine the pages displaying the analyses for each of them. For your preliminary list from within that subject *sub*division, glean all of the periodicals which you recognize as scholarly journals, or which have "journal" in their titles, or which appear to be associated with academe, published in your language or nation, and which are indexed. The data for periodical indexes, if any, appear at the end of each display. *Ulrich's* is also useful for the list of cessations, or defunct periodicals, which each edition provides.

It is possible to have a computer-assisted literature search made in your behalf of the contents of *Ulrich's International Periodicals Directory,* and interim supplements, which have been stored on-line and can be searched in many libraries. Consult the reference librarian. The more specific you can be about the information you seek, the better. Your print-out will provide the same data as a hand search of the printed volumes. Frequently, better information is generated because the interim data are included, and in the hands of the professional searcher who is familiar with the process, the search itself can be more focused, if she or he interviews you and if you are prepared to describe what you need. There may be a small charge. Funding for searches for this purpose might well be included in professional development enabling services for nontenured faculty.

Although the *Directory of Publishing Opportunities in Journals and Periodicals* has not been updated since the fifth (1981) and final edition, it can be included among the basic tools supporting selection of journals because it provides manuscript information and editorial description. (See figures 2:2A and 2:2B.) But it is absolutely essential that current journal issues be examined, especially for the editors' names and addresses. Specialized journals and conference proceedings which accept submissions in English are included in its scope. For each journal, there is a brief description of contents or editorial purposes, the audience to whom it is addressed, and specific subject areas covered, including any topical, geographic or chronological limitations. Other types of useful information included are manuscript requirements, information regarding payment and reprints, and a time frame disposition. The journals are organized into subject-chapters which include Medical And Health Sciences (General), Native America Studies, Black Studies, Hispanic Studies, and Women's Studies (pages 493–496). The only limitations are its failure to list titles of periodical indexes in which the journals are analyzed, and its age.

GERONTOLOGY [3715]
International Journal of Experimental and Clinical Gerontology
S. Karger AG
P. O. Box
CH-4009 Basel, Switzerland
061-390880

SUBSCRIPTION DATA
Previously entitled *Gerontologia,
Gerontologia Clinica.*

Issues and rates: Published bimonthly. One annual volume with 6 issues. Average issue contains 10 articles. Circulation 1,050. Annual rate(s): SFr. 212.00; approx. $120.00 per volume.
Main Editors: F. Bourlière, Paris; H.P. von Hahn, Basel; J. Andrews, London

EDITORIAL DESCRIPTION
Publishes experimental and clinical research results concerning the processes of aging and age-related diseases; features a Clinical Section where recent progress receives comprehensive review through reports on the clinical aspects of aging and on the clinical application of research results. An Experimental Section reports on the latest research results in the fields of biology, biochemistry, physiology and experimental psychology of aging. Particular significance is placed on those areas which have a direct bearing on clinical practice.

MANUSCRIPT INFORMATION
Manuscript requirements: Style sheet sent on request. See latest issue for style requirements. Preferred length 6 printed pages at 3,800 characters. Submit 2 copies and abstract, with 3-9 key words. Mss. accepted in English.

Author information and reprints: No payment. Simultaneous submission is not permitted. Periodical holds exclusive rights after acceptance. Copyright held by publication. Reprints available at cost. Charge for additional printed pages. Query letter not necessary.

Disposition of manuscript: Receipt of manuscript is acknowledged. Rejected manuscript is returned, criticized.

Submit to: Dr. H. P. Von Hahn
Stiftung Füi Experimentelle
Alternsforschung
Felix-Platter-Spital
Ch-4055 Basel, Switzerland

RESOURCES FOR FEMINIST RESEARCH/DOCUMENTATI-ON SUR LA RECHERCHE FÉMINISTE [2604]
formerly the Canadian Newsletter of Research on Women
Sociology Department
Ontario Institute for Studies in Education
252 Bloor Street West
Toronto, M5S 1V6, Canada
(416) 923-6641, ext. 278

SUBSCRIPTION DATA
First published in May 1972.

Issues and rates: Published 4 times per year. Annual rate(s): $15.00, U.S. $18.00, Institutions $25.00.

EDITORIAL DESCRIPTION
Strives to improve communication among people doing research in women's studies; publishes information on the status of women in institutions and countries; provides for exchange of ideas about courses on sex roles or women. Regular sections on research reports, periodicals, book reviews, bibliographies, abstracts, etc.
Audience: Research oriented

MANUSCRIPT INFORMATION
Subject field(s): Only book reviews, bibliographic review essays, and bibliographies are accepted from outside sources. Balance of material is solicited. Books must have been published since 1975, both internationally and Canadian (excluding U.S.), dealing with sex roles or about women.

Manuscript requirements: No specific style guide. See latest issue for style requirements. Preferred length maximum of 5 double-spaced pages. Submit 1 copy. Abstract not necessary.

Author information and reprints: No payment. Simultaneous submission is permitted. Periodical does not hold exclusive rights after acceptance. Copyright held by publication. Reprints available at cost. Query letter is necessary.

Disposition of manuscript: Receipt acknowledged. Decision in 1 month. Published 3-6 months after acceptance. Rejected manuscript is not returned.

Submit to: Carol Zavitz, Mary O'Brien, Editors

It may be useful to consult less focused directories of periodicals. *Writers Market* is one of the many books found in public libraries' reference collections directed at "working writers," who usually write magazine articles and novels. A comparison of the treatment of *Signs* or another journal in your field in each tool you consider can be helpful. The 1986 *Writers Market* collection of "women's magazines" does not list *Signs* among writers' market periodicals.

MIMP: Magazine Industry Market Place is an annual compilation supportive of free-lance publishing in periodicals which are magazines, that is, selling to them. It does, however include some journals, and has more potential utility here than *Writers Market* publications, including information related to the author's approach to the journal. *MIMP* does not indicate whether the periodical is indexed by any standard abstracting tools; it sometimes indicates whether the magazine accepts unsolicited articles and lengths of articles which are sought. Another *MIMP* feature is a section listing publishers of multiple periodicals, which identifies all or many of the journal titles published by each consortium, conglomerate, multiple publisher, university press, or umbrella listed.

The *Standard Periodicals Directory* claims to be the largest authoritative guide to United States and Canadian periodicals; it is "the" periodical directory in many libraries' reference collections. The 1985–1986 edition provides information on more than 65,000 periodicals, organized into subject and other categories, one of which is newspapers. Women's Interests includes *Signs* journal and refers to it as "a women's studies magazine." The *Gale Directory of Publications* (formerly Ayers) also lists newspapers, magazines, journals, and related publications for the United States and Canada.

A way of identifying and knowing more about periodicals which are likely to provide congenial placements for feminists' contributions is the quarterly current contents serial, *Feminist Periodicals: A Current Listing of Contents*.[36] Table of contents pages from current issues of major English-language feminist journals from throughout the world are reproduced, preceded by a comprehensive annotated listing of all journals. While not all currently published feminist periodicals are scholarly journals, the user can get so much up-to-date information about each journal in addition to its current issues that *Feminist Periodicals* also provides directory-like support. The annotated listing provided for each journal includes: year of first publication; frequency of publication; United States subscription prices; subscription address; current editor; editorial address; ISSN; locations where the journal is held in the University of Wisconsin system; tools in

Figures 2:2A (opposite, left) and 2:2B (opposite, right). *Directory of Publishing Opportunities in Journals and Periodicals, 5th Edition*

which the journal is indexed; and a subject focus/statement of purpose of the journal. Feminist Periodicals can also provide the professionally young scholar new to research writing and getting published with an idea of current disciplinary concerns, ways to construct titles, and topics which are receiving thematic or special issue concentrations.

Summary of Some of the Advantages and Disadvantages Generally Associated with Submission of Unsolicited Articles to Refereed/Nonrefereed Journals

Refereed Journal

Disadvantages

Author risks use or discussion of article with others, more so than with submission to a non-refereed journal.

Referees may review for more than one journal in author's field; another journal might send rejected article to the same reviewer.

Process takes longer.

Referees do not know identity of author.

Editor screens out submissions (decides) first anyway, i.e. not all articles are referred to reviewers. Editor screens which referees, as well as whether to refer the article.

Advantages

Referees do not know identity of author.

"Expert" referees.

Prestige.

Advice, assistance, feedback generally associated with refereed journals.

Possibility of encouragement to revise and resubmit even if article is rejected.

Nonrefereed Journal

Disadvantages

Editor knows identity of author.

Advantages

Process may not be as long; faster decisions possible.

Editor knows identity of author.

Editor will read or scan manuscript.

Judgment of only the editor or editorial board possible.	Identity of members of the editorial board may be known.

Usually not as prestigious.
Normally no advice, assistance, feedback.

Take your menu of journal titles to the shelving area for current and recent periodicals in a university library. (Major public libraries may have some of them.) Examine the current or most recent available issue of each of your journals. University libraries usually shelve periodicals in three zones, with the *current* issue on racks (or kept at the desk) or on open shelves in a browsing area. *Recent* issues may be in a nearby stacks section, alphabetically arranged by titles. "Recent" may mean up to a year or two, depending on the frequency of the periodical itself, e.g. weekly, monthly, quarterly (many journals), semiannual, and even annual, as well as irregular or "occasional." And ultimately, bound, numbered volumes of *back* issues are usually in the library stacks arranged by classification call number, and possibly on microfilm. Today you need the "current," i.e. the most recent received by and available in the library, or most recent available issues of each of the titles on your list of journals. At some point in this process it may be useful to invest a day's trip to a large university campus which has numerous subject-specialized libraries and librarians. Before you go, check the schedule as well as when the subject-specialist reference or collection development librarian will be on duty for a consultation.

After you have taken your list of approximately twelve journals to the library shelves and examined the current issues to confirm and complete the information you have assembled, reread the recent issues of periodicals to which you submit manuscripts. If necessary, send for author's instructions. Select "one best" journal in terms of your article's contents and the journal's reputation scope, subject matter and audience.

● ● ●

"... most people, no doubt, when they espouse human rights, make their own mental reservations about the proper application of the word 'human'. . . ." Suzanne LaFollette (1889–1983). United States. *Concerning Women*, 1926. Arno 1972 reprint.

Many journals have prepared procedures for submitting articles and perhaps book reviews and other types of submissions. Instructions to prospective authors usually appear in the preliminary pages of each journal issue, at the end of the issue, once in each volume (which generally encompasses a year), are available from the editorial office upon request, or are nonexistent . . . suggesting perhaps that unsolicited contributions are not actively sought. Also note whether the names of the editorial board are provided. They may review articles, or evaluate in a preliminary screening, or participate in a final decision. For your own edification, note whether the makeup of this judgmental group is representative of the demographics of the readership or association membership. The time may come when you will have the opportunity to contribute to this type of professional endeavor.

After you have obtained professional reaction to the content and organization of your paper by having a colleague go over it, and perhaps sharing it at a conference or other presentation, and after you have judiciously applied suggestions you receive, it is ready to prepare for submission to *The Right Journal*. Your article should be organized according to the protocol of your field or discipline and the type of article it is, and it should be prepared according to the requirements of the journal to which you submit. The possibility of seeking counsel regarding what you have in mind or have written from a journal editor before you submit the article is suggested by some, but I do not commend this, mainly because I do not think it will be forthcoming.

Article formats vary according to the field and article type, but there are organizational aspects which they have in common. Make sure that you can describe your article's major point or focus, and that it is of particular interest to the journal's readership. This will involve provision of several "sub"-points. Break the article's organization down into an outline whose parts you mentally label.

Incorporate in your article's title all the keywords related to its retrieval when using standard and on-line tools. Consider an attractive, but not cute, relatively short preliminary title, plus a subtitle which is more descriptive and probably longer. For example, "Two Martinis and a Rested Woman: 'Liberation' in the Sunday Comics" by Linda Mooney and Sarah Brabant (*Sex Roles; A Journal of Research* 17 [October 1987]:409–20), "Amazons, Hermaphrodites, and Plain Monsters: The 'Masculine' Women in English Satire and Social Criticism from 1580–1650" by Susan C. Shapiro [Atlantis: *A Women's Studies Journal/Journal dÉtudes súr la Femme* 13 [fall 1987]:66–77), and "The Gender/Science System: Or Is Sex to Gender as Nature Is to Science?" by Evelyn Fox Keller (*Hypatia: A Journal of Feminist Philosophy* 2 [fall 1987]: 37–50.)

An abstract is a brief summary that gives the essential points of an article, dissertation, book, etc. It is not, or it should not be, evaluative or critical. Prepare it after you have completed the article. The overall theme, together with one or two subpoints, should be identified in it. Many computerized abstracting tools input journal article titles' *and* abstracts' keywords. Some professional journals are no longer reproducing the author's abstract at the heading of the article. Instead, they provide a statement from the editor summarizing the article and perhaps how it came about, e.g. the *Journal of the National Association for Women Deans, Ad-*

ministrators and Counselors. Science journals continue to provide abstracts at the heading of the first page of the published journal article.

To prepare an abstract of your submission, determine the maximum number of words or lines the journal requires or permits. The maximum length will usually be indicated in terms of the number of words — one hundred fifty or so. If there is no indication, do not exceed one page. Spell out acronyms. State purpose, method, results, conclusions. Do not cite others' titles unless your study is a replication or evaluation of another's work. Do not include information that is not contained in the articles, or it will not be an abstract. Keep in mind that the abstract's main purpose is to serve a busy readership. Scan a copy of your article. Tentatively delete all descriptive words and elaborative phrases and sentences. Extract from the remaining phrases what you need in order to summarize the *essence* of the article. A topical sentence should state what was found. Follow with some details; place general statements, if any, at the end. Differentiate between hypothesis and experiment. Use short but complete (not cryptic) sentences.

The abstract provides a condensed version of the article's content, without comment or evaluation, and it should rely on the words in the article. An annotation is not an abstract. Strictly speaking, an abstract of a publication does not use such annotative or descriptive phrases as "the author points out" or "the article consists of." It is not easy to prepare a functional abstract. It should serve someone in communicating whether the article which follows will be relevant to her or his needs and should be read in its entirety. Or, when using an abstracting service, whether the journal issue containing the article should be retrieved from the library's collection so it can be read in its entirety. You are providing prospective readers of the article (and frequently users of secondary services such as the abstracting tools which adopt the author's abstract) with the essence of the document. It should contain no added interpretation or criticism or words, and it should not be possible to determine who the abstract preparer is by reading the abstract.

The abstract will appear after the title and just before the beginning of the article when it is published in the journal issue. It may also be used by abstracting tools which index that journal, such as those listed at the conclusion of the *Ulrich's* entry for that journal. You may have noticed in abstracting tools attribution credit to the abstractor is by means of initials in parentheses at the end of the abstract. Sample abstracts appear in Chapter Four.

The introduction to the article should lead the reader easily into the central points in the body. Make clear early in the article that your purpose is a new approach to this topic or a significant contribution to it. A review of the literature for this purpose is not a conventional exhaustive survey nor a list of landmark titles such as a guide to the literature of your field usually provides. Mention titles which pertain to this article's genesis and to its main points in the context of the background or takeoff point which the literature review can provide. You might need to document little or inadequate previous work or to refer to publications with which you disagree. This review of pertinent literature does not consist of a bibliography, although the titles to which you refer should be provided with full bibliographic citations. Utilize your review of the pertinent literature to enable you to present the body of your article, findings, and conclusions.

In the body of the article, describe your method if it is a report of a study or experiment. Your analysis should be a clear, convincing argument. It may be an analysis of findings, observations, or contentions, depending on the discipline and type of article. Demonstrate that this topic is worth investigating, your research is sound, you have considered and are aware of all relevant sources and points of view, and that this is something new. Make clear that it is a contribution to the field. Put it all together so that your article does not exceed the length requirements of the journal and conforms to the journal's instructions. Apply the style manual the journal requires authors to use or which is discipline appropriate. Many journals no longer specify style manuals, and simply commend systematic reference to a single, appropriate style guide.

The manuscript should follow the journal's format guidelines closely. If there are none:

- Adjust the length to that of the typical article currently published in the journal, or perhaps twenty manuscript pages.
- Use wide margins.
- Type doublespace using 12 pitch type (12 strokes to the inch).
- Use subheadings generously.
- Prepare a cover sheet on a separate piece of paper, with your name, article title, date, address, and affiliation. If there is more than one author, determine who is the primary author and place that name first.
- On the first page of the article itself, put "Page 1 of [#]" at the top, and proceed to number in one sequence all pages.
- Proofread carefully, including at least once after several days have elapsed.
- All numbered notes and references should *follow* the article—i.e., no footnotes at the bottom of pages.
- Avoid appendices; you might summarize a unique-but-lengthy, very relevant questionnaire within the article.

In the absence of other instructions, your package should consist of:

- A one-page transmittal letter, on a letterhead if possible, in which you include your telephone numbers and mailing address and convey any information which could enhance the possibility of publication and clarify any pertinent matters, e.g. that the research was done while abroad, a grant was associated with it, status of authorship when more than one name is listed, etc. The writer should be the primary author. Do not refer to "joint authorship."

- Two copies of the article. Some journals require the original and copies.
- An abstract no more than one page in length.
- Author biography no more than one page in length on a separate page which focuses on your credentials for researching or reporting on the material in your article.
- A self-addressed stamped post card. Some journals require a stamped self-addressed envelope in which to return the manuscript. If you mail overseas, enclose International Reply Coupons, which you purchase at the post office.

Mail your package first class in a flat envelope so that the pages are not folded. Spending money on a return receipt from the post office is unproductive. I advise against sending it to the editor at her or his residence. Some getting-published books suggest delivering it personally.

Put in on your calendar. If you have not received acknowledgment of receipt within four weeks, write or telephone to inquire. Keep a copy of the manuscript you submit, and maintain another copy on which you make notes and apply minor revisions in the long interim. The journal may assign your manuscript a number and record the dates it was received and a decision reached. It may or may not have a policy or goal regarding the amount of time which can elapse until the author is informed. You should be prepared to wait from three to six months, and much longer is quite possible. Some journals now provide the sequence of dates with the published article. For example, Basow and Silberg presented their research on student evaluations of college professors in March 1985 at an association meeting. Later they submitted a paper on which the publishing journal suggested some revisions. The sequence appears in the *Journal of Educational Psychology* September 1987 issue, in which the article was published:

[Research presented at Association meeting	March 1985]
Manuscript received by *Journal*	July 1986
Revisions received by *Journal*	February 1987
Article accepted by *Journal*	March 1987
Article published in issue dated	September 1987[37]
[Issue delivered	October 1987]

If you have not received a decision or reaction beyond acknowledgment after six months, do not tell yourself No Answer means No. Write and inquire about its status. As a matter of routine or pride, it appears that most journals will expect you to make some changes in your article, particularly if you are unpublished. Many authors do so from need, weariness, or habit.

Relatively new, less prestigious, or regional journals may need articles. Your article's topic may happen to fit well into a journal's publishing plan or to touch on a subject which is sought for some other reason. A journal may even be looking for representative topics and authors. Think positive, but after six months, begin your preparations so you will be ready to send the article to the next journal on your list. Do not send it to another journal until the first has actually rejected it, preferably in writing. If the editor tells you the bad news by phone or at a meeting, request that the conversation be followed up by letter and that some suggestions be provided. Better still, request copies of all of the reviewers' comments. If, however, the editor suggests revisions *and* the possibility of resubmission (and you are willing to apply the suggested requirements), respond immediately that you will do so, and immediately get to work on the revision. The journal editor and referees may realize the temptation to attempt to place the article elsewhere during their lengthy interim, and they will definitely be miffed if you return to them later as a last resort.

When your article is accepted and until it appears, list it on your publications list or resume under "In Press." The journal may send you galleys to proofread, in which case, give your personal attention to them immediately.

But suppose your article is rejected. It is important that you understand the criteria for evaluating journal articles and recognize the potential problems for women. Presumably journals are concerned with content, readability, and impact or relevance. Presumably the double blind refereeing process has provided the author with several expert critiques and suggestions, opportunity to revise and perhaps even encouragement and guidance by subject specialists who do not know the author nor her or his characteristics. If you have not received statements of referees, write and ask how many reviewers considered it and request copies of all of their comments. Editors may assume that you will not do so, but that if you do, you will accept the standard nonspecific reasons, which include backlog, recent issues having had information or articles on this subject or "covered it," or no reason. Editors are evasive about how many persons reviewed an article because copies of all their reviews are less likely to sustain a completely negative response, one that does not provide any encouragement nor encourage the writer to apply a reviewer's suggestions or to resubmit. Some journals now simply report that they have decided not to accept "it" for publication, and that "comments from referees are available to you upon request." Serious comments should be seriously considered.

Notes

1. *Ulrich's International Periodicals Directory, 26th edition, 1987–1988.* New York: Bowker, 1987. p. vi.

2. *[Ulrich's International Periodicals Directory,] Irregular Serials and Annuals, 13th edition, 1987–1988.* New York: Bowker, 1987. p. vi.

3. *Gale Directory of Publications,* 12th edition, Volume 2. Detroit, Michigan: Gale Research, 1988. p. viii.

4. Katz, William. *Introduction to Reference Work, 5th edition, Volume 1: Basic Information Sources.* New York: McGraw-Hill, 1987. p. 31.

5. Masters, William, Virginia Johnson, and Robert Kolodny. *Crisis: Heterosexual Behavior in the Age of AIDS.* New York: Grove, 1988. "Sex in the Age of AIDS" (excerpt) *Newsweek* 111 (March 14, 1988). Special Report begins on p. 42.

6. *Directory of Women's Media.* Edited by Martha Leslie Allen. Washington, D.C.: The Women's Institute for Freedom of the Press, 1988. The Institute is located at 3306 Ross Place, N.W., Washington, D.C. 20008. Also listed are publishers, news services, columns, radio and television groups and programs, video and cable, film and writers' groups, editorial and public relations people, speakers' bureaus, distributors, media organizations, bookstores, and mail order sources throughout the world.

7. "One in ten of *New England Journal of Medicine* manuscripts are [sic] published." Dr. Arnold S. Relman, Editor. May 4, 1988, "MacNeil-Lehrer News Report," a PBS broadcast.

8. Katz, William. *Introduction to Reference Work, 5th edition, Volume 1: Basic Information Sources.* New York: McGraw, 1987. p. 31.

9. Astin, Helen S., and Diane E. Davis. "Research Productivity Across the Life and Career Cycles: Facilitators and Barriers for Women." In *Scholarly Writing & Publishing: Issues, Problems and Solutions,* pp. 147–60. Edited by Mary Frank Fox. Boulder, Colorado: Westview, 1985.

10. Katz, Bill. "Publishing, Serials." *The ALA Yearbook of Library & Information Services: A Review of Library Events, 1986,* Volume 12, pp. 254–56. Chicago, Illinois: American Library Association, 1987. p. 256.

11. Rush, Ramona R., Carol E. Oukrop, and Sandra W. Ernet. *More Than You Ever Wanted to Know About Women and Journalism Education.* Paper presented before the Division of Minorities and Communications at the convention of the Association for Education in Journalism, Carbondale, Illinois, August 1972. Referenced by Nancy W. Sharp et al. *Faculty Women in Journalism and Mass Communications: Problems and Progress.* Syracuse, New York: Gannett Foundation, 1985. pp. 29–30.

12, 13, 14. Sharp, Nancy W., et al. *Faculty Women in Journalism and Mass Communications: Problems and Progress.* Syracuse, New York: Gannett Foundation, 1985. p. 30, p. 31., p. 34.

15. Blum, Debra E. "Black Woman Scholar [Sondra A. O'Neal] at Emory University Loses 3-Year Battle to Overturn Tenure Denial, But Vows to Fight On." *Chronicle of Higher Education* 34 (June 22, 1988): A15–A16.

16. International Congress on Peer Review in Biomedical Publication, Chicago, Illinois, May 10–12, 1988. Correspondence from the American Medical Association, 535 North Dearborn Street, Chicago, Illinois 60610.

17. Lloyd, James E. "Selling Scholarship Down the River: The Pernicious Aspects of Peer Review." *Chronicle of Higher Education* 30 (June 26, 1985): 64.

18. Ceci, Stephen J., and Douglas P. Peters. "Letters of Reference: A Naturalistic Study of the Effects of Confidentiality." *American Psychologist* **39** (January 1984):29–31. Four years later, University of Chicago Press *Social Service Review* editor John R. Schuerman's declaration that "these days, deception in social research is almost universally condemned" was quoted by the *Chronicle of Higher Education* in its reportage that begins, "The editors and reviewers of a number of journals in social work and related fields have been stung." Reference is made to Schuerman's "rejecting the paper and offering her a chance to respond to the charge of plagiarism." My requests of both *Chronicle of Higher Education* and *Social Service Review* editors for further information, sharing of the embarrassing "multiple sub-missions," or forwarding my request were not answered. (34 [February 3, 1988]: A4). "Her" identity remained unknown until the *Chronicle of Higher Education* reported that William B. Epstein had submitted the "bogus article" to journals as part of a study of review procedures. (35 [November 2, 1988]: A1, A7).

"Selling Scholarship Down the River: The Pernicious Aspects of Peer Review." *Chronicle of Higher Education* **30** (June 26, 1985): 64.

20. Lloyd refers to David F. Horrobin's "Peer Review—A Philosophically Faulty Concept Which Is Proving Disastrous For Science." *Behavioral and Brain Sciences* **5** (1982): 217–218.

21. Armstrong, Jon. "Barriers to Scientific Contributors—The Author's Formula." *Behavioral and Brain Sciences* **5** (1982): 197–99.

22. Lloyd, James E. "Selling Scholarship Down the River: The Pernicious Aspects of Peer Review." *Chronicle of Higher Education* **30** (June 26, 1985): 64.

23. Stieg, Margaret F. "Refereeing the Editorial Process: The *American Historical Review* and Webb." *Scholarly Publishing* **14** (February 1983): 99–122.

24. *Guidelines for Authors, Editors and Publishers of Literature in the Library and Information Field.* Adopted by ALA Council, 1983. Prepared by the ALA Library Information Literature Membership Initiative Group. 5 pp.

25. Stanton, Domna C. "What's In A Name? The Case for Author-Anonymous Reviewing Policies." In *Women in Print, Volume II: Opportunities for Women's Studies Publication in Language and Literature*, pp. 65–78. Edited by Joan E. Hartman and Ellen Messer-Davidow. New York: Modern Language Association of America, 1982.

26. Luey, Beth. *A Handbook for Academic Authors.* "Journal Articles," pp. 7–22. New York: Cambridge University Press, 1987.

27. When both worked full-time year-round, the average American woman earned 64¢ for every dollar received by the average American man in 1984. ["20 Facts on Women Workers." *Fact Sheet* No. 86–1, U.S. Department of Labor, Women's Bureau, 1986.] Despite increases in women's labor force participation, education, or experience levels, the wage gap actually widened between 1955 (when women averaged 65 percent of men's earnings) and 1981 (when women averaged only 59 percent). At 63.5 percent in 1983, the wage gap was wider than it had been thirty years earlier. "If women were paid the same wages that men of similar qualifications earn, about half the families now living in poverty [in the United States] would not be poor." [June 1, 1988, communication from the Women's Economic Agenda Project, 518 17th Street, #200, Oakland, CA 94612. pp. 1, 2.]

28. In March 1985, 79 percent of women 25–64 years of age with four or more years of college were in the labor force, whereas only 44 percent of women with less than four years of high school were labor force participants. [*Fact Sheet* 86–1.] Data comparing educational attainment and monthly income of women and men as of spring 1984 showed an average monthly income of women of $734.00 and of

men $1,620.00; 0.2 percent of the adult women surveyed held the doctorate, but insufficient data exist to determine their monthly income. Monthly income of the men doctorates (9.7 percent) was $3,667.00. Women holding the master's degree (3.0 percent) earned $1,645.00 while master's degree males (3.8 percent) had monthly incomes of $2,843.00. ["Educational Attainment and Monthly Income." *Chronicle of Higher Education* **34** (October 14, 1987):A36.]

    29. College and university athletic directors showed a 53.4 percent differential favoring males' median salaries in 1985–1986; library service directors, 25.8 percent; library and information sciences deans, 15.6 percent; food services directors, 34.3 percent; student health services directors who are physicians, 18 percent; development and alumni affairs directors, 30.4 percent; and social work deans, 19.7 percent differentials favoring males in each case. [College and University Personnel Association's 1985–1986 Administration Compensation Survey.]

    30. *Chronicle of Higher Education* **33** (January 14, 1987).

    31. "Information for Authors" announcement of *Psychology of Women Quarterly*, undated.

    32. "Instructions for Authors" announcement of Haworth Press: *Women & Politics*, undated.

    33. Turner, Judith Axler. "U.S. Research Libraries Search for Ways to Combat Spiraling Subscription Costs of Scholarly Journals." *Chronicle of Higher Education* **34** (June 8, 1988): A4, A6.

    34. MIMP: *Magazine Industry Market Place 1986*. "Publishers of Multiple Periodicals" section.

    35. *Chronicle of Higher Education* **34** (January 13, 1988): A4.

    36. *Feminist Periodicals: A Current Listing of Contents*. Madison, Wisconsin: Office of the Women's Studies Librarian-at-Large, University of Wisconsin System, 1981– .

    37. Basow, Susan, and Nancy T. Silber. "Student Evaluations of College Professors: Are Female and Male Professors Rated Differently?" *Journal of Educational Psychology* **79** (September 1987): 308–14.

Bibliography

In addition to many of the titles cited in the Notes, the following publications and mentioned tools within the Resources section should be consulted.

Arnold, June. "Feminist Presses and Feminist Politics." *Quest: A Feminist Quarterly* 3 (1976): 18–26.

Bridgewater, Carol A., et al. "Pretenure and Posttenure Productivity Trends of Academic Psychologists." *American Psychologist* 37 (February 1982): 236–38.

Bunch, Carol A., et al. "Feminist Journals: Writing for a Feminist Future." In *Women in Print, Volume II: Opportunities for Women's Studies Publication in Language and Literature*, pp. 139–52. Edited by Joan E. Hartman and Ellen Messer-Davidow. New York: Modern Language Association of America, 1982.

Casewit, Curtis W. *Freelance Writing: Advice from the Pros, New Rev. Edition*. New York: Collier, 1985.

Cole, Jonathan R., and Harriet Zuckerman. "The Productivity Puzzle: Persistence and Change in Patterns of Publication of Men and Women Scientists." In *Women in Science, Volume 2: Advances in Motivation and Achievement*. Edited by Marjorie W. Steinkamp and Martin L. Maehr. Greenwich, Connecticut: JAI, 1984.

According to sociologist Cole in his *Fair Science: Women in the Scientific Community* (New York: Free Press, 1979), "The measurable amount of sex-based discrimination against women scientists is small. The data do not require that we modify prior conclusions that the scientific stratification system is basically universalistic." Karen Oppehheim Mason found the data did not support Cole's conclusion. (Mason's book review appeared in *Science* **208** [April 18, 1980]: 277–78.) Later, Cole summarized his empirical studies (*American Scientist* **69** [July–August 1981]: 385–91), saying that there is "significant gender-based discrimination in the promotion of female scientists to tenure and high academic rank." Although women scientists have as high intelligence quotients as their male colleagues do, the women publish less than the men. One reason for this, Cole says, may be that "many women continue to be excluded from the very activities that allow for full participation and growth, or productivity . . . the informal activities of science — the heated discussions and debates in the laboratory, inclusion in the inner core of the invisible colleges, full participation in the social networks where scientists air ideas and generate new ones."

Ferguson, Marjorie. *Forever Feminine: Women's Magazines and the Cult of Femininity.* London: Heinemann, 1983.

Forscher, Bernard K. "The Role of the Referee." *Scholarly Publishing* **11** (January 1980): 165–69.

Harman, Eleanor, and R.M. Schoeffel. "Our Readers Report." *Scholarly Publishing* **6** (July 1975): 333–340.

Katz, Michael J. *Elements of the Scientific Paper.* New Haven, Connecticut: Yale University Press, 1985.

Kroenfeld, Jennie J. "Publishing In Journals." In *Scholarly Writing & Publishing: Issues, Problems and Solutions*, pp. 17–32. Edited by Mary Frank Fox. Boulder, Colorado: Westview, 1985.

Maddox, Robert C. "'We Still Have Quite a Backlog of Articles.'" *Scholarly Publishing* **6** (January 1975): 127–35.

Penaskovic, Richard. "Facing Up to the Publication Gun." *Scholarly Publishing* **16** (January 1985): 136–40.

Reitt, Barbara B. "An Academic Author's Checklist." *Scholarly Publishing* **16** (October 1984): 65–72.

Sachs, Harley L. "The Publication Requirement Should Not Be Based Solely on 'Refereed' Journals." *Chronicle of Higher Education* **35** (October 19, 1988): B2.

Scal, Marjorie. "The Page Charge." *Scholarly Publishing* **3** (October 1971): 62–69.

Wheeler, Helen R. "A Feminist Researcher's Guide to Periodical Indexes, Abstracting Services, Citation Indexes, and Online Databases." *Collection Building: Studies* . . . **5** (Winter 1983/1984): 3–24. Also, 1988 edition.

Whitsitt, Julia. "From Observed Courtesies to Glib Unconcern: 35 Years of Scholarly Writing, MLA Style." *Chronicle of Higher Education* **32** (March 5, 1986): 104.

Woolf, Patricia K. "'Pressure to Publish' Is a Lame Excuse for Scientific Fraud." *Chronicle of Higher Education* **34** (September 23, 1987): A52.

Chapter Three

Sword Blades and Poppy Seed: The First Book Publication

"All books are either dreams or swords. You can cut, or you can drug, with words." Amy Lowell (1874–1925). American poet and critic. *Sword Blades and Poppy Seed*. Macmillan, 1914; reprinted by Haskell.

Unlike Mary Daly, Angela Davis, Betty Friedan, Germaine Greer, Barbara Jordan, Kate Millett, Toni Morrison, Jehan Sadat, and others whose reputations within and outside the academy include good and best-selling book publications, *you* must take the initiative in getting a recognized publisher's interest and a contract. Even before writing a book, the women just mentioned are able to expect much more of a publisher in contractual provisions and marketing guarantees than are other scholar-writers. Usually the unpublished author struggles merely to get the manuscript of her first book examined by a faceless publishing house. When she gets a contract, she may also have to contend with such tenure committee members' comments as "I never heard of ABC Press," and "not scholarly" when the book is published. Usually a first book is well underway when a contract for publication is signed by publisher and author. If this is your first book publication, you will likely need to have a completed manuscript in hand, as they say, *and* to take initiative. There is no law that requires you to peddle your manuscript, and you *should* aspire to being able, someday, to get a contract and an advance from a publisher and *then* write the book!

Returning to the present, you need to have a clear picture of what will be in your book and to what market it is addressed, and to have completed the groundwork research. There are five steps to publication of this book:

- *Prepare* your proposal package.
- *Identify* the right publisher(s).
- *Contact* publishers and get a contract.
- *Prepare* the manuscript for publication.
- *Follow-up* during and after production.

71

The fact that books by relative unknowns are not usually afforded the attention and consideration given to books by scholars who have already established their name and academic reputation is due to both low visibility of the author and the problems novice authors have with book publishing companies.[1] Professionally young scholars may be unaware of the many publishers in their field. They may rely on such hit-or-miss methods as roaming the exhibits area at conferences and conventions, where vendors and sales representatives operate. It is possible for a publisher with an impressive number of new books each year and a significant number of titles in print not to have instant name recognition and perhaps not to have a conference booth.

It is not unacceptable to contact publishing house editorial and acquisitions editors at a conference to discuss a contract for publication of your manuscript on a subject in which they publish, especially if you are located at great distance from publishers. It may be more productive to write to them beforehand to inquire about the possibility of an appointment during the conference, which communicates that you consider the publisher's time and your book worth making such arrangements. Do not expect a publisher to read your manuscript during the conference, although you should bring along a copy you can spare. Your strategy here is to sell the idea of publication of your book. You want a *contract* for a book which you have completed or which you will complete shortly. Before signing a contract with you, the publisher will expect to see an outline and at least the first and last chapters, possibly all of the book, in manuscript form. If interest is aroused, you may be encouraged to mail a proposal and what you have completed. Do this at once, with a cover letter reminding her or him of your meeting at ABC Association conference and the encouragement you received.

In a paper intended to orient newcomers, one faculty member has identified four types of personal and professional needs to be met at conferences and conventions: recognition, affiliation, audience, and power. In the "Fun and Games" section of her article, Anderson lists Game #2, "Know a Publisher," among social games she has observed being used to meet the need for affection and status.[2] Her suggestion that one visit the exhibits, as convention displays consisting largely of vendors' wares and salespeople are referred to, in order to "wangle an invitation to the company suite" does have some potential for getting published, however. It is not necessary to be in awe of a publisher or university press officer. The publishers portrayed in novels, motion pictures, and television—Shepherd "Shep" Henderson (James Stewart) of John Van Druten's *Bell, Book and Candle* . . . Gus LeRoy (Hal Holbrook) in Mary McCarthy's *The Group* . . . and Sir Theodore Allen Mourne of Ernest Raymond's *Gentle Greaves*—tend to be fictional types, men of the past.

There are several facts about publishers of trade books, including university presses, which you need to know in order to select the most appropriate ones to receive your proposal package and to structure the most judicious submission. Some of this information can be obtained from directories and a publisher's catalog or special list in your discipline, usually available at professional conferences. The publisher may include individual persons on a mailing list, and you can request that your name be placed on it; there may be a list on which to sign up in the conference exhibits booth. Some publishers rely on other channels to publicize their books and do not maintain mailing lists. They may focus on selling mainly to libraries or other audiences and markets and utilize mailing lists which they purchase or structure based on such job-titles as United States and Canadian college library acquisitions librarians or teachers of English. One of the bases on which to select a publisher is titles of books published in the last few years. If you are unable to acquire a publisher's current catalog to examine, consult the *Publishers' Trade List Annual* in the library reference department. The *Literary Market Place* lists many publishers and most of their concentrations and specializations, but not book titles. There are several aspects of a publisher's program which you need ideally to confirm before you approach any publisher. They include:

- whether unsolicited proposals for book publication are considered
- the language (and nation) in which it publishes and distributes
- the function of the publishing house. It might be an outlet for a professional association (e.g. Modern Language Association of America); an independent small press (e.g. South End); a university press (e.g. University of California Press); a textbook publisher which is part of a conglomerate (e.g. CBI Publishing Company, a subsidiary of Van Nostrand Reinhold Company, Inc., a division of the International Thomson Organisation); an independent feminist press (e.g. Cleis Press); or may have overlapping functions.
- its declared subject, professional, and other specializations, e.g. history, education, physics, scholarly books, textbooks, bibliographies, professional books, translations, etc.
- its market(s), e.g. subject-specialized audiences, bookstores, libraries, colleges, schools, professional people and groups, etc.
- its reputation . . . its regard as prestigious, respectable, well known, acceptable, "the" publisher in its and your field . . . generally *and* on your campus
- in addition to a publishable manuscript, anything else that is expected of the author, such as a "subsidy"
- the number of book titles the publisher is able to keep in print and the number of book titles published last year

- characteristics of titles, subjects, and authors published recently
- whether advances on the author's royalties are provided, and how often they are paid and accounting provided
- their version of the "standard contract," and how it would be adapted to your book and you
- whether they actively promote sales of books they publish, including advertising
- when the press was founded
- corporate and subsidiary relationships to other publishing entities, companies, and groups.

You need a publisher whose name on your resume and dossier will be irrefutable (read any of the following: scholarly, respected, acceptable, major, recognized) in the judgment of the beholder. Discuss this with your colleagues. Search for publishers combining characteristics relevant to your book and your goals. For starters, compile a list of publishers which:

- specialize and publish in your field, discipline, profession. Their records show it, or they declare commitment to it. They publish books for specific educational levels, audiences, or readers, and they publish formats appropriate to your book, e.g. instructional materials, reference books, textbooks, translations, bibliographies.
- publish in English (or your language) for distribution in English- (or other-) speaking and reading nations and populations
- seriously consider unsolicited proposals and submissions. Their records show that they are not restricted to inhouse staff or commissioned writers. They have taken chances and have published unknown authors and "first books." They are not dependent on blockbusters.
- promote their authors' books. They advertise. You may find that you have to relinquish this criterion first.

Do not eschew publishers because they are unknown to you or because they appear to be small. Many publishing entities which do not have name or size recognition are sturdy, reputable parts of the marketplace, not always part of a conglomerate structure. Types of publishers of books include:

- small presses, often associated in the past with "fine books"; today they are often regional or alternative presses. Most of the thousands of United States book publishers are very small.
- alternative presses, usually committed to ecology, social responsibility, humanism, and worthy causes, currently include several formerly "feminist" publishers
- feminist presses, a term not necessarily equivalent to women's studies

lines, women's books (books for women), or women's reading (reading for women)
- scholarly presses, perhaps overlapping "university presses"
- university presses, often combining the qualities of academe and trade publishing. Many publish "women's studies" books in traditional disciplines, although ". . . they could become more daring by seeking out books that are interdisciplinary and those that are more openly critical of prevailing modes of thought. Some of the most exciting books in the latter category are feminist critiques of science."[3]
- general trade publishers.

Trade books have traditionally been hardcover books aimed at general audiences and sold through normal trade outlets. Many trade books appeal to special audiences as consumers rather than professionals. So many special-interest works are published and sold to both general and special audiences that the term "trade book" has come to mean a book that carries a trade or long discount to booksellers and jobbers. There are now also paperbound trade books.

A useful family of reference books published by the R.R. Bowker Company consists of *Books in Print* and *Publishers' Trade List Annual*. *Books in Print* (BIP) is an annual listing of currently available, regardless of when published, English-language books. It has separate author, title and subject (using Library of Congress subject-headings) access volumes. *Publishers' Trade List Annual* (PTLA) consists of the contents of many publishers' catalogs which have been reprinted and alphabetically bound together. Note also the separate, small collection of small publishers' catalogs together at the beginning of the first PTLA volume.

Books which are out of print (OP) are no longer available on the open market, mainly because the publishers have ceased making further printings. It is often possible to purchase a new copy of a book which has recently become OP, even though the book is no longer listed in the current BIP, because there may be supplies in vendors', jobbers', and wholesalers' warehouses. In order to have its books included in the current BIP, a publishing house must publish at least three titles within a year (university presses and publishers of dictionaries, encyclopedias, atlases, and braille books are excepted), and the books must be available to the trade and for single copy purchase; imported books must have a sole U.S. distributor. The 1987–1988 BIP lists approximately 750,619 titles available from 22,500 United States (including Puerto Rico, Guam, and U.S. Virgin Islands) publishers.[4] Most nations have comparable books-in-print tools, e.g. *British Books in Print, Libros en Venta . . .*, etc. Many book titles are never retailed in bookstore outlets, although your bookstore may be willing to special-order a copy of an in-print book you request.

The vision of a bookstore display of books in colorful dustjackets and the expectation of almost any book being obtainable at any bookstore located within five minutes of campus are unrealistic. Some people will tend to judge your book based on their opinion of the publisher; some of them may also be the judges of your academic credentials. The only objection expressed in writing to Sharon Leder's scholarship when she challenged her denial of tenure was that Greenwood Press was "a nonscholarly press" and that her book would have to be published and receive "positive reviews in responsible journals." After she met the original criteria and had been offered a publisher's contract, the board insisted that she meet new criteria. The book? *The Language of Exclusion: The Poetry of Emily Dickinson and Christina Rossetti.*[5]

Some women scholars charge that, ultimately, evaluations of women's scholarly work—such as the criticism of Nancy Shaw's research as journalistic—are not true evaluations but an automatic response to what is seen as a commitment to a cause.[6] The ranking of book publishers has been considered by Arnold, and much of what she concludes also applies to journal publishing:

> A feminist might have a manuscript that is actively sought after by a prestigious academic publisher, but wish to place it with a feminist press. In this case, she may find that while the manuscript would be an impressive item on her publication record with an academic publisher, it would well be "discounted" with a feminist publisher.[7]

While it is not possible to guarantee which publishers will be deemed scholarly by your department, review board, or chancellor, it is sometimes possible to infer the names of acceptable publishers by checking book titles reviewed positively by academicians in periodicals such as *Choice*, the Association of College and Research Libraries' conservative review journal, which identifies reviewers' names and their affiliations in academe.

The publishing industry is going through change attributed variously to production costs (said to represent 25 percent of sales), computers, conglomerates, and competition. In 1986 Bertelsmann, a German publisher, became a giant of world publishing when it acquired Doubleday for a reported $475 million. Simon and Schuster and its parent company, Gulf + Western, remained the biggest United States book publisher, with revenues of more than $920 million for the year ending July 31, 1986.[8]

Distributors, wholesalers, vendors, and booksellers are parts of the mass media experiencing pressure for change, which ultimately influences authors, readers, scholarship, and libraries. Not all books being published can ever be stocked by a bookstore. Independent booksellers lack the advantages of higher discounts and promotional allowances which chain stores rely on. Millions of people who have money are *a*literate—they can but do not read. Many of the people who can afford to buy books, especially those who have recently acquired credit status, regard books and reading as luxury items. Public libraries have always been perceived as custodians of culture, respectability, and *books,* despite the efforts of socially responsible librarians to get recognition of and support for their provision of *information* in addition to tomes and programs combating illiteracy, which in the United States is growing by 10 percent every year.[9]

The move to multiple ownership of mass media has affected publishing houses. Conglomerate influence filters down to authors, buyers, and readers. For example, Scarecrow Press, founded in 1950 as an independent publisher, is now a subsidiary of Grolier, Inc., itself a recent acquisition of France-based Hachette; Grolier was ordered in the late 1970s by the Federal Trade Commission to cease and desist unfair sales practices.[10]

Whereas an author could in the past expect to receive an advance on her or his royalties, advances are no longer as forthcoming. Dissatisfaction among authors with the prices of scholarly publications and time lags in the publishing process is widespread.[11] Professional standards are lowered when publishers contract with authors who meet their contracted deadlines and hold the manuscript for a year before beginning actual production. This is yet another Big Business situation impacting on women with disparate effect, for the publisher and its parent companies have, not merely an attorney, but a firm of legal publishing industry specialists, and a woman is least likely in any adult population to have legal resources.

Publishers of all sizes and types—not just university presses—subject women authors to the delay-divide-discredit syndrome which the academy as an employer imposes in its practices with women who respond to discrimination or otherwise step out of their feminine role. If they are established authors whose track records belie innuendo, publishers are quick to acknowledge their being "bright" (young) or "feisty" (old). As in college and university life, the buddy system functions well across town-and-gown campus and publishing house borders.

Women in academe who have recognized and responded to sex discrimination have reported that one of the aspects of tangential retaliation and harassment is disparate treatment of their publications. The media have occasionally published reports of failure to retain, promote, or tenure a woman academic based on the *merit* of her book publications and her publisher, i.e. not on the fact that she had not published a book. A variation on this put-down is the failure to acknowledge and celebrate publication of a woman or feminist faculty member's new book, which on some campuses is a chummy routine.

Of the more than six thousand United States publishers' companies, 3.3 percent controlled 70 percent of the industry's volume in 1976.[12] West noted in 1978 in her contemporary classic, *The Passionate Perils of Publishing,* that even then a handful of large, brand-name companies controlled almost all the books produced in the United States. What's wrong with all this? Imperfect competition results in a few large firms producing *and* selling books. The trend toward consolidation in the book industry has led to takeovers. Marketing is centralized from wholesaler to the chain bookstore, like the oil business. When trusts come in, social responsibility goes out, prices go up. Conglomerates focus on higher profits through publication of books which are evaluated as most likely to be made into big blockbusters, which often exploit violence and personal insecurities. Authors who provide sensationalism, gothic escape, torrid historical novels, and formula genres are able to get agents who work on publishers to pay highly inflated prices, selling their author or book to the highest bidder. Some writers perceive conglomerate publisher tie-ins with war games, repressive governments, and the corporate crimes to which multinational firms seem prone.[13] By 1985, fifty male-controlled book, magazine and broadcasting conglomerates, newspaper chains, and film and recording studios dominated United States communications. Of the thirty book publishers controlling 70 percent of the market, two were headed by women, and these were owned by the Newhouse newspaper chain and Gulf + Western.[14] Ben Bagdikian reported in 1987 that twenty-six companies owned the majority of media outlets in the United States.[15]

Employees of publishing houses often have an acute case of what West describes as "identifying with the oppressor." Union organizing of an elitist "glamour" profession that is not perceived as a factory is difficult.[16] Like employer colleges and universities, many publishing houses have had female-sex discrimination in employment charges filed against them. There are basics which, until publication of Abramson's *The Invisible Woman,* had not even been touched on in the literary marketplace.[17] Her San Francisco–based publisher did not hesitate to say scornfully to me that "she peddled that manuscript up and down the West Coast." (Consider the possibility of a comparable statement by a company president about the author of a book documenting discrimination based on race.) There is a strong tendency to perceive female-sex discrimination as somewhat distinct among the several classes encompassed by the Civil Rights Act and Amendments. It is indeed different — so ingrained, historic, and pervasive as to be invisible to most males and some females. And institutions associated with academe are not more "professional" employers merely because they are viewed as more respectable, pointing up the handicap of assumptions and stereotypes. The university itself employs all types of workers in substantial numbers—clerical, technical, publishing, reprographics, communications, printing, and media. Abramson's next book, *Old Boys—New Women: The Politics of Sex Discrimination*, was published by Praeger, part of Holt, Rinehart & Winston, a subsidiary of Harcourt Brace Jovanovich, Inc., distributed by Gessler Publishing Company and distributor for Dryden Press—all owned by CBS Educational and Professional Publishing, a division of CBS, Inc.[18] I asked her to describe her experience getting it published.

What publishers did you approach?
    I can't really remember any longer which ones I approached. I remember there were many.
How did you go about getting a contract with Praeger?
    I approached them, as I approached others, with a query letter explaining who I am and what my book was about and asking whether they would care to see a sample chapter.
How did your publisher deal with you?
    Not very well—but through no fault of my original editor. I was the victim of a purchase of Praeger/Holt Rinehart & Winston by CBS. Promises made by Praeger for advertising and distribution went down the tubes after the CBS purchase.
Did you have or consider having an agent?
    No. I've dealt with agents in the past and found them more of a hindrance than a help for this type of book.
Did the WEEA or HEW do anything towards getting the book published?
    (Abramson had been the recipient of a small, individual grant under the United States Department of Health, Education and Welfare Women's Educational Equity Act, which had partially enabled creation of *Old Boys—New Women*.)
    In fact I'd say they were a negative in my case on everything except the money. The grant funds were at least half of what made the book possible. My grant was for $15,000, and I probably spent twice that much in producing the book. But it would have been impossible without at least that level of financial support. The other half of what made the book possible was the willingness of many very fine women to share their experiences with me. Without them there would have been no book.
What would you do differently?
    The only thing I might do differently would be to keep control over page proofs. Praeger wanted to turn out the book after galley proofs only (in the name of reaching the market with speed). They weren't any faster anyway. And the final book is riddled with typographical errors since I did not get a chance to look at page proofs and, apparently, no one at Praeger bothered to do so either.
Did you approach Jossey-Bass (publisher of her previous book)?
    No. My reason was that Jossey-Bass did no bookstore distribution and very little advertising for my 1976 book, *The Invisible Woman*. As it turns

out, despite promises, Praeger did even less than Jossey-Bass. So the book did not sell as well.

Did you prepare a proposal?

In a way, I did. As I said, my method was to send a query letter. For those publishers who responded positively, I sent an outline and two sample chapters. This way, I was able to query many publishers at once, which saves time. And time saving is quite important with this kind of book.

When did you get your WEEA grant?

I believe it was 1977. I traveled and did interviews throughout 1977 and wrote the book in 1978.

What differences were there between the grant product and the book?

The grant product was the book.

Did the grant enhance the publishers' perception?

Probably not, but it is hard for me to judge. In my case, I think my past publishing record was more important.

Did you have an editor at Praeger?

Not really. My editor left with the CBS purchase, and I was left to sort of float. (I had an excellent editor with Jossey-Bass.)

Did Praeger retain the copyright?

Yes, this is the usual case.[19]

Be prepared for impressive claims of incredible numbers of manuscripts submitted to a publisher by unpublished authors. Women may tend to accept readily (and to repeat) such overwhelming statements. Most "over the transom" proposals come to publishers from men. Statistics such as the University of California Press' publishing two hundred of six hundred proposals received each year should be kept in perspective. Many university presses operate as trade publishers, for profit. Association with academe may carry prestige, but a university press is not necessarily more respectable nor professional than the rest of the marketplace. Just as a college or university administration may like to brag that it has more applications from qualified students than it can accommodate, so academic press acquisitions management may paint pictures of business success which include many more manuscript submissions than can be considered for publication. The fact is that most of the 22,500 United States trade publishers are constantly searching for suitable manuscripts. Many houses, including smaller ones, select management personnel because they are "extremely well-connected" (a phrase used by one company president in admiration of a competitor's new vice president, editorial) whose strengths include ability to bring with them, attract, locate, and sign up authors, manuscripts, and projects. These company officers and managers may themselves not be successful academicians, university administrators, or authors of published books. One press's manuscript acquisitions code lists three categories or modes of consideration: author-initiated contact with the publishing house; author having had previous ties to the house or referred by someone who had some connection with it; and manuscript acquisition due to editor's initiative or contacts.[20]

Get systematic. Browsing bookstores and advertisements and prowling conventions and conferences are not systematic. Here is one model for generating a list of at least six publishers suited to your goals. The *Literary Market Place* (LMP) is an annual reference book in public and academic libraries which provides sections describing United States and Canadian publishers. Use the current LMP volume, arranged in several useful sections. The first and major section is a list of United States publishers, alphabetically arranged, from A.B. Cowles Company to Zondervan Publishing House. For each publisher, there are several types of basic information provided in a consistent display arrangement. Three indexes to these publishers make it possible to access them by subjects published, by fields of activity or types of publications, and by geographical location. Figure 3:1 is a reproduction from the alphabetical United States Book Publishers section of the 1988 LMP.

We would, however, first consult the classified indexes, and *then* move to the alphabetical list of publishing houses. The Book Publishers Classified by Subject Matter section provides numerous lists of publishers organized under such academic subjects as anthropology, archaeology, art, biological sciences, economics, government and political science, history, literature and literary criticism, music and dance, philosophy, physics, psychology, and social sciences and sociology. Publishers of books related to inter-disciplinary concerns are identified under such headings as Asian Studies, Black Americans, Foreign Countries, Public Administration and Urban Studies, Third World Studies, and Women's Studies. Publishers of books related to professions, often part of university higher education offerings, are identified under such headings as Architecture and Interior Design, Business and Marketing, Child Care and Development, Communications, Computer Science and Data Processing, Criminology and Law Enforcement, Education, Finance and Investments, Human Relations, Journalism and Writing, Labor and Industrial Relations, Library and Information Sciences, Medicine-Nursing-Dentistry, and Public Administration and Urban Studies.

"Women's studies" is the umbrella term adopted by some publishers and used instead of "women's interests." Many publishers refer to their "women's studies" books and journals; a small number have arrangements such as Routledge & Kegan Paul's Pandora Press and Pergamon Press's Athene Series. Locate and check out at least three subject categories, especially if yours is an interdisciplinary book. You may not always find a subject list which sounds sufficiently specific, or the "nearest" list may consist of relatively few publishers. Broaden a bit.

```
┌─────────────────────────────────────────┐
│                                         │
│        US Book Publishers (1)           │
│                                         │
│                                         │
│  The University of Michigan Press       │
│  Box 1104, 839 Greene St, Ann Arbor, MI │
│    48106                                │
│  SAN: 202-5329                          │
│  Tel: 313-764-4394                      │
│  Dir: Walter Sears                      │
│  Ed-in-Chief & Rts & Perms: Mary C Erwin│
│  Man Ed & Prodn Mgr: LeAnn Fields       │
│  Prom: Margaret Haas                    │
│  Nonfiction, textbooks, paperbacks; behavioral │
│    & biological sciences, anthropology, ecology │
│    & women's studies.                   │
│  1986: 40 titles. In print: 501 titles  │
│  Founded 1930                           │
│  ISBN Prefix(es): 0-472                 │
│  Imprints: Ann Arbor Paperbacks; Ann Arbor │
│    Science Paperbacks                   │
│  Foreign Reps: Feffer & Simons Inc (world │
│    exc Canada); Fitzhenry & Whiteside Ltd │
│    (Canada)                             │
│                                         │
└─────────────────────────────────────────┘
```

Figure 3:1 *Literary Market Place 1988*, page 148.

For a book about the subject(s) gerontology, gender, aging, and ageism, begin by considering publishers under Social Sciences and Sociology, Women's Studies, and Behavioral Sciences. Expand to Public Administration and Urban Studies, Education, Health and Nutrition, and Government and Political Science lists. Consider Black American, Ethnic, and Gay & Lesbian. At present there are no Asian-American or Hispanic-American lists but publishers with these authors and titles can be located if you persevere—e.g. consider Asian Studies.

There are two other LMP indexes to consult as part of the first step. Be sure to examine the Book Publishers Classified by Fields of Activity section in terms of your book's format or genre. Those with the most potential will probably be Bibliographies, Foreign Language and Bilingual Books, General Trade Books, Professional Books, Scholarly Books, Textbooks, and University Presses. (Occasionally this strategy might be supplemented at this point by checking the BIP subject volumes, in this case, under AGED WOMEN, and gleaning the frequent publishers.) Now move to the alphabetically arranged first section of the LMP: United States Book Publishers, and locate the displays for the publishers you have noted. Examine each entry overall to determine its potential relevance to your book and you. Transcribe the crucial data. In a large firm, there may be an editor responsible for your field; for example, Praeger's LMP listing identifies a Women's Studies and Sociology editor. For a smaller press with two or three executive titles listed, transcribe the name of the editor-in-chief.

Some publishers do not wish to identify their editors in print, e.g. Jossey-Bass. You can telephone the number listed here and request the name of the person who is presently acquistion editor for books in your field. There is a list of publishers' "800" telephone numbers elsewhere in this LMP edition, and the BIP Publishers' Volume (1987–1988, Volume 7) has a publishers' toll-free numbers section. There is, however, considerable other information in each display.

Suppose your manuscript relates to an aspect of nurses as professional managers and pay equity, or comparable worth. In the Subject Matter index section you could start by checking the Medicine-Dentistry-Nursing, Women's Studies, Management, Business, Economics, Education, Human Relations, Social Sciences and Behavioral Sciences in that order. You might quickly compile a list consisting of Human Sciences Press, Praeger, Saunders, and Springer publishers, each of which appears in the Professional Books list in the Activities and Types of Publications classified index section. Then you would study the individual display for each in the publishers' displays section to confirm your impression and to get further information and contact-data for each.

Some independent, scholarly, and university presses view disciplinary professional conferences, although convention-like, as a means of contacting prospective authors of books and authors with manuscripts which are in their specialized areas. The appropriate acquisitons editor may contact potential authors she or he has heard about before the conference. Not all publishers are located in New York City; some have several locations throughout the United States. It is also useful to use the LMP Book Publishers Classified Geographically section in order to take advantage of your being in or near a publisher's city and such conference cities as Atlanta, Chicago, New York and San Francisco. It is important not to assume that a publisher is small or does not have subject-specialized acquisitions editors on its professional staff, based on a relatively brief LMP display with few names and seemingly little information.

The LMP Imprints, Subsidiaries, and Distributors section can help to clear up some of the potential overlapping, inbreeding, conglomerate-related problems, so that you can avoid approaching what appear to be two distinct and unrelated publishers. An imprint is a publisher's line, e.g. Simon & Schuster's *Ourselves, Growing Older* is a Touchstone Book imprint. Not all publishers have separate imprints. Usually books published under a publisher's imprint have something in common. Simon & Schuster's *The New Our Bodies, Ourselves* was also a Touchstone imprint. The lists of literary agents and of awards, contests and grants are two of the other useful LMP provisions.

In January 1986 I provided technical assistance in getting published for United States Department of Education Women's Educational Equity Act

April 17, 1986

Dear:

    Disabled women have the highest unemployment and underemploy-
ment rate of men and women, disabled and nondisabled. In fact, four out
of five disabled women are unemployed. Research shows this group has
a great need for more appropriate career preparation. We are pleased to
tell you about a book we have written addressing this critical need,
*Reaching the Hidden Majority: A Leader's Guide to Career Preparation for
Disabled Women and Girls.* This book is a comprehensive guide to disabled girls' and women's career preparation.

    The authors collectively have over 25 years of experience in career
preparation for special needs populations; hold degrees in special education, vocational rehabilitation, and guidance and counseling. We have
been co-directing the Career Education for Disabled Women Project at
University of Wisconsin–Stout since 1983. This project is federally funded
through the Women's Educational Equity Act Program. We have conducted extensive literature reviews to locate similar books, including
ERIC and Psychological Abstract searches. While a variety of books have
been published which address career preparation for women, e.g. *How
Women Find Jobs: A Guide for Workshop Leaders* by V. Norwood and
Career Planning for Minority Women by S.M. Jackson, they do not address
the unique needs of women and girls with disabilities. Other books such
as *Planning Your Job Search: Making the Right Moves* by Aves and Anderson address employment for the disabled, but not disabled women. The
vast majority of career related books for women or the disabled are self-
help manuals rather than leader guides. The few books specifically addressing disabled women's issues, e.g. *Voices from the Shadows* by G.F.
Matthews focus on personal/social issues rather than career development.

    According to Richard Harris, National President of the Association on
Handicapped Student Service Programs in Post-Secondary Education,
and Coordinator of Handicapped Student Services at Ball State University,
our book "would be a valuable resource for service providers. The book
provides detailed instructions in providing a program of career preparation to help disabled women overcome the dual discrimination they will
encounter in the job market. I strongly endorse this publication because
of the expertise of the authors and importance of the topic."

    This book should be made available to a broad range of service pro-
viders. It would be advertised in guidance and counseling, career education, special education, and vocational rehabilitation trade journals such
as *Journal of College Student Personnel, Journal of Learning Disabilities,
Mainstream, Disabled USA, Exceptional Children, Teaching Exceptional*

**Figure 3:2. Query sent to fifteen publishers by the authors of *Reaching the Hidden
Majority*. Including the abstract, this query ran three pages and was sent out on
the authors' university letterhead.**

Children, and *The Advocate*. It could also be advertised through newsletters circulated by women's disability organizations; and direct mailings to members of associations such as Handicapped Organized Women, Women's Educational Equity Act Projects, Transition from School to Work Projects, and the Association for Handicapped Student Services in Post-Secondary Education.

An abstract of the book is included for your review. We would be happy to send you Table of Contents and sample chapters. Thank you in advance for considering publication of *Reaching the Hidden Majority: A Leader's Guide to Career Preparation for Disabled Women and Girls*.

We look forward to your response. We can be reached at (715) 232-1310 or (715) 232-1181, or write to The Career Education Project, 430 EHS, UW–Stout.

Sincerely,

Mary Hopkins-Best, Ed.D.
Associate Professor

Shirley Murphy, M.S.
Training Coordinator
Career Education for Disabled Women

Ann Yurcisin, Ed.S.
Director
Services for Students with Disabilities

*Reaching the Hidden Majority: A Leader's
Guide for Career Preparation of
Disabled Women and Girls*

Abstract

This book was written in response to the critical need for comprehensive and specific career preparation for disabled girls and women. The book is divided into eight topic chapters: Conquering Career Stereotypes; Utilizing Your Legal Rights; Assessing Your Career Potential; Asserting Yourself; Exploring Nontraditional Careers; Breaking the Barriers; Seeking Employment; and Balancing Personal and Professional Roles. Additionally, an annotated bibliography is included for each chapter topic and supplemental suggestions are included for conducting a workshop or class. Each chapter is divided into specific training activities

including time, group size, resources, learner objective, leader procedures, and evaluation. A broad variety of activities are included, e.g.
questionnaires, games, group discussions, self-directed activities, and lec-
tures. The majority of activities cost nothing to implement as student
materials are included in the book. The activities have been successfully
field tested with a wide range of disabilities and age groups. The activities
can be used individually or collectively for a workshop, class or counseling
situations.

   The book is intended for use by any individual or group providing
career training to girls and women who have a disability. This includes, but
is not limited to: guidance counselors, teachers, tutors, coordinators of services for students with disabilities, vocational rehabilitation staff, Private
Industry Council staff, employment services staff, parents, local vocational
education coordinators, work experience coordinators, and corporate
training staff.

(Figure 3:2 continued.)

grantees. Workshop participants from the University of Wisconsin–Stout
had titled their grant proposal *Career Education for College Women Who
Are Disabled.* In 1988 the resulting book, titled *Reaching the Hidden Majority: A Leader's Guide to Career Preparation for Disabled Women and
Girls,* was published by Carroll Press, which, according to its LMP listing,
publishes textbooks and reference books for school and personal counselors
with emphasis on career guidance. This press is listed under the subjects
Social Sciences and Sociology, Self-help, Psychology and Psychiatry, and
Education. The authors' initial three-page overture (Figure 3:2) was
directed to fifteen publishers. Four requested sample chapters, and the
authors then narrowed it to Carroll Press.

   The LMP includes a section listing foreign publishers with United
States offices and has a Canadian Book Publishers section. The *International Literary Market Place* is a LMP counterpart volume covering one hundred sixty nations. *Cassell's Directory of Publishing,* published in England,
lists British Commonwealth publishers and provides a Women's Studies
list. The *Small Press Record of Books in Print* has a companion volume, the
International Directory of Little Magazines and Small Presses. Details of
these and other reference books with some of this information are provided
in the Resources section. Professional associations and levels of government
sometimes publish. The *Encyclopedia of Associations,* which is available in
print form and for on-line searching, includes organizations which publish.
Some, like the American Association of University Professors and the Older
Women's League, are not listed in LMP. The word "association" does not
always appear in a group's title.

After you have groomed your list of publishers, it may be possible to arrange them in a priority order. You may still eliminate some from consideration by examining their catalogs or special brochures of current books in your field. To request a catalog from a publisher, use your letterhead. While writing, perhaps also request a copy of the publisher's guidelines for its authors. If you cannot obtain a copy of a publisher's current catalog, consult the PTLA. Small and large publishers can represent both advantages and disadvantages for authors and for women's studies books. Small publishing houses are more likely to sign unknown authors with interesting proposals, and they can keep a book in print longer. But they tend to provide the author with smaller and even no advances on her or his royalties and to put out less on promotion and even nothing on advertising.

The chart on pages 90–106 identifies book publishers (self-) listed in the 1988 LMP and PTLA as having a women's studies subject-specialization, typically among other subject-specializations, and publishing English-language books. Interestingly, only six of these publishers appear in both the LMP's and PTLA's women's studies lists: Greenwood Press, Llewelyn Publications, Modern Language Association of America, and the University of Michigan, North Carolina, and Oklahoma presses. Keep in mind in using this list that some publishers have not self-listed under the LMP women's studies subject-category, but do have a women's studies line, i.e. more than a token woman-sounding title. There are many small publishers not included in LMP and some not even in PTLA. This is not intended to convey a comprehensive or authoritative list of "women's studies publishers," which would be difficult to define as well as compile. Keep in mind that there are other women's studies book publishers worth considering, but they are not listed here for any number of reasons. For example, some publishers are simply not listed in LMP or even PTLA, or they might be listed in these and other directories but not identified under women's studies subject-specializations, e.g. Mayfield is a publisher of college level texts designed to serve undergraduate course programs and has published all editions of Freeman's *Women: A Feminist Perspective;* the Calyx Editorial Collective has produced *Women and Aging* (1986) and *Asian-American Women's Anthology* (1987); and Cleis Press's *Sex Work: Writings by Women in the Sex Industry* (1987) illustrates this feminist press's output. Some publishers do not identify any of their specializations. Refer to the Women's Institute for Freedom of the Press *Directory of Media* and to the *International Literary Market Place* for many of the women's studies publishers and feminist presses located in English-speaking nations and throughout the world, e.g. Hecate Press (Australia), Women's Educational Press (Canada), Editions des Femmes (France), Verlag Frauenoffensive (Federal Republic of Germany), Kali for Women (India), Attic Press (Republic of Ireland), and Shoukadoh Booksellers (Japan).

A sample nonfiction title published in the 1980s by each publisher has been provided wherever possible. (Space limitations require that only the surname of the primary author be listed.) Clearly "women's studies" can mean many things to these publishers and their authors! Other categories applicable to each publisher's major output — including trade, textbook, scholarly and professional books, bibliographies, and translations, which are especially relevant to nonfiction book publishing in academe — are identified as well as some subject areas for each publisher.

Submitting Your Proposal

Do not send a book manuscript to a publisher out of the blue. Wait until you have discussed it with a company representative and been encouraged to send it. Then address it to the person with whom you spoke, and mention your correspondence or conversation. Offer to send more than one copy, which will facilitate an outside review process. It is more likely, however, that you will be sending a proposal package consisting of two parts:

- A cover or conveyance letter addressed to the appropriate job-title person, by name if possible.
- An enclosure, which is the proposal, sometimes referred to as a prospectus.

Some authors prefer to send a cover letter which includes considerable information or even to build the proposal into letter form. An example is Figure 3:2. I suggest a relatively brief, typed cover letter *and* a separate detailed proposal covering the background of the book, its audience, prospective market, related and competitive titles, and author's qualifications, and including a detailed outline.

Although this may be your first book, you have some things going for you which you should highlight in your proposal. You are probably "affiliated" — on the faculty of, employed by, or a graduate student or research center associate at a college, university, or education-related agency, so use this title and this letterhead. You may have been involved in a related project or begun the work on the research, report, or book based on some enabling. If you have been funded or had a grant, consider this as recognition and worth mentioning in your cover letter or including among your qualifications to write this book described within the proposal. There may be a published author on the team involved in that project, or one of several persons authoring the book may be published. She or he may be the writer of the cover letter and should possibly be identified throughout the publication process as primary author.

The cover letter should not exceed one page in length. Telephone numbers with area codes and when you can be reached at them, as well as when a tape will record a message, should appear in the vicinity of your mailing address. Type at the top of your letter "Re [Book Title]." Address the person at the first publishing house on your list by name and title. Request her or his consideration of your book in terms of "a contract for publication." Point out that you are approaching this publisher first, or only this publisher at this time, if this is the case. Refer to the enclosed prospectus containing full information about your proposed book, and point out that a detailed outline is part of the prospectus; offer to send a chapter. Mention your personal availability and interest in discussing a contract at a forthcoming conference if you are not located in the same city, making clear that you have in mind an appointment (rather than an unscheduled encounter). Think in terms of at least an hour. You may have already acquired a copy of this publisher's manuscript preparation and submission guidelines and editorial policies, but if not, request them now, probably at the end of the letter. Keep a copy of the guidelines, and start your book's file with it.

I prefer to cover the following in the prospectus, although you can initiate them in your cover letter effectively if you do not exceed one page. Mention anything special. Perhaps the book is the result of a grant, in which case, clarify the copyright situation. Need for this book publication may be endorsed by Professor Big Name, an expert or practitioner in the field, or your doctoral or dissertation advisor or a dissertation committee member. If your book is to be a trade revision of your doctoral dissertation, emphasize that, while this book is related to your doctoral work, it is not the dissertation itself. It has been or will be revised and supplemented with several case studies, for example. If there is more than one author, clarify that you are the primary author. If you plan to use a word processor, describe the equipment. Indicate when the book will be completed, and provide a date when you anticipate being able to provide a complete manuscript. This date may appear in the contract. While an estimate, it should be realistic and specific.

Your prospectus is the enclosure, the proposal itself. It should be typed double-space, perhaps six pages in length. Your working title should contain all the key words and consist of a catchy preliminary title possibly followed by a dash, semicolon, or colon and a descriptive, longer subtitle. It is important to provide a statement of the problem or topic and the rationale for this book. If it is a textbook, indicate the grade-level span or other audience. If there is potential for course adoption *[continued on page 107]*

Book Publishers in the United States Associated with "Women's Studies" Publications

Publisher and Recent Title	ABC-Clio — Iglitzin, *Women in the World, 1975–1985: The Women's Decade.* 1986.	Abingdon Press — Kilgore, *The Intimate Man: Intimacy and Masculinity in the 80s.* 1984.	Alicejames Books — Aguero and Goodman, *Thirsty Day & Permanent Wave.* 1977.
Fields of Activity			
TRANSLATIONS, BILINGUAL, FL*			
TEXTBOOKS (MAINLY COLLEGE)	●	●	
BIBLIOGRAPHIES	●		
PROFESSIONAL PUBLISHER	●		
SCHOLARLY PUBLISHER	●	●	
UNIVERSITY PRESS			
TRADE PUBLISHER		●	●
WOMEN'S STUDIES PUBLISHER	●	●	●
Subject Areas	Library and information science; political science.	Theology and religion; music program; learning and multimedia; psychology and psychiatry.	Poetry primarily by women.
Also Publishing in:			
BUSINESS, ECON, FINANCE			
HISTORY	●	●	
SCIENCE			
SOCIAL/BEHAVIORAL SCIENCE	●		
COMMUNICATIONS			
LITERATURE, CRITICISM, ESSAYS			
GOVERNMENT/POLITICAL SCIENCE	●		

*FL: Foreign Language Publications

Alyson Publications
Adelman, *Long Time Passing: Lives of Older Lesbians*. 1986.

Gay and lesbian fiction and nonfiction.

Antelope Island Press
Luchetti, *Women of the West*. 1982.

Arte Público Press
Castillo, *Women Are Not Roses*. 1984.

Biography; Hispanic-American authors.

Beacon Press
Martin, *The Woman in the Body: A Cultural Analysis of Reproduction*. 1987.

Theology and religion; anthropology; philosophy; psychology.

Bergin & Garvey
Hamilton, *Women and Nutrition in Third World Countries*. 1984.

Third World; anthropology; child care and development; education; maternity; Jewish studies; gerontology.

Branden Publishing Co.
King, *Sarah Miriam Peale—America's First Woman Artist*. 1987.

Religion; naval and maritime; psychology and psychiatry; aviation; art; ethnic; biography; child care and development; language arts; music and dance.

Brookings Institution
Steiner, *Abortion Dispute and the American System*. 1983.

Education; foreign policy.

Chandler & Sharp
Kikumura, *Through Harsh Winters: The Life of a Japanese Immigrant Woman*. 1981.

Anthropology; psychology and psychiatry.

Also Publishing in:

	Cherry Valley Editions	City Lights Books	Cornell University Press	Crossing Press
BUSINESS, ECON, FINANCE				
HISTORY			●	
SCIENCE			●	
SOCIAL/BEHAVIORAL SCIENCE				
COMMUNICATIONS				
LITERATURE, CRITICISM, ESSAYS	●	●		●
GOVERNMENT/POLITICAL SCIENCE			●	

Subject Areas

Cherry Valley Editions	City Lights Books	Cornell University Press	Crossing Press
Poetry.	Third World; anthropology; biography; religion.	Anthropology; religion; music.	Feminist and gay topics; health; birth.

Fields of Activity

	Cherry Valley Editions	City Lights Books	Cornell University Press	Crossing Press
TRANSLATIONS, BILINGUAL, FL*	●	●		
TEXTBOOKS (MAINLY COLLEGE)				
BIBLIOGRAPHIES				
PROFESSIONAL PUBLISHER				
SCHOLARLY PUBLISHER	●		●	
UNIVERSITY PRESS			●	
TRADE PUBLISHER	●		●	●
WOMEN'S STUDIES PUBLISHER	●	●	●	●

Publisher and Recent Title

Cherry Valley Editions
Peters' Black and Blue Guide to Current Literary Journals. 1983.

City Lights Books
Hayton-Keeva, *Valiant Women in War and Exile*. . . . 1987.

Cornell University Press
Lamphere, *From Working Daughters to Working Mothers*. . . . 1987.

Crossing Press
Johnson, *Going Out of Our Minds: The Metaphysics of Liberation.* 1987.

Publisher / Entry	Subject	1	2	3	4	5	6	7	8
Curbstone Press Rasmussen, *If It Really Were a Film.* transl. 1982.	Poetry.	•							
Diemer, Smith Publishing Stephenson, *Women's Roots, Status and Achievements in Western Civilization.* 1986.	Anthropology.		•						
Duke University Press Cohn, *Romance and the Erotics of Property: Mass Market Fiction for Women.* 1988.	Americana; blacks and Afro-Americans.			•					
East Rock Press				•	•	•			
Exposition Press of Florida Childs, *Fabric of the Era.* 1982.	Anthropology; behavioral sciences; East-West relations; East Asia.				•	•	•		
Fairleigh Dickinson University Press Adler, *Women of the Shtetl. . . .* 1980.	Religion; anthropology; music; naval maritime; psychology and psychiatry.			•	•	•	•		
Feminist Press at the CUNY Howe, *Everywoman's Guide to Colleges and Universities.* 1982.	Music; religion; psychology and psychiatry.						•		
Firebrand Books Randall, *This Is About Incest.* 1987.	Education; biography; children's books.							•	
Ford Foundation Stimpson, *Women's Studies in the United States.* 1986.	Third World; lesbian studies.								•

Publisher and Recent Title

Garland — Miller, *The Hand That Holds the Camera.* 1988.

General Hall — Fields, *Future of Women.* 1985.

Georgia State University, College of Business Administration. Henderson, *Job Pay for Job Worth.* 1981.

Greenwood Press — Zaimont, *The Musical Woman: An International Perspective, 1983.* 1984.

Growing Pains Press — Hunter, *The Rest of My Life.* 1981.

Subject Areas

Publisher	Subject Areas
Garland	Architecture; medicine; technology.
General Hall	Black studies; philosophy; education; theater.
Georgia State University	Advertising.
Greenwood Press	Psychology & psychiatry; music; blacks and Afro-Americans; music.
Growing Pains Press	

Fields of Activity

	Garland	General Hall	Georgia State	Greenwood	Growing Pains
TRANSLATIONS, BILINGUAL, FL*					
TEXTBOOKS (MAINLY COLLEGE)		●			
BIBLIOGRAPHIES				●	
PROFESSIONAL PUBLISHER				●	
SCHOLARLY PUBLISHER	●	●		●	
UNIVERSITY PRESS					
TRADE PUBLISHER					
WOMEN'S STUDIES PUBLISHER	●	●		●	●

Also Publishing in:

	Garland	General Hall	Georgia State	Greenwood	Growing Pains
BUSINESS, ECON, FINANCE	●				
HISTORY		●		●	
SCIENCE	●	●			
SOCIAL/BEHAVIORAL SCIENCE		●	●	●	
COMMUNICATIONS		●		●	
LITERATURE, CRITICISM, ESSAYS		●			
GOVERNMENT/POLITICAL SCIENCE		●		●	

Guilford Press
Brodsky, *Women and Psychotherapy.* 1980.

Behavioral sciences; audiovisual materials; geography & geology; psychology & psychiatry; neurosciences.

G.K. Hall
Weitz, *Femmes: Recent Writings on French Women.* 1985.

Art; library and information science; humanities.

Harcourt Brace Jovanovich
McCarthy, *How I Grew.* 1987.

Psychology; education; medicine, dentistry and nursing.

Harrington Park Press
Golub, *Health Needs of Women as They Age.* 1985.

Behavioral sciences; psychology and psychiatry; gay, feminist.

Holmes & Meier
Berkin, *Women, War, and Revolution.* 1980.

Blacks and Afro-Americans; humanities; Judaica; art and costume

Hudson Hills Press
Carmean, *Sculpture of Nancy Graves: A Catalogue Raisonné.* 1987.

Archaeology; art; biological sciences; photography.

Human Sciences Press
Lesnoff-Caravaglia, *World of the Older Woman: Conflicts and Resolutions.* 1983.

Education; medicine, dentistry and nursing; behavorial sciences; religion.

I L R Press
Cook, *Working Women in Japan: Discrimination, Resistance and Reform.* 1980.

Blacks and Afro-Americans; law and legal; personnel management; labor and industrial relations.

Also Publishing in: / **Subject Areas** / **Fields of Activity** / **Publisher and Recent Title**

Publisher and Recent Title	Fields of Activity	Subject Areas	Also Publishing in:
Ide House — Templeton, *Woman in Yorkist England.* 1984.	TEXTBOOKS (MAINLY COLLEGE); PROFESSIONAL PUBLISHER; SCHOLARLY PUBLISHER; WOMEN'S STUDIES PUBLISHER	Behavioral sciences; black Americans; education.	HISTORY
Impact Publishers — Phelps, *Assertive Woman: A New Look.* 1987.	WOMEN'S STUDIES PUBLISHER	Child care and development; parenting; assertive behavior.	
Indiana University Press — Andrews, *Sisters of the Spirit: Three Black Women's Autobiographies of the 19th Century.* 1986.	SCHOLARLY PUBLISHER; UNIVERSITY PRESS; TRADE PUBLISHER; WOMEN'S STUDIES PUBLISHER	Blacks and Afro-Americans; philosophy.	HISTORY; LITERATURE, CRITICISM, ESSAYS
Institute for Policy Studies — *Legislative Handbook on Women's Issues.* 1976.	SCHOLARLY PUBLISHER; WOMEN'S STUDIES PUBLISHER	Economics; Third World; international affairs; foreign policy.	GOVERNMENT/POLITICAL SCIENCE

Fields of Activity categories: TRANSLATIONS, BILINGUAL, FL*; TEXTBOOKS (MAINLY COLLEGE); BIBLIOGRAPHIES; PROFESSIONAL PUBLISHER; SCHOLARLY PUBLISHER; UNIVERSITY PRESS; TRADE PUBLISHER; WOMEN'S STUDIES PUBLISHER

Also Publishing in categories: BUSINESS, ECON, FINANCE; HISTORY; SCIENCE; SOCIAL/BEHAVIORAL SCIENCE; COMMUNICATIONS; LITERATURE, CRITICISM, ESSAYS; GOVERNMENT/POLITICAL SCIENCE

International Publishers
Reetz, *Clara Zetkin as a Socialist Speaker.* 1987.

Blacks and Afro-Americans; contemporary Marxism-Leninism.

Johns Hopkins University Press
Forster, *Woman's Life in the Court of the Sun King.* 1985.

Anthropology; blacks and Afro-Americans; psychology and psychiatry.

Labyrinth Press
Ferrante, *Woman as Image in Medieval Literature.* 1985.

Philosophy; theology.

Llewellyn Publications
Stein, *Women's Spirituality.* 1987.

Astrology; occult; New Age sciences.

Louisiana State University Press
Budick, *Emily Dickinson and the Life of Language.* 1985.

Regional; music.

McFarland & Company, Inc., Publishers
Martin, *The Servant Problem: Domestic Workers in North America.* 1985.

General reference; library and information science; performing arts; humanities and social sciences.

Macmillan Publishing Company
Badinter, *Mother Love: Myth and Reality.* 1981.

Anthropology; blacks and Afro-Americans; music; medicine, dentistry and nursing; religion; naval and maritime; psychology and psychiatry.

Meyer Stone Books
Berryman, *Liberation Theology . . . Latin America.* 1987.

Theology and religion; Third World.

Publisher and Recent Title	Business, Econ, Finance	History	Science	Social/Behavioral Science	Communications	Literature, Criticism, Essays	Government/Political Science	Subject Areas	Translations, Bilingual, FL*	Textbooks (Mainly College)	Bibliographies	Professional Publisher	Scholarly Publisher	University Press	Trade Publisher	Women's Studies Publisher
Modern Language Association of America — Stringer, *Stepping Off the Pedestal: Academic Women in the South.* 1982.				●		●		Blacks and Afro-Americans; education; journalism and writing.	●	●	●		●			●
Morning Glory Press — Lindsay, *Pregnant Too Soon: Adoption Is an Option, Rev. Edition.* 1987.			●													●
William Morrow — Janeway, *Cross Sections: From a Decade of Change.* 1982.	●	●	●					Blacks and Afro-Americans; naval and maritime.							●	●
Naiad Press — Potter, *Lesbian Periodicals Index.* 1986.								Lesbian; feminist; fiction.	●		●					●

Column group headers: "Also Publishing in:" (Business through Government/Political Science), "Subject Areas", "Fields of Activity" (Translations through Women's Studies Publisher).

New American Library
Jong, *Parachutes and Kisses* (novel). 1984.

Anthropology; blacks and Afro-Americans; music, psychology and psychiatry; religion.

New Society Publishers
Goodman, *No Turning Back: Lesbian and Gay Liberation for the 80s.* 1983.

Education; Third World; ecology; nonviolent actions; anti-nuclear issues.

Northeastern University Press
Newman, *Gertrude Stein and the Making of Literature.* 1988.

Law and legal; music and dance; philosophy; psychology and psychiatry.

Ohio University Press
Andelin, *Mrs. Trollope: The Triumphant Feminine in the Nineteenth Century.* 1974.

Americana; philosophy.

Pantheon Books
Strasser, *Never Done: A History of American Housework.* 1982.

Sports and athletics; art; Americana.

Pathfinder Press
Borge, *Women and the Nicaraguan Revolution.* 1982.

Labor; philosophy; Afro-American, Chicano and women's liberation studies.

Pergamon Press, Ltd.
Haavio-Mannila, *Unfinished Democracy: Women in Nordic Politics.* 1985.

Behavioral sciences; psychology and psychiatry.

Persea Books
dePizan, *Book of the City of Ladies.* 1982.

Art.

Praeger Publishers
Varro, *Transplanted Woman: A Study of French-American Marriages in France.* 1988.

Behavioral sciences; international relations; psychology; military studies.

Also Publishing in:

	Random House	Reference Service Press	Lynne Reinner Publishers	Rémi Books	Rice University Press
BUSINESS, ECON, FINANCE	•				
HISTORY	•				•
SCIENCE	•				•
SOCIAL/BEHAVIORAL SCIENCE			•		•
COMMUNICATIONS			•		
LITERATURE, CRITICISM, ESSAYS					•
GOVERNMENT/POLITICAL SCIENCE	•		•		

Subject Areas

Publisher	Subject Areas
Random House	Drama and theater; music; psychology and psychiatry.
Reference Service Press	Blacks and Afro-Americans; education; ethnic.
Lynne Reinner Publishers	Third World; agriculture.
Rémi Books	Psychology and psychiatry.
Rice University Press	Americana; Texana; photography.

Fields of Activity

	Random House	Reference Service Press	Lynne Reinner Publishers	Rémi Books	Rice University Press
TRANSLATIONS, BILINGUAL, FL*	•				
TEXTBOOKS (MAINLY COLLEGE)	•		•		•
BIBLIOGRAPHIES		•			
PROFESSIONAL PUBLISHER			•		
SCHOLARLY PUBLISHER	•		•		•
UNIVERSITY PRESS					•
TRADE PUBLISHER	•				•
WOMEN'S STUDIES PUBLISHER	•	•	•	•	•

Publisher and Recent Title

Random House
Pagels, *Adam, Eve, and the Serpent*. 1988.

Reference Service Press
Schlachter, *Directory of Financial Aids For Women, 1987–1988*. 1987.

Lynne Reinner Publishers
Leahy, *Development Strategies and the Status of Women* . . . . 1986.

Rémi Books
Maxtone-Grahame, *Pregnant by Mistake*. 1987.

Rice University Press
McMillan, *Legend of Good Women*. 1987.

Routledge: Pandora Press
Wandora, *On Gender and Writing.* 1983.

Education; anthropology; psychology and film study; archaeology; architecture; Oriental studies; occult and mysticism; philosophy.

Rowman & Allanheld
Trebilcot, *Mothering: Essays in Feminist Theory.* 1983.

Art; computer science; geography; medical and nursing research; philosophy; statistics.

Scarecrow Press
Handy, *International Sweethearts of Rhythm.* 1983.

Art; music and dance; library science; film and television.

Seal Press
An Everyday Story: Norwegian Women's Fiction. 1984.

Self-help; fiction.

South End Press
Weinbaum, *Pictures of Patriarchy.* 1982.

Environment and ecology; radical history

Spinsters/Aunt Lute Book Co.
Kuzwayo, *Call Me Woman.* 1985.

Novels and nonfiction by women.

Springer Publishing
Lerman, *A Mote in Freud's Eye.* 1980.

Health and nutrition; behavioral sciences; medicine, dentistry and nursing.

SUNY Press
Afshar, *Women, State, and Ideology: Studies from Africa and Asia.* 1987.

Education; Middle East, Jewish, and Asian studies; philosophy; religion; public policy.

Summa Publications
Lewis, *The Literary Vision of Gabrielle Roy.* 1984.

Drama and theater; blacks and Afro-Americans; humanities.

Also Publishing in:

	Syracuse University Press	Thor Publishing	Thunder's Mouth Press	Transnational Publishers
BUSINESS, ECON, FINANCE				
HISTORY	•			•
SCIENCE				
SOCIAL/BEHAVIORAL SCIENCE				•
COMMUNICATIONS				
LITERATURE, CRITICISM, ESSAYS				
GOVERNMENT/POLITICAL SCIENCE				•

Subject Areas

- **Syracuse University Press:** Education; Americana; Middle East; Irish and medieval studies.
- **Thor Publishing:** Sports and athletics; self-defense; physical education.
- **Thunder's Mouth Press:** Blacks and Afro-Americans.
- **Transnational Publishers:** Law and legal; international law.

Fields of Activity

	Syracuse University Press	Thor Publishing	Thunder's Mouth Press	Transnational Publishers
TRANSLATIONS, BILINGUAL, FL*				
TEXTBOOKS (MAINLY COLLEGE)				•
BIBLIOGRAPHIES				
PROFESSIONAL PUBLISHER				•
SCHOLARLY PUBLISHER	•			•
UNIVERSITY PRESS	•			
TRADE PUBLISHER	•		•	
WOMEN'S STUDIES PUBLISHER	•	•	•	•

Publisher and Recent Title

Syracuse University Press
Callaway, *Muslim Hausa Women in Nigeria: Tradition and Change.* 1987.

Thor Publishing
Tegner, *Self-Defense and Assault Prevention for Girls and Women.* 1977.

Thunder's Mouth Press
Sanchez, *Homegirls and Handgrenades.* 1984.

Transnational Publishers
Stockland, *Creative Women in Changing Societies.* . . . 1982.

Twayne Publishers
Scharnhorst, *Charlotte Perkins Gilman.* 1985.

Music and dance; biography of world leaders.

University of Illinois Press
Callaway, *Gender, Culture, and Empire: European Women in Colonial Nigeria.* 1987.

Film; American and black studies; folklore; music.

University of Massachusetts Press
Lovenduski, *Women and European Politics: Contemporary Feminism and Public Policy.* 1986.

New England, American and Afro-American studies; art and architecture; philosophy; environment.

University of Michigan Press
Buss, *Dignity: Lower Income Women Tell of Their Lives and Struggles.* 1985.

Biological sciences; behavioral sciences; anthropology; environment and ecology.

University of Nebraska Press
Lecompte, *Emily; The Diary of a Hard-worked Woman, Emily French.* 1987.

Agriculture; natural resources; anthropology; musicology; philosophy; psychology; wildlife; Trans-Missouri West.

University of North Carolina Press
Rosenfeld, *Farm Women: Work, Farm, and Family in the United States.* 1985.

Americana; public administration and urban studies; regional

University of Oklahoma Press
Boyd, *Prioress's Tale, by Geoffrey Chaucer.* 1987.

Americana; anthropology; archaeology; music; naval and maritime; psychology and psychiatry.

University of Tennessee Press
Lauter, *Feminist Archetypal Theory: Interdisciplinary Re-visions of Jungian Thought.* 1985.

Blacks and Afro-Americans; anthropology; regional.

University Press of New England
Rohner, *Women and Children in a Bengali Village.* 1988.

Art; religion; environment and ecology; music; blacks and Afro-Americans.

Utah State University Press
Brooks, *Emma Lee.* 1984.

Americana.

Volcano Press
Greenwood, *Menopause, Naturally.* . . . 1984.

Health and nutrition; medicine, dentistry and nursing; psychology.

Wayne State University Press
de la Barre, *Women's Voices From Latin America.* . . . 1988.

Medicine, health and nutrition; psychology and psychiatry; research.

Wesleyan University Press
Birnbaum, *Liberazione Della Donna: Feminism in Italy.* 1986.

Drama and theater; religion; blacks and Afro-Americans.

Whitson Publishing
Lumpkin, *Women's Tennis: A Historical Documentary of the Players and Their Game.* 1981.

Drama and theater; education; humanities; anthologies.

Markus Wiener Publishing
Baxter, *Women's History.* 1984.

Biography; accounting; management.

Women-In-Literature
Dallman, *Woman Poet – The South.* 1987.

Women's Legal Defense Fund
Essentials of Child Support Guidelines Development. 1987.

Law and legislation.

Publisher and Recent Title

Worldwatch Institute
Newland, *The Sisterhood of Man.* 1979.

Yale University Press
Bartlett, *Sarah Grimke: Letters on the Equality of the Sexes and Other Essays.* 1988.

Fields of Activity

	Worldwatch Institute	Yale University Press
TRANSLATIONS, BILINGUAL, FL*		
TEXTBOOKS (MAINLY COLLEGE)		
BIBLIOGRAPHIES		
PROFESSIONAL PUBLISHER		
SCHOLARLY PUBLISHER		•
UNIVERSITY PRESS		•
TRADE PUBLISHER	•	
WOMEN'S STUDIES PUBLISHER	•	•

Subject Areas

Worldwatch Institute: Agriculture; environment and ecology; energy.

Yale University Press: Anthropology; music; religion; psychology and psychiatry.

Also Publishing in:

	Worldwatch Institute	Yale University Press
BUSINESS, ECON, FINANCE		•
HISTORY		•
SCIENCE	•	•
SOCIAL/BEHAVIORAL SCIENCE		
COMMUNICATIONS		
LITERATURE, CRITICISM, ESSAYS		
GOVERNMENT/POLITICAL SCIENCE		•

or supplementary reading, show how you know this is so. Indicate the antic-
ipated length of the manuscript, the estimated number of manuscript pages
in each chapter, and the relative number of pages of illustrations and bibliographic support. You can allow twenty manuscript pages for the index.

A delineation of your unique approach is important. You should be able
to describe your point of view in three hundred words. Think about all of
the books which have been written, or just those titles in print which sound
as if they are on the same subject or do what you are doing! Your premise
is that there *is* nothing else like your book, so it is needed, so it will sell.
But go on to demonstrate your awareness of the literature (the competition,
as it were) by referring comparatively to several other books—others who
have (not) done it. How is yours different—strengths and weaknesses of
others, what's unique and competitive about this content and your treatment of this material? In the case of research reportage, it might be your
methodology. Refer to your sources of data. If appropriate, clarify whether
this book is a collection of original or previously published articles, or a
single author study.

A list of at least ten periodicals to which review copies might be
dispatched will demonstrate further your knowledge of the market (audience) as well as need for the publisher to send out review copies. Another
list of perhaps twenty journals to receive announcements of the book's
publication, and reference to any specialized mailing lists to which you have
access, would also be impressive. These lists should include reviewing
media (e.g. *Choice*), scholarly journals in your field which publish book
reviews, "responsible journals," and newsletters with significant circula-
tions that announce new books. A list of nations where it would sell well
may be appropriate. Many publishers have cooperative arrangements with
others abroad. Communicate this in your proposal as a "plus," and make
sure that your contract provides you language rights throughout the
world.

Professor Big Name should be an authority in this field or subfield. If
she or he is willing to endorse your proposal or write a brief foreword for
the book, state this in the prospectus. Or perhaps you can recruit someone
of magnitude and direct relevance to the book's focus—as was Jessie Bernard to Theodore's *The Campus Troublemakers*—to write a brief foreword.
If possible, provide a list of six persons (at least half in academe), with their
titles and affiliations, whose subject-expertise and other characteristics
qualify them to evaluate this book proposal. One publisher's request for
"the names of at least three senior scholars (with their affiliations) who have
not read your manuscript, but who are working in your field and are
qualified to read and evaluate the manuscript for the Press" is typical.

An outline with descriptions of each chapter's contents, form, and
length is an important part of the prospectus.

Your credentials for authorship of this particular book will probably include degrees and institutions, previous publications, professional affiliations, and recognitions. Stress those things relevant to the proposed book. If you are a so-called reentry woman, I advise not including dates your degrees were received, and of course date of birth is rarely relevant to *anything*.

Keep a copy; put it in your file. Send your proposal package first class mail, and start a "watch" on your calendar.

Summary of What to Include in a Book Proposal

I. Cover or Conveyance Letter

Typed. On a letterhead. Keep a copy; start a file. No more than one page in length.

To appropriate person, job title, and by name.

Request consideration of your work in terms of a contract for publication.

Refer to enclosed prospectus containing full information.

Possibly:

Point out that you are approaching them first.

Request a gratis copy of their author's guidelines.

Conclude by:

Offering to send a chapter.

Indicating how much is completed and when the final copy will be completed.

Mentioning your personal availability to discuss the matter.

Optional in letter, but should appear in prospectus or letter:

Anything special, e.g. this work is the result of a grant from Major Foundation or other recognition, in which case, clarify the copyright and primary authorship.

Need for this book has been endorsed by Professor Big Name.

II. Prospectus (The Enclosure)

Typed. Double-space. Keep a copy; add to file. Six pages?

Working title.

Estimated date of completion of manuscript and how much of the work is completed.

Estimated length of manuscript.

Statement of problem or topic, importance and need (rationale) for the book.

Your unique approach, content, methodology, or design.

Primary and secondary audiences, potential market, users, readers
(level).
The literature. The competition; relate this to other books.
Titles of relevant periodicals for review copies and journals for an-
nouncements.
Authority's endorsement desirable.
A list of suggested evaluators.
Outline with description of each chapter's content, form, treatment,
length.
Author's credentials for this particular book.
Miscellaneous:
> Word processing.
> Your requirements for illustrations, maps, appendices.

Dr. Susan Pharr shares with us her experiences with university presses
and with getting her first book published. Pharr is Professor of Government
and Director of the Harvard University United States–Japan Relations Program. She received the Ph.D. degree from Columbia University in 1975.
Her doctoral dissertation was titled *Sex and Politics: Women in Social and
Political Movements in Japan.* Her book, *Political Women in Japan: The
Search for a Place in Political Life,* was published by the University of
California Press in 1981. When she contacted the Press, she had a com-
pleted manuscript.

> . . . The road to publishing a book for the first time is filled with difficulties
> for many people, and I was no exception. I initially approached the editor
> of a major academic press at the annual meeting of the Asian Studies
> Association, asking whether I might send my book manuscript to her when
> I completed it. The editor was pleasant, but non-commital. When the
> manuscript was ready, I then dispatched a single copy to the press, for
> which I was thanked, and told that a review would ensue. . . . After a full
> eighteen, anxiety-producing months, I finally decided that I had to
> withdraw the manuscript from the press. Before doing so, however, I had
> discussed the publication process with a friend who had already published
> a book with University of California Press. He told me that his experience
> with University of California Press had been excellent and suggested that
> I submit my manuscript there. Therefore I dispatched a letter to Phil
> Lilienthal, then head of the Asia list for the Press, and asked if I could
> speak with him at the Asian Studies Association meeting to discuss the
> possibility of sending them my manuscript. By that time I had learned from
> my colleague that I should ask for "simultaneous review"—something I
> hadn't even known about before. Since presses normally require two
> reviews in order to decide on publication, they have the option of either
> requesting reviews sequentially or requesting reviews simultaneously.
> Obviously, the first process is extremely time-consuming, since they wait

for the first reader's report to come in, and only then decide if the manuscript merits a second review. It is, in every sense, preferable to an author to get simultaneous review to avoid this riskier and more time-consuming route. I later learned that the first press to which I had submitted my manuscript would have undertaken a simultaneous review had I only sent them two manuscripts! Had I but known, I would have inundated them with copies of my manuscript. . . . At any rate, I requested simultaneous review of the manuscript this time. I found Phil Lilienthal extremely cordial at the AAS meeting. He asked me to send the manuscript as soon as I had withdrawn it from the other press (I had given him the full story). So, as soon as I had settled things with university press one, I dispatched two copies of the manuscript to California. They received it in early May, and by September had gotten back two favorable reader's reports and had accepted the manuscript. The volume came out approximately a year later.

Based on my experience, there are several words of advice that I would offer to anyone contemplating publishing their first book manuscript.

1. Talk to someone in your own field about the process. Things vary according to field, and it is good to talk to someone who has published with the press to which you are contemplating submitting a manuscript.

2. Always request simultaneous review of the manuscript if that option is available. It will greatly expedite the review process.

3. Ask the press if you can submit names of possible reviewers. In the case of California, if I remember correctly, I gave them a list of some 7–10 persons whom I regarded as potentially good reviewers of my manuscript. This came at my suggestion, not theirs, but it presented a marvelous opportunity, from my standpoint, to list the people whom I felt would be the best possible reviewers of a manuscript.

4. Also ask the press if you can mention people who would *not* be suitable reviewers. Particularly in the case of manuscripts that involve issues relating to women and gender, this is a prudent step, because as we all know, there are some scholars who are simply closed to research that deals with these types of issues. If the press is willing, in effect, to let you veto one or two persons whom you might be concerned about getting the manuscript, this will certainly ease your own mind. . . . California Press used one person from my list, and one scholar whom I had not listed.[21]

You may receive a form post card or other acknowledgment promptly. If nothing is received in six weeks, follow up with a letter which makes clear that you are inquiring whether your mailing has reached the publisher and that you do not expect a reaction at this point. If you do not receive a response within six more weeks, telephone. Some publishers never respond; most do. You may receive a form letter and questionnaire which seems to ask for all the information you have already provided. Whether you want to pursue this dubious routine is up to you. It depends on the questions, how many other publishers you have on your short list, and how much time you have.

There are several variables which may influence a publisher's interest.

Paperback format is not necessarily cheaper to produce. If there is a reason for your book's being relevant to the user in a particular format, then you should make this point in your proposal or as soon as it becomes apparent. Unusual size might be appropriate to the function of a book. An 8½ x 11" format is not usual, but it is possible. (The average book is 22 centimeters tall as it stands on the shelf.) For a book, you need a minimum of two hundred fifty typed double-space manuscript pages, and it is better to think in terms of three hundred fifty pages. Five hundred manuscript pages is probably the maximum today, and might involve discussion with the publisher. There are twenty-five sixty-character lines (about two hundred and fifty words) per manuscript page. Reference is usually made in terms of twelve-pitch type, i.e. twelve strokes to an inch. (Typewriters are ten-, twelve-, and fifteen-pitch.)

In making your list of publishers to approach, avoid overlapping publishers, subsidiaries, and distributors. Unlike journals, book publishers usually do not consider it heresy to approach more than one of them simultaneously about your manuscript or idea, but neither do they bless the practice, so do not stress that you have submitted it to other publishers.[22] However, begin by approaching only the first publisher on your systematically developed and prioritized list, and point out in your cover letter that you are contacting only them. The publisher's questionnaire which you may receive in lieu of a response may ask whether you are submitting it to another publisher at this time. When you receive a firm offer, which is a contract signed by the publisher, and if and when you sign, date, and return it, also write to any other publishers to whom you have sent the proposal.

Dear Ms./Mr. Doe:

Some time ago I forwarded for your consideration a proposal for my book, _____. I have heard nothing from you in the interim, and I am now withdrawing it from consideration. Please discard or return the prospectus. Thank you for your continued interest.

Very truly yours,

A publisher may send the proposal package to an outside, paid reader-evaluator, whose response and identity may or may not be shared with you. The reader, the process, and the press usually take an inordinant amount of time. When or even before you have established a relationship which includes reference to readers evaluating your manuscript, offer to send the publisher an additional copy or copies, which may facilitate the outside review process. ("How to get the best reviewers for book manuscripts" was one of thirteen topics considered at the 1988 Society for Scholarly Publishing annual meeting.) Some publishers will make their decision in-house. A decision based on *one* evaluator's expertise is to some extent based on opinion. Request "simultaneous review" if you have reason to believe that they normally use more than one outside evaluator. Feel free to request an additional reader if the manuscript is said to be turned down on the basis of one reader's reaction. A copy of the evaluation should be provided you. Request it if it is not provided. These evaluations, when provided, are often not anonymous. I urge you to invest a little more in the process by writing to thank the publisher for their consideration and to request their counsel in the form of a critique which might help you to revise your work. Ultimately you may receive a negative decision with no explanation. "Does not fit into our plans" is not an explanation, and yet many first-book authors are not even accorded this much. You and I may not consider "while your proposal is an interesting and worthy one, it is not suited to our present publishing program" an explanation either.

The first book is generally the most difficult: Nothing succeeds like success, you have to have money to get a loan, ad infinitum. For publishers, almost every book is an unknown before it is marketed, and a new author is yet another unknown. The record shows that yours is likely to be a more difficult process if you are a woman scholar or your topic is gender-related, so keep these good-news statistics and views in mind when dealing with rejection until you get that contract (and you will): United States book publishers' sales in 1986 reached almost ten and a half billion dollars, an increase of 5.8 percent over the previous year. Their pre-tax profits exceeded one billion dollars. Even small publishers reported improved profit margins.[23] Scholarly presses are publishing more and more.[24] The opportunity for publication of women's studies is increasing as the field evolves, matures, and stabilizes as part of academe.[25]

Contracts for book publication vary. Publishers tend to respond to first-book authors' royalty and contract-related questions with a brief, vague reference to a "standard contract" as if it were in the realm of common knowledge. Short of, "Don't give me that," your response should be "Please send me a copy." If they do, you will discover the standard contract has several now-blank, fill-in portions. Even with a signed contractual agreement, publishers basically have the upper hand, but at least negotiate before you sign. Regardless of any aspects of the publisher-author relationship (this is your first book, you're just glad to get a publisher, he's such a nice young man, they published Such and Such and So and So), if you have access to an attorney, go over the offered contract with her or him before signing.

Possible sources for locating qualified, available attorneys include the local Women's Yellow Pages, the national association of feminist or women lawyers, which may be able to refer you to a nearby group of women lawyers, advertisements in feminist periodicals, and the International Federation of Women Lawyers.[26] Lawyers who advertise in telephone company Yellow Pages under ATTORNEYS — CONTRACT LAW or PATENT, TRADEMARK AND COPYRIGHT LAW headings are often associated with firms representing publishers rather than individual authors; advertisers listed under ATTORNEY REFERRAL SERVICE typically charge a fee, which is neither necessary nor appropriate. (County, state, and other bar and medical associations typically provide names of practitioners who are inexperienced or newcomers seeking clients.)

The contract actually means little as a legal instrument requiring the publisher's and author's fulfillment of an agreement. The author may be a resident of one state and the publisher located in another. Attorneys, indeed, law firms are accessible to and sometimes retained by publishing groups, and even a small press may be part of a trade conglomerate. Rarely does a woman have an attorney in the old, family retainer sense. A book contract between a publisher and an unpublished woman can work out for her much as a conventional marriage agreement often does. She may find it is less feasible to respond to his deviations, which appear to be more tolerated by society. In a context regarded somewhat like a domestic matter, she risks being considered "difficult" if she writes to the top of the pyramid. Currently, it is almost impossible to identify lawyers who will involve themselves in gender-related matters other than *class actions* or sensational, potentially lucrative matters. This is a situation familiar to feminists, and as such, should be responded to by us and them.

The move towards unionization of free-lance "working authors" includes professional and academic persons. Their concerns include legal representation and the significance and implementation of contracts with publishers. A recent National Writers Union survey of book authors asked about their worst problems experienced with publishers. Responses included publishers "sitting on manuscripts" after contracted manuscripts have been received, and simultaneous publication of a book as a double journal issue and a hardcover book, which frequently results in lower book sales and thus lower royalties, with no payment for the journal article other than ten offprints, royalties being paid only on hardcover sales. One university press director has characterized repackaging issues of journals as books as an example of publishers contributing to "too much for the sake of a buck," which exploits the library market, confuses efficiency with laziness, and dilutes the "prestige accorded to the book as a scholarly achievement."[27] Proper remuneration to editor-compiler-author has become a contemporary contract-related matter. Massive mutilation, as one author referred to it in the survey, of text without consultation or forewarning by publishers is another. Responses to "What are the most important things the National Writers Union could be doing for you?" included: keep going; investigate, rate, and otherwise influence delinquent presses and journals to reform their pay and editorial practices; lobby nationally and globally for authors' rights and freedom; oppose government disinformation and secrecy, as well as privatization of public libraries and data bases; and publicize and "legitimize" alternative presses since mainstream media are hopelessly corporate centrist.

Read a contract carefully. Compare it, if possible, with others from the same publisher and other publishers. They *do* vary. If there is something in it that you do not like, ask the publisher to discuss, adjust, or delete it before you both sign it. Add to it in your own words. If, for example, the contract does not prohibit the publisher from making specific changes in your manuscript, then add a clause in your own words which obligates the publisher to ask the author before making specific changes. Keep in mind that there is no such thing as one "standard" book publishing contract. You end up signing based on your bargaining position and your convincing arguments. Your contractual obligations to deliver a satisfactory manuscript by the manuscript delivery date provide publishers with the ultimate control because they define what satisfactory is.

Helen Hayes is said to have gotten out of a theatrical contract based on an "act of God" when she got pregnant. The Authors Guild trade book contract refers to an author being slowed by "illness, accident or military service." In a statement like, "Given full cooperation by the author, the publisher will publish within eighteen months of receipt of a satisfactory manuscript or will notify author of an unavoidable delay in a timely manner," the publisher has the opportunity to define "full cooperation" as well as "satisfactory manuscript," and ultimately, "unavoidable delay," whereas the onus is on the lone scholar to attempt to respond to the publisher's failure to publish within eighteen months of receipt of her or his manuscript. Similarly, a phrase like a publisher's "moving into production" might consist of very little movement indeed. The National Writers Union provides trade book contract guidelines for members. Bunnin and Beren include before-and-after-negotiations contract samples in their contract book.[28,29,30]

If you write a book which is published, the world will assume that you are regularly receiving royalties from your publisher and even that you have had assistance and encouragement in the writing and pre- and post-publication phases. More realistic would be the picture of a woman scholar whose royalties for her first book are negligible and largely consumed by the expenses of getting a contract for publication and by pre- and post-publication procedures which do not include an advance on royalties, a secretary, or a wife, but do involve preparation of the index and proof reading the work before it goes to the printer, as well as some of the post-production promotion.

Provisions of any contract agreement for publication of a book which a new author should cogitate include:

- royalties (basis; frequency and accounting; advances)
- in addition to royalties, what else is forthcoming? (number of author's copies and discounts on others; sharing in subsidiary rights)
- when the book will be published
- rights and responsibilities the publisher retains
- when the author agrees to provide a satisfactory manuscript
- alterations the author is permitted to make
- copyright arrangements
- author's production-related obligations and responsibilities

When you receive or discuss a contract, the main thing with which you are usually concerned is the royalties! They may be expressed in terms of net receipts (gross minus actual returns) *or*, less likely, the list price of the book, which can be preferable depending on other aspects of the contract and the publisher's reputation. Royalties are computed in percentages of the net *or* of the retail price of the book. Clearly a retail price of anything is greater than its wholesale or discounted price. But royalties paid on book sales are *also* computed in terms of numbers of copies sold, and the percentages change after a given number have been sold. The percentage on which your royalties are computed may change after the first 1,500 copies are sold. The first printing for most hardcover books consists of 10,000 or fewer copies. The list or cover price of a book is the retail price charged in the bookstore, which appears in the publisher's catalog and sometimes on the dustjacket, if the book has a dustjacket.

For a book with a $30.00 list price on which the contract provides for a 10 percent of retail per copy royalty, you would receive $3.00. Most specialized publishers, however, including some trade publishers, base royalties on the *net* price of a book. The net price of a book refers to the discounted amount which the publisher receives for the book as a result of quantity arrangements with distributors, vendors, wholesalers, and bookstore chains. If booksellers buy your $30.00 book from the publisher at their standard 40 percent discount, they pay $18.00; when your royalty rate is 10 percent of the publisher's net receipts, your royalty becomes $1.80 per copy.

If you have an agent, she or he will endeavor to get a royalty scale which will be based on list price, or if not on list price, then a scale which will generate the equivalent in royalties for you and for her or him.

First-book authors usually hesitate to negotiate aspects of a contract, successful authors bargain a bit, and agents of best-selling authors bargain.

Frequency and accounting of royalty payments are among the worst problems with publishers that book authors identify. They refer specifically to yearly, rather than semiannual, royalty statements and payments, and failure to pay royalties altogether, or failure to report sales after an initial royalty statement, claiming that sales were too low and the royalty "too insignificant" to be worth sending a check!

Will the publisher provide an advance on *your* royalties? It will probably not be mentioned in the contract. Ask about it anyway. How much and when. Advances on your royalties are not necessarily associated with such authorship-related expenses as illustrations and data gathering. If you have authored books for the same publisher previously, the possibility of getting an advance on your royalties may or may not be enhanced. Times change, or you may fall from grace. Changes in policies may be associated with change in ownership and management, but "inconsistencies" cannot. The only recourse most women authors have is to move to other publishers. Publishers who declare categorically that they never provide advances on authors' royalties usually make exceptions.

You will probably receive ten copies of your book at the time it is published. You may use most of them to give to people who have participated indirectly in the work, such as the person who contributed the foreword and Professor Big Name who commended to the publisher-friend the potential of your dissertation. Before you use up your supply, ask your publisher to assume these responsibilities and the mailing process.

The contract may specify conditions pertaining to publication options on future manuscripts by the author. This provision usually works mainly to the publisher's advantage.

You should share in subsidiary and foreign rights, i.e., payment from them. The contract should specify that you be notified of reuse of your book.

When will the book get published? The date of publication should appear in a contract, but it probably will not. At best, a time limit will be provided. Ask about this, and insist that it be included. The grievances which are easiest to deal with are based on signed contracts. Next best is a letter confirming a verbal agreement, signed by both parties. So log your telephone calls (the information goes into the book's file) and immediately mail to the publisher a followup summary of your impression of a conversation which relates to contractual matters. If necessary, ask permission to tape a telephone conversation, and have equipment ready. Although in most jurisdictions a recording of a telephone conversation made without permission is not legal, it is always possible to draw from your personal shorthand notes of a conversation. Make a note of the corporate name and address, bank, and account number before you deposit the publisher's check.

Set a time limit—within no more than ninety days following receipt of the manuscript—for the publisher to notify you of anything which is unsatisfactory, why, and what changes are proposed. Otherwise, when the publisher objects to something about the manuscript (and usually proposes as a solution or improvement that you delete it), you will be able to respond to a form of retaliation which consists of delay in publication while the manuscript becomes staler. Logically, the publisher cannot profit by such tactics; clearly the goal is to get you to initiate cancellation of your part of the contractual agreement or to go off in a huff.

Unless you initiate it, the contract may not allude to the publisher's obligation to go into production and get it onto the market, let alone a deadline. A contract which calls for the publisher to go into production within a year of receipt of a satisfactory manuscript enables him to hold your manuscript for fifty weeks and then to budge slightly.

Usually the contract states that the publisher agrees to pay royalties and to register the copyright. It should also describe the terms under which the agreement may be cancelled by either the publisher or the author. Rights and obligations of both parties when publication of the book is discontinued (no longer maintained in print by the publisher) may be spelled out in the contract. The publisher may also prohibit the author from involvement with competing books. All in all, the contract tends to focus on the publisher's rights and the author's responsibilities.

Avoid submitting a manuscript on which your work is tentative or with which you are not entirely satisfied. Prepare it so that it will not be susceptible to major changes. If you have done your work well, you will discover few changes you would like to make in it as you proofread the galleys or proof pages. Of course something may develop which you would like to add or correct, particularly when the publisher fails to move promptly into publication and much time has passed. Most publishers and editors will cooperate in normal updating and corrections, inasmuch as they enhance the book's utility, and thus its sales. Some problems can be avoided by keeping in touch with your editor, if one is assigned, or the publisher. Your contract may limit you to making changes only at the time of proofreading, which might suffice if you have an experienced editor and have previously worked with her or him. The contract will surely limit you to the number and extent of such changes, however. A few will be permitted, but they will be counted, and the cost beyond the number of alterations provided in your contract will be deducted from your royalties. (The contract for this book permits author changes other than corrections of publisher's errors on twenty-five pages of the proofs.) The author should not request substantial changes requiring costly "author's alterations" after the manuscript has been typeset or otherwise composed.

In order to obtain copyright registration, two copies of every book published in the United States must be sent to the Register of Copyrights in Washington, D.C. All copyrighted materials are then reviewed for eligibility for Library of Congress cataloging and subsequent listing in the *National Union Catalog* and the Library of Congress' MARC tapes. It is customary for the publisher also to send copies of books to the R.R. Bowker and H.W. Wilson companies so that they will be listed in the *Weekly Record, American Book Publishing Record,* and *Cumulative Book Index.*

In reading about contracts and copyright, be sure that your references are up-to-date, themselves recently copyrighted. (When your sources for any research are revisions of previously published references, keep in mind that a revised edition of a book does not necessarily guarantee that every page has been updated.) The copyright of your book should be in your name. Publishers use the contract phrase, "The Publisher will obtain the copyright in the name of the Author, who will hold it for the benefit of the Publisher so long as the book remains in print." The publisher will insert the copyright notice in the book on the verso of the title page. If in doubt, particularly if the publisher is clearly not moving into production, you might consider getting your own copyright. If you check *Forthcoming Books in Print* and find the book has not been announced for publication within the period of time to which the publisher has made a contractual commitment, you may have reason to be concerned.

The intellectual content of the manuscript is the property of the author, and the copyright is in your name unless you have made an agreement which *employs* you to write. People may contact you or your publisher(s) for permission to quote from your book(s). You may wish, as a matter of convenience, to give the publisher the right to grant permission to people requesting the privilege of photocopying portions of the work, mainly for instructional classroom purposes. You should, however be compensated for their reproduction of your articles, chapters, and parts of books within their commercial works.

The author's production-related obligations will usually include proofreading galleys and indexing the book. You may, in fact, prefer to be responsible for these, which are two aspects of the book's appeal and crucial to its utility. They may not be specified in the contract, and the publisher will simply send you the galleys or instruct you to provide the index. An author's time writing a book is paid for in the royalties earned from its sale. The publisher's responsibility is presumed to be production and distribution of the book. If the author is involved in other ways in its production, a flat fee payment should be provided, and if predictable, stated in the contract. The author can incur numerous related expenses before the manuscript goes to the publisher and after signing the contract, e.g. those related to getting permissions to quote and to reproduce illustrations and prepare camera-ready copy. Do not hesitate to ask for financial underwriting for expenses after you have signed your contract — need for a questionnaire which would enhance the book might develop or become apparent after the contract is signed, for example.

Chapter four of the *Chicago Manual of Style* includes Rights and Permissions, a very useful section about the author's responsibilities. If you adhere to the "doctrine of fairness," you should have no trouble in this respect. Avoid lengthy quotations (more than four hundred words) in your book in any event; it is not a dissertation. Quotes are in aggregate: fifty scattered twenty-word quotes all from one source is 1,000 words. Book contracts usually have provisions for the author's responsibility so that the publisher cannot legally be involved in libel or violation of copyright. Obtain permissions for quotes which are not in the public domain or copyrighted, *before* using them or proposing a book in which they are essential. Enclose copies of permissions with your manuscript. Your publisher may ask about them as a result of reading your proposal. Periodical and book publishers are generally willing to provide authors with permission to reproduce an excerpt or to quote from their publications, but you should allow for the possibility that they will charge a preposterous fee, and you should allow time for the process of obtaining permission. Write a specific request in which you identify the exact page or portion of a page, from what book or journals, and for what purpose you wish to use it; include the title of your book and, if known, its publisher. If you have not settled on a final title, refer to your "working title." Some publishers have permission forms available for their authors' use. Avoid charts and illustrations derived from others' work as part of your manuscript; they should be used only when absolutely essential to the points you are making and to the book's purpose. Obtain and follow your publisher's instructions for their inclusion.

Your obligation to obtain permissions to quote, reprint, and reproduce from others' work is part of your contract, and it is also an additional cost for you to plan on. Surely other writers are deserving of just compensation for their original and copyrighted works. And, for the future, remember that you may have this aspect of potential sisterhood at your disposal: respond promptly and affirmatively to requests which reach you. (See also: Chapter Four: Anthologies.)

Some publishers perceive their postproduction responsibilities as distribution, rather than promotion. They may be willing to provide the author with supplies of an announcement or blurb of the book. Many authors are themselves now mailing these to journals, editors, educational administrators, librarians, women's centers, etc., of whom they are aware. In some cases the publisher will reimburse the author for the postage. On the other hand, there are publishers who promote and publicize their books and authors to the extent that their author's questionnaire asks about willingness to participate in television and radio interviews!

Having signed a contract with a book publisher, you should meet all deadlines and follow any instructions which are provided for preparation and delivery of the book manuscript. Unless instructed differently, type your surname and the first keyword of the title at the top left of each and every page of the manuscript. At the right, record the page number, with "Page 1 of [total] #" on the first page, and number the pages consecutively from the first straight through to the last page of the manuscript. Consistent application of an appropriate style manual is important in preparation of nonfiction book manuscripts as well as journal articles. Proofread the manuscript (including printouts) at least twice, several days apart. Pages should be loose; do not use weighty and costly (for you), cumbersome (for the publisher) staples, clips, binders, etc. Make at least two copies for yourself, and mail your manuscript first class. The same day put into the mail elsewhere a note to the publisher indicating that you have just dispatched the manuscript. Some contracts call for more than a single copy of the book or for the "original."

Publishers now utilize for some or all of their books the "camera-ready" method of page production. Camera-ready books are reproduced exactly "as is," which should justify a word processor. An example is Searing's *Introduction to Library Research in Women's Studies*, published by Westview Press in their Guides to Library Research publisher's series.[31] Westview makes "Guidelines for Authors" and "Preparing a Camera-Ready Typescript" available to its authors.

Your responsibilities continue during production and after publication of your book. Publishers can get a good manuscript into book form in a matter of months (even weeks for blockbusters by best-selling politician authors) if they wish to do so. But you can allow about a year. During that time, you and your book may be assigned an inhouse editor who will go through your manuscript to correct your stylistic errors and perhaps make suggestions which will enhance the book. For my 1972 and 1975 *Womanhood Media* books, for example, I was assigned an editor who, before the manuscripts were returned to me with galley proofs for correcting, wrote me a few times with appropriate questions and suggestions. I recall disagreeing with him on something which I cannot recall and writing to explain what I had in mind. (He is now president of McFarland & Company, Inc.) Times change, and a recent book received neither this type of expert conferring nor an advance on my royalties. The galleys simply arrived for me to correct the typists' many errors, i.e. more than in the 1970s decade. Your publisher will probably provide you with instructions as to how to record your corrections when you proofread. If not, consult the *American Heritage Dictionary* under "Proofreaders' Marks." For more detailed information, there are numerous publications and portions of books.[32] Plan ahead as the time for proofreading galleys approaches, so that you will be able to set everything aside to concentrate on this work and to return them as quickly as possible. Record *corrections* in typography and the few *changes*, or alterations, you make in two clearly different ways. Keep a record of your changes, if any.

When your manuscript goes to the publisher and production is underway, add the book's title to your publications list with "in press" or "forthcoming," the publisher's name, and the date of publication. If there is criticism of this practice in your department, delay until it is cited in *Forthcoming Books in Print*.

Begin your preparation for the book's indexing at this time. I suggest getting a carton of used 3″ x 5″ scrap catalog cards, which are being discarded by many libraries these days. Go through your copy of the manuscript for all references to at least three types of information: titles of publications, subjects (subject matter), and people-as-authors to whom you refer. Record each on a separate card. Whether you decide on one interfiled index or three separate ones for each type of entry should depend on how you view your readers' needs and approach to the book. It will also depend on what type of typography your publisher can provide.

As the book moves closer to publication, you will probably be contacted by a member of the promotion department of your publishing house, or the promotion person at a small house. You may be asked to prepare two hundred words or so describing the book for use in announcements about it. Recognize this as an opportunity rather than a chore. The autobiographical material which you provided as part of your proposal may or may not be suitable for this situation, and considerable time may have passed. Read publishers' blurbs for other books which will compete with yours; ask your publisher for some sample blurbs. This type of announcement accompanies a book when it is sent by the publisher to reviewers. It may be available at the publisher's booth at conference exhibits. The information may be utilized in the publisher's brochures listing new and related titles, and it would be a source for the material printed on the book's dustjacket, if any, or on the cover of a softcover book.

On balance, I believe that, having sold the book to the publisher, you are also able to construct an announcement which will sell the book to the audience for which you wrote it. Describe the book and highlight the aspects which make it competitive and unique. These may include its organization, arrangement, scope, special features, possibly a relationship to another publication by you or someone else. Promotion material prepared before publication of the book might include a very brief excerpt from Big Name's foreword. Later it should be revised to include excerpts from reviews. Authorship information is usually briefer than the information about the book, but in that space, focus on credentials which are acknowledged as qualifying you as *an*, if not *the*, expert to write this particular book. In writing about yourself, do not say, "She *attended* XYZ College" if you *graduated;* do not say you graduated if you did not.

Return to your prospectus list of periodicals appropriate to receive review copies and announcements. Prepare a revised list which includes any titles which have come into existence in the interim, with their current editorial address and the name of the book review person, if any, or editor. It is standard operating procedure for periodicals to review and announce new books. Unless your publisher's request for such a list restricts you to a certain number, send as long a list as you consider appropriate. It may be useful to mark for review copies *Booklist, Choice, Chronicle of Higher Education, Library Journal, NWSA Journal,* the NWSA regional newsletter(s), *New Directions for Women, Studies on Women Abstracts, Women Studies Abstracts,* and the scholarly journals of your discipline which publish reviews and announcements. Your publisher's promotion person may be aware of all of these and others.

Your responsibilities to your book continue after it is published. Consult the LMP Awards, Contests and Grants section, which includes prizes, and try to get your book nominated or submitted for relevant recognition. Try to get it adopted for course use or supplementary reading, reviewed or at least listed in periodicals, stocked in bookstores, and displayed at conferences if your publisher has not covered these or is no longer doing so. Mailing announcements from the supply which your publisher provides to individuals whom you judge to be prospective purchasers is not efficient. First, go for the big picture . . . recommendation, purchase, reading, and use of your book will take place if it is reviewed or listed in periodicals which are read or scanned by many people and displayed at conference gatherings. Your publisher may be willing to provide you with a supply of announcements of your book and to reimburse you for postage involved in dispatching them. Some publishers ask whether you want the edited copy of your manuscript ultimately returned to you; be sure to inform the publisher early on that you do indeed want it back.

"She Was Damned Nice Before She Got Ambitious."

Of Gertrude Stein, Ernest Hemingway commented that "It's a funny racket, really. But I swear that she was damned nice before she got ambitious." (Bill Henderson. *Rotten Reviews: A Literary Companion, I and II.* Wainscott, New York: Pushcart, 1986 and 1987.)

After your book manuscript has gone to the publisher and you have set up the index and worked with a company editor who may be assigned to you and your manuscript, and later with the promotion person, you can take a breather while you await reviews! How soon reviews appear depends on (1) whether, and in what numbers, and how rapidly, the publisher dispatches review copies, (2) whether periodical editors choose to review your book, and (3) the frequency of the periodicals publishing the reviews. Scholarly journals are typically quarterly publications with backlogs of books for review. Review periodicals and other types of periodicals are not as slow. (The *New York Times* reviews about one tenth of the 20,000 trade books sold each year.)[33] Book review excerpts may provide good quotes for enhancing promotional materials, especially if your book does not have a foreword by a Big Name from which you might draw.

But what if reviews do not appear in recognized journals? Suppose the book . . . and you . . . get rotten reviews. Bill Henderson's *Rotten Reviews* will take on a whole new meaning for you.[34] While his compilations are quotes from literary reviews, with few women authors' works involved, some are notable here. ". . . It is a pity that Mrs. Friedan has to fight so hard to persuade herself as well as her readers [of *The Feminine Mystique*, Norton, 1963] of her argument. In fact her passion against the forces of the irrational in life carries her away," appeared in no less than the *Yale Review*. In the *New York Times Book Review:* "To paraphrase a famous line, 'the fault, dear Mrs. Friedan, is not in our culture, but in ourselves.'" "Bores aid no revolution," wrote the *Library Journal's* reviewer of Germaine Greer's *The Female Eunuch* (McGraw, 1971). No matter. As a major publisher pointed out to me, *any* LJ review increases sales.

After one of my books was published and I had received lots of good reviews, I was unprepared for a negative review. I probably *felt* (note the feminine emotional verb) that I needed to defend myself and to point out the lack of qualifications of the person who had received the assignment and clearly had not read the book, the personal ax to grind, etc. I wrote my reaction to my publisher. He promptly and calmly responded along the lines of (it is now many years ago), "Forget it — for some reason, they do this to our books. It doesn't matter. Don't concern yourself; we don't. . ." It was good advice. But, as Kolodny has observed, "Most faculty members are not acquainted with the scholarship in women's studies. They don't read it, so they don't know what it is or even how to evaluate it."[35]

The importance of your up-to-date list of periodicals to receive review copies can be seen. Give close attention to compiling the list of scholarly journals in your field which publish book reviews or list books received or are themselves review journals for your publisher's promotion person's use. It is unwise for an author to attempt to influence a periodical book review editor to assign or route her or his book to a particular reviewer. Even though it might be helpfully innocent, it would inevitably be misunderstood by someone.

Review periodicals consist almost entirely of reviews of books and sometimes of other media forms, as well as bibliographical essays on timely topics which may function as literature reviews. Examples of review serials to which books might be dispatched by your publisher and in which an advertisement might be placed include *Academic Library Book Review, Belles Lettres, Booklist, Books in Canada, The Bookwatch, Choice, Feminist Bookstore News, Kirkus Reviews, Library Journal* Reviews, *New Directions for Women, New Women's Times Feminist Review, News and Reviews of the Small Press, New York Review of Books, New York Times Books, Publishers Weekly,* and the *Women's Review of Books.* These are in addition to the numerous discipline-related journals and newsletters such as *Contemporary Psychology: A Journal of Reviews, Current Literature on Aging, History: Review of New Books, Law Books in Review, NWSA Journal, Review of Education, Reviews in American History, Reviews in Anthropology, Science Books & Films,* and *SciTech Book News.* Advertisements in the *Chronicle of Higher Education* and *New Directions for Women* are always productive for books by women scholars, women's studies personnel, and gender-related topics.

Your publisher's promo person may send you copies of reviews and possibly "mentions" of your book, and both of you will inevitably discover some which the other person does not. Mark each with the source, date of issue, volume and page numbers, and save them. Use one of your copies of the book as a "master" in which you mark any errors you discover and record updating information.

If anyone doubts that current and dormant doctoral dissertations constitute a vast amount of primary research material and potential for nonfiction books about all aspects of females and gender, much of it done by competitively qualified women of their and our days, consider that computer-assisted searching generated more than twelve thousand dissertations completed between 1870 and 1983 at United States, British, and Irish universities in many disciplines on hundreds of topics.[36] Or simply examine the University Microfilms International current catalog of doctoral dissertation researches in the women's studies subject area, or the women-related dissertations within the other subject catalogs UMI issues: anthropology, the arts, black studies, communications, ecology and the environment, ethnic studies, Latin America, music, nursing, petroleum and geology, philosophy and religion, political science, and United States history.[37] Most doctoral dissertations accepted in the United States and Canada since 1861 are bibliographically accessible by an on-line computer-assisted or hand search of *Comprehensive Dissertation Index;* the abstracts for some of them are available in the counterpart tool, *Dissertation Abstracts International.*

"Dissertation" is used to refer to a lengthy and formal treatise or discourse, especially when written by a candidate for a doctoral degree at a university. "Thesis" is now used more outside the United States, where doctoral dissertation and master's thesis—or essay—are heard. The two terms, have, however, become almost synonymous in their usage by many people. The title of one of Kate Turabian's perennial style manuals is *A Manual for Writers of Term Papers, Theses, and Dissertations.* In a dictionary sense, a thesis is primarily a proposition that is maintained by argument. Its secondary meaning is as a dissertation advancing an original point of view as a result of research, especially as part of the requirements of an academic degree. Thesis is more comprehensive and may apply to both master's and doctoral papers. A dissertation research report typically includes an extensive bibliography, surveys and reports the related literature, or reports on the state of the art.

Theses and dissertations may both be required in partial fulfillment of graduate academic degrees, and they constitute a significant segment of the academic literature in all fields. They are usually unpublished typescripts, duplicated as necessary in microform or by other photocopying processes. Before World War II, many institutions required that a supply of printed copies of the dissertation be provided by the author. The University of California, Berkeley, in 1896 required the Ph.D. candidate to provide one hundred fifty copies; by 1926 it was down to two copies.

One's doctoral dissertation work should be considered a source of ideas and publishable material for one's journal articles or for a book. As "book" signifies monograph, so does it mean a single author, and for maximum worthiness, "primary author" short of "*the* author." And the dissertation has going for it a single very primary author! Women's book publications based on their doctoral work generally appear on the book market about five or more years after receipt of the degree, whereas men's tend to be marketable in less than five. This may relate to motivation, time, ability to do the rewrite and rework which is involved, or to any number or combination of factors. Warren Farrell's Random House book, *The Liberated Man: Beyond Masculinity: Freeing Men and Their Relationships with Women,* was published in 1974; his doctorate was awarded the same year, with a dissertation titled *The Political Potential of the Women's Liberation Movement as Indicated by Its Effectiveness in Changing Men's Attitudes.* Robert "Man-From-Uncle" Vaughn's Putnam book, *Only Victims: A Study of Show Business Blacklisting,* was published in 1972; his doctorate was awarded the year before, with a dissertation titled *A Historical Study of the Influence of the House Committee on Un-American Activities on the American Theater, 1938–1958.*

Rarely will a woman scholar combine the merit and luck to be able to use her doctoral dissertation work as the basis of a best-selling trade book publication. But it happens. Kate Millett's Ph.D. in English and comparative literature was awarded by Columbia University in 1970, with her dissertation titled *Sexual Politics*. Her book of the same title was published by Doubleday the same year. Her faculty appointment in the Barnard College experimental program was then "phased out."[38]

In the past, persons with new doctoral degrees might have gotten their dissertations published, with little or no review, by a university press. It is different now. The resources of university presses are said to be more restricted. Graduate students in some fields are turning to narrower topics than in the past, and these may be less publishable as books. A dissertation usually has a limited purpose and a small audience. Most dissertations are available in microform or photocopy and by interlibrary loans. As presses have become more selective, the quality of scholarly books has usually improved. But some tenured academicians and administrators are unwilling to empathize with problems of publication faced by younger faculty in general and by women, feminists, and gender-related topics in particular. Many dissertations are written by literate people knowledgeable in their discipline who are simply unable to write. Peyre's list of common dissertation faults is often cited: length, repetitiousness, slowness of pace, monotony (especially in synopses of novels, plays, and earlier critical works), defensiveness, dogmatism, inaccessibility, too many footnotes, and jargon.[39]

The purpose of the doctoral dissertation is generally considered to be provision of the opportunity for the scholar to demonstrate researching ability, writing ability, mastery of an aspect of the discipline, and these things in combination. Some would add opportunity to contribute to knowledge, or perhaps to offer a new perspective. The ultimate goal becomes satisfaction of requirements, committee, and the university . . . getting that degree.

With a trade book publication, everything is different. *You* are now the subject specialist, and your book's purpose is to communicate ideas to a different audience, one which is also a market. So you should consider your readership's knowledge of the subject. It is likely to be different from that of doctoral committee members, so it is necessary for you to widen your focus on the topic and to make your presentation more accessible. To accomplish this, you can incorporate footnote information and eliminate the technical nomenclature to which Peyre refers as jargon. In essence, you retitle it, free yourself up so that you can have a literal re-vision (more than seeing), get rid of the footnotes, shorten it, and scrap the technical lingo. In the course of doing this, the book will usually become shorter than the dissertation, if you do not supplement it in some way, and the title will be enhanced. For example, my doctoral dissertation, titled *The Community College Library: An Appraisal of Current Practice*, became *The Community College Library: A Plan for Action*. This suggests that, freed of academic restraints, as they say, one may find that she has the opportunity to say more in less space. A comparison of the titles of a few women's doctoral dissertations—on gender-related topics, as it happens—and what was then usually their first book publication may further illustrate (note that even in these relatively recent pairs, there tend to be time lapses between the dates of the dissertation and the book which are greater than those generally observable for men):

Baker, Melva Joyce. *Images of Women: The War Years, 1941–1945: A Study of the Public Perceptions of Women's Roles as Revealed in Top-Grossing War Films.* Ph.D., University of California, Santa Barbara, 1978. Became *Images of Women in Film: The War Years, 1914–1945.* UMI Research Press, 1980.

Matthews, Sarah. *Social-Psychological Aspects of Being an Old Widowed Mother in American Society.* Ph.D., University of California, Davis, 1976. Became *The Social World of Old Women: Management of Self-Identity.* Sage, 1979. Sage Library of Social Research 78.

Mulhern, Chieko Ireie. *Koda Rohan: A Study of Idealism.* Ph.D., Columbia University, 1973. Became *Koda Rohan.* Twayne, 1977.

Paul, Diana Mary. *A Prolegomena to the Srimaladevi Sutra and the Tathagatagarbha Theory: The Role of Women in Buddhism.* Ph.D., University of Wisconsin, Madison, 1974. Became *The Buddhist Feminine Ideal.* American Scholars Press, 1980.

Sacks, Karen Helen Brodkin. *Economic Bases of Sexual Equality: A Comparative Study of Four African Societies.* Ph.D., University of Michigan, 1971. Became *Sisters and Wives: The Past and Future of Sexual Equality.* Greenwood, 1979.

Sapiro, Virginia. *Socialization to and from Politics: Political Gender Role Norms Among Women.* Ph.D., University of Michigan, 1976. Became *Women, Biology and Public Policy.* Sage, 1985. Volume 10 Yearbook in Women's Policy Studies.

Shakeshaft, Carol. *Dissertation Research on Women in Academic Administration: A Synthesis of Findings and Paradigm for Future Research.* Ph.D., Texas A & M University, 1979. Became *Women in Educational Administration.* Sage, 1986.

Shibamoto, Janet Sutherland. *Language Use and Linguistic Theory: Sex-Related Variation in Japanese Syntax.* Ph.D., University of California, Davis, 1980. Became *Japanese Women's Language.* Academic Press, 1985.

After you receive your doctoral degree, if your advisor or a dissertation committee member has commended your work to a publisher, then start the necessary revisions immediately. But if this is not the case, the ideal situation would be to start an afterthought and corrections file, and to set it aside for a while. Perhaps during the interim, you could talk to the dissertation advisor for an endorsement of your dissertation as a book. Not all scholars are able to be leisurely about their livelihood. As Pharr pointed out,

Many months passed. Since I was then an assistant professor facing, eventually, the tenure gun, I began to grow increasingly anxious. Basically, the reader [at the press] hadn't gotten around to reviewing the manuscript and the press was prepared to wait it out. I will not go into all the details of this saga, but I can report that after a year had passed, the editor began to avoid my phone calls. Lest someone think I am paranoid, I can report that the person answering the phone at the press would put a hand over the receiver and then come back on the line to tell me that the editor was unavailable at that particular time. After a full eighteen, anxiety-producing months, I finally decided that I had to withdraw the manuscript from the [first] press.[21]

Contact the university press where you obtained your doctorate or where you are now employed. While this approach may not result in a book contract, it might provide a consultation and suggestions on how to proceed. When you propose a book which is to be a trade revision of your doctoral dissertation, emphasize that, while this book is related to your doctoral work, it is not the dissertation itself. It has been or will be revised, expanded, or perhaps supplemented with several case studies. A growing number of journals now list or review doctoral dissertations in their fields. The *International Journal of the History of Sport*, for example, reviews both books and dissertations. A portion of such a review may be quoted as part of the book-publication proposal.

An alternative is to utilize the dissertation as the basis for journal articles and presentations. It is also possible that some of the research and writing which took place during your doctoral work, although not necessarily appearing in the dissertation, may be publishable. In describing it, you can refer to its coming out of your work for the doctorate.

Especially in the humanities and social-behavioral sciences, the doctoral dissertation is relatively narrowly focused, impersonal (not written in the first person singular), repetitious, unconcerned about an audience other than the dissertation committee, and contains jargon and an extensive review of the literature. Often changes are required for publication of the dissertation in book form. Revised as a nonfiction trade book, it is broadly focused, personalized (occasional use of the first person singular perhaps), written with its audience in mind and thus containing no jargon and only a selected bibliography of essential references.

Because a doctoral dissertation is now almost automatically "reprinted," later, in the tenure process, stress that your newly published or contracted book is "based on work done for the doctorate" or "for the doctoral dissertation," i.e. it is a trade book revision with its own life, published (ideally) by a scholarly press.

A publisher may approach a scholar who recently received a doctoral degree at a prestigious university and whose dissertation was on a timely topic or one about which very little has been published, or which received accolades. You can contact a publisher before a professional conference and request a brief appointment with an editor to discuss the possibility of trade revision of your doctoral dissertation on a subject in which the publisher specializes. I would not expect her or him to read your dissertation and provide a prognosis at the appointment, although you should bring along a copy you can spare. Your strategy on this occasion is to sell the idea of a contract to revise the dissertation into a book. You are not proposing to sell it to a publisher to reprint, which would communicate naivete to the publisher and represent less than nothing to most departmental committee members. In the United States, your dissertation was probably made available in reprint form by the Xerox Company at the time it went to University Microfilms for recording access in microform, an automatic arrangement with numerous doctoral-granting universities in English-speaking nations.

You may be able to obtain encouragement and interest in the potential of the dissertation revised, in which case you must make a decision because they want to see a manuscript. You can proceed to revise it and resubmit it, or you can pursue other publishers with the hope that you will be able to obtain a contract before you revise it, which *might* include a small advance on your royalties and assignment of an editor to counsel as you proceed, and it would provide in the interim a few professional merit points.

•   •   •

After you have gotten your first book published and especially if you are writing fiction, consider the possibility of an agent. Consult colleagues with similar interests about their agents as well as reference books which list them. Many authors discover that it is difficult to locate an agent who has expertise in the area of their needs *and* who is available to take them and their creations on.

The term literary agent underscores their services often in relationship to stories, novels, and popular nonfiction. Agents and consultants are accustomed to attempts to pick their brains for gratis critiques of "work in progress." Should you decide that this relationship is for you and you have located an agent in whom you are interested who is interested in you and your work, you should consider the list of questions to ask about an "agent's personality and credentials" and steps to a clear understanding with your agent provided by Larsen.[40] This relationship should relate to a percentage commission, rather than to fees or expenses, and it also involves a contractual agreement. If your agent provides editorial help, her or his percentage will be greater.

Some publishers approach scholars about books on which they have heard they are working. They might be books on timely topics about which very little has been published in book form or on which every publisher has at least one, or associated with major awards or grants, or recommended by professors or experts. A publisher's representative might approach an established scholar to edit a book series and to recruit writers for chapters of a book, e.g. G.K. Hall's now-defunct *Women's Annual* series. An initiative might originate with the university press associated with your employing institution or studies. Accept an invitation to discuss the matter. If the publisher and you are located at considerable distance but your expenses for such a safari are not mentioned, counter with a reference to a conference you will be attending. The publisher should provide some specific information once you have demonstrated that you have written or will be completing an attractive marketable manuscript. If contractual arrangements are not discussed at some level of specificity, ask about contractual details then and there.

What has been referred to as *vanity press*, in which persons have paid to have their books published or their biographical data included in reference books, is not a thing of the past. And there is another approach to which you should be alerted. You have probably noticed its advertising in such periodicals as *Atlantic Magazine*, the *Chronicle of Higher Education*, and the American Association of University Women's *Graduate Woman*. The results are ultimately much the same. You pay someone to print and disseminate your book. This form of publication is likely to be discounted in terms of scholarship-enhancing professional advancement. The *subsidy publisher* does not offer a contract to publish your book in the conventional sense, although the advertising rhetoric sounds the same. It might begin "Authors wanted by New York publisher. Leading subsidy book publisher seeks manuscripts of all types, fiction, nonfiction, poetry, scholarly, and juvenile books, etc. New authors welcomed. Send for free, illustrated brochure." One subsidy publisher seeking authors' manuscripts is Vantage Press, not to be confused with Vintage, which is a Random House imprint, or with Viking Press. A classified magazine advertisement under the Literary Interests heading queries, "Looking for a publisher? Learn how you can have your book published, promoted, distributed. . . ." It is true enough to say that a subsidy publisher prints, distributes, and promotes a book. Persons experienced in this area point out that the promotion can consist of mailing announcements to a list provided by the author and gift copies to libraries. A glossy copyrighted free brochure refers to "a specialized plan for the publication and promotion of your book." With it is a "Dear Author" letter in which "the nation's largest publisher of books by new authors" is described as having attracted authors prominent in a variety of fields and in many walks of life including homemakers and retired people.

A "publication fee is required . . . [and] in many cases is tax deductible. . . ." Choice of a bonus gift is provided with submission of a full-length manuscript. A *New York Times Book Review* clipping (lacking issue, date, or page citation) is enclosed, implying that the article endorses or at least relates to this business in particular or subsidy publishing in general; neither, however, is mentioned in the article. This type of mass media advertising is fraudulent and insults the groups of persons most susceptible to it. Book titles published by one subsidy publisher include *The Adventures of Tildy and Hildy in Story Land Forest; How to Stay Youthful All Your Life; For Each a Woman; The Ugly Woman; A Bachelor Defends American Women; To Hell with the Circus; The Galley Slave Cookbook; God Was, God Is, God Shall Be; The Pony That Lost Her Neigh; The Scars of the Cross; Who's Who in Thoroughbred Racing;* and *How to Shoot Crap to Win.*

How does this business of subsidy publishing work? The author pays to get published, the amount of the publishing fee varying with each manuscript depending upon its length "and other factors" contributing to production costs. "We issue an annual catalog in which your book is described; this catalog goes to bookstores and libraries all over the nation. We submit your book for listing in the standard trade publications such as *Books in Print* and *Publishers Trade List Annual.* When suitable, your book is called to the attention of educators, journalists, columnists, scholars, government officials, and other molders of public opinion . . . But please be realistic. Most books by new authors do not sell well, and most authors do not regain the publishing fee."

The names of famous writers, some of whose works are said to have been published by means of subsidized publishing, are scattered through the pages of one brochure. They are not contemporary authors, and most date from the era when literary works were typically handled by one and the same printer-seller. Not surprisingly, a series of illustrations of production stages from copy-editing to design and production shows these roles filled by males, while the majority of authors' names and photographs are of females. One subsidy press's advertising declares that its reviews appear in many scholarly journals. Clips of reviews (some are mere mentions, rather than book reviews) from *Comparative Education,* the *American Bar Association Journal,* and *Science* appear without issue, date or page citations.

The heading of another type of business's advertisement reads "Looking For A Publisher? XYZ is interested in unpublished manuscripts or class notes suitable for publication as softcover primary texts or supplementary texts. Author must guarantee adoption for his/her classes of 150 copies in the first year. Standard royalties. Attractive production. Standard contract terms. No subsidy is expected or required." A unique manufacturing process is said to enable this organization to publish your book within one month of receipt of manuscript. Correspondence is addressed to "Dear Professor" (which is a rank, not a generic). This is not exactly subsidy publishing nor vanity press, in that a forthright fee to be paid up front is not mentioned. Printing costs are said to be absorbed from revenues generated by sales of your writing or compiling. It is assumed that the author is currently employed, with teaching responsibilities on the faculty of a college or university. Does the author receive royalties? Of course, *but* "your royalty will depend upon the quality of your manuscript. That's an individual decision and we will be happy to talk to you about it . . . Unfortunately, the texts most professors would like to write cannot generate — at least in their first printings — these large scale sales, so many students cannot benefit from the very special emphasis and expertise each professor brings to his classes. . . ."

Subsidy publishing (as distinguished from subsidiary rights, mentioned in a contract for publication) is perceived by many as another designation for vanity publishing, in which a book is produced with little regard to the merit of the work, at the author's expense, and at no risk to the publisher. But the term subsidy publishing is also used to refer to the publishing of works of specialized interest to a relatively small group, e.g. a corporation or institution for which a grant or fund is provided, in which case it may be called a *sponsored book*, especially if the sponsoring organization or person guarantees to purchase ("acquire" may appear in a grant proposal) a significant number of copies. Reference is also made to the provision of *subsidies* in connection with publication of scholarly works in behalf of faculty publishing, especially by university presses. ("Subsidized publishing" is to be avoided.) Luey's 1987 handbook for academic authors, published by a university press, uses the term *subventions* and devotes several pages to subventions *by authors* and as a grant of money from the author to defray costs of publication. This is presented as not being vanity publishing because a vanity press will publish anything an author pays for, and a university press asks only that the author share costs! Luey refers to Smith's 1977 survey which declared an average subvention of $1,000-$2,500 required by university presses, not to enhance their profits but to enable them to publish books that otherwise would not make economic sense.[41,42]

A more recent survey suggests that universities and colleges offer more support for publishing in the humanities than may be generally recognized and describes a "diversity of subsidizing policies" followed by colleges, universities, and university presses. Germano reminds us that, typically, state university personnel contend that their faculty members' book publications cannot be subsidized because they do not have the wealthy endowments of private universities, which in turn refer to the large tax-supported budgets of the public institutions. He surveyed one hundred ten departments concerning the availability of and criteria for subsidies for publication of faculty books. Approximately half of the responding institutions reported "special programs for such purposes." They may be endowed programs, designated as publications funds, lines in the administrator's budget, or derived from research funds or general operating lines. Of the reporting state institutions, 29 percent follow a policy of granting subsidies to their university presses if their institution has a press. "The only definite criterion seems to be the quality of the project; beyond that, few generalizations hold." Such "off the top," not generally known, discretionary policies and uses of monies are conducive to maintenance of the status quo — gatekeeping. One administrator suggested "an ambitious overhaul of the present system of disbursement. 'I would rather see subsidies (for first books at least) funded from a general pool supplied by universities, on recommendation by the university presses and review by an impartial committee, so that the element of vanity publishing could be totally avoided, and so that prospective scholars from richer or more generous universities would not have an unfair advantage.'" Who, then, *is* subsidizing faculty publication, asks Germano. "A diverse number of institutions, state and private; more, perhaps, than scholars or publishers have suspected; fewer than are needed to make every outstanding manuscript publishable."[43]

Subsidy publishers are aware of the women's studies market. One university press's representative appeared on a conference publishing–related panel, where she handed me a business card and an announcement. When these were read carefully, it became clear that this press pays no royalties to authors for books published in its scholarly series because it reasons that writers by trade live from earnings generated by their writing, whereas scholars "usually live by faculty salaries — and their salaries tend to be increased when they publish. So scholars are paid by increased salaries, not by royalties. . . ." Some scholars have noted a *déjà vu* effect in their dealings with trade publishers. One responds to proposals with an "Author's Questionnaire," which asks, "Are there any funds available to assist with the cost of publication and/or are there any organizations or groups which might purchase your book in quantity? (Special prepublication bulk order rates are available.) If so, please provide details." Another press responds with an "Editorial Data Sheet" which has a "Marketing: Advance Sales and Subsidies" section in which one is asked, "Will you have need of substantial quantities of your book which can be ordered in advance of publication at a 50% discount? Approximate number of copies? Will the funding agency for your project or other relevant organizations be interested in prepublication purchase of your book at 50% discount? Approximate number of copies? Name of organizations?"

A classified advertisement in a publication associated with university women and headed Publications reads, "Publish it yourself! Save $100. — $1,000. Free brochure." Technically this relates to another process —

self-publishing. Self-publishing and desk-top publishing are useful for anyone who wants to disseminate information, but recognition in academe generally involves getting a contract with a recognized publisher. For people who have written and want to see their work and themselves in print, self-publication can sometimes be satisfying and even profitable. But before undertaking this approach, consider it in terms of time, skills, and contacts needed to coordinate, manufacture, ship, promote, and do the bookkeeping related to publishing a book.

Rarely will a tenure committee acknowledge "just a bibliography" as a scholarly publication, a book, or a major contribution to the field, despite the fact that a book-length bibliographic publication can provide scholarly enabling and fill a void for many of the writer-compiler's own peers. A scholarly publisher's or editor's overture to you (in writing) might be helpful in justifying a place among your credentials for such lesser works as bibliographic publications, chapters, and books of which you are not the primary author.

The standard definition describes a *bibliography* as an organized list of books which are related in some way, e.g. subject-matter, authorship, time period covered, location, function. It may be helpful to read the material provided by Sheehy regarding bibliography and guides. Note the many titles in his *Guide to Reference Books* index which begin with the words *Bibliographies* and *Bibliography,* and their non–English language counterparts, as well as those beginning *Guide To,* their coverage, and where subject gaps seemingly exist.[44] Selective, as distinguished from comprehensive, bibliographies are likely to fill a need and purpose which can be defined. "Comprehensive" tools tend to be sponsored and carried out by archivists, documentalists, and librarians. A *guide to the literature* and research of a subject field should be distinguished from a bibliography, although it usually includes bibliographic support among its provisions.

Bibliographies provide for two kinds of needs. The user who needs to find out something about a particular publication must track down a specific book in order to *verify* its existence, characteristics, location, etc. – i.e., to ascertain the author's full name, edition, publisher, date of publication, what library has it (a union list is bibliographic), wording of the title, etc. There is also the need to *select* a book, periodical, periodical article, essay, chapter, etc., to meet a particular informational need, which usually involves the user compiling a list (bibliography) of several titles to provide *subject information* regardless of the type of format. The first user usually needs a comprehensive list (e.g. *Books in Print, Comprehensive Dissertation Index*). The second may select from a rather comprehensive list or directory or go directly to a selective list already prepared by an expert such as Farley's *Academic Women and Employment Discrimination: A*

Critical Annotated Bibliography or Franzosa and Mazza's *Integrating Women's Studies into the Curriculum: An Annotated Bibliography.*[45] The expert is thereby subject to the risks of criticism, disagreement, and omission.

Titles which include the word *guide* (and sometimes *handbook*) are often all or partly bibliographic in nature, particularly a guide to the literature or resources or researching of a discipline, field, or subfield. These often become stale within a few years of publication. A comprehensive bibliography can usually be updated by supplement(s) for a while, imposing multiple searches on the user in the interim until the next edition or cumulation. There is no single method for preparation of a bibliography nor for getting it published. Bibliographic citations should be functional. A press which publishes bibliographies may have format guidelines it requires compilers to use. In preparing (selecting) titles for a specific purpose, consider the users' needs. For example, scholars are researching and needing to know about researching the subject of aging and ageism as they relate to females. But would such a bibliography be intended to enable social and behavioral sciences (gerontology) or medical, science, health, physiology (geriatrics) people, or both? Consider the possibility of integrating the titles of the selected publications in such a bibliography, regardless of whether they are books, chapters, essays, speeches, proceedings, government publications, journal issues, journal articles, articles from other types of serials, "reference books," etc., based on their function — their provision of needed subject information. For such a tool, the compiler might consider inclusion of fictional as well as nonfictional works, probably separated into two "collections." For a published bibliography which is intended to serve current needs, consider the importance of including or emphasizing available titles, i.e., books which are in print or otherwise readily obtainable.

Searing's *Introduction to Library Research in Women's Studies* is an extreme example of a book which might be perceived by the inexperienced academic or hasty evaluator as an annotated list of library reference books. The use of "introduction" and "library" modifying "research" may result in some users bypassing such a book. The publisher's series title, *Westview Guides to Library Research,* conveys its role as a *guide.* Examination of this book confirms the presence of cross-references, useful annotations which are not merely descriptive, and in-depth indexing. Several chapters of valuable narrative material precede the bibliographic portion. There would not be much difference between this book and a guide to the literature of women's studies at the time it was published.[31] This type of tool, which is comprehensive *and* in a way selective, requires organizational ability as well as "broad" knowledge of the field which consists of numerous specialized interests. Interdisciplinary bibliographies are always subject to extra problems and scrutiny.

A resource *guide* in a specialized aspect of a field provides an overview at the beginning in one "chapter." The compiler-author should demonstrate and explicate a way of reorganizing that subfield. For example, a guide to the literature or resources of females and aging might, depending on the specific intended users, be organized, not by books and articles, but by information in groups of titles related to women as caregivers, displaced and reentry women, sexuality of older women, nutrition and skeletal disorders, self-image and societal attitudes toward old women, images of middle-aged and old women in the mass media and art, aging of women in cross-cultural perspectives, support communities, public policy including pensions, and a variety of other ways which would not include the use of cosmetics, diseases of older women, women as caretakers of elderly parents, the role of the older woman in the family, protection of the older woman, and other dubious proscriptive and assumptive assignments. To be useful in scholarship, such a resource guide for academicians, professionals, and graduate students would provide an indication of the titles which are classics, e.g. Sontag's "The Double Standard of Aging," and landmarks, e.g. *Ourselves, Growing Older*, regardless of when published, and the basic tools of research, e.g. *Women Studies Abstracts* and *AgeLine*.[46,47,48,49]

I do not commend guides to a literature to the neophyte author. Rather, perhaps begin with selective bibliographies and compilations which are the resources in your campus libraries' collections to support a course or seminar, which is far from looking under a few keywords and happening on subject headings in the card and on-line catalogs and then scanning a periodical index.

What might be unique about your bibliographical publication? What might justify its publication? A need which you can demonstrate and articulate or which a publisher may have already recognized, *and* your qualifications for accomplishing it. To be functional and publishable it must evidence expert selectivity, utilitarian annotations and other aspects of guidance, and accessible organization which you uniquely are able to provide, particularly in professional fields.

For example, Hesslein's *Serials on Aging: An Analytical Guide* has been mentioned in Chapter Two. I commend its organization as a model in several ways. Hesslein presents her rationale for this specialized, directory-like publication in the book's introduction, and she provides a logical, serviceable overall arrangement. The bibliographical portion of the book itself is organized into five parts identifying three hundred and seventy-five serials. The first part lists ninety-six magazines on diverse subjects published primarily for older adults. The majority of the serials is approximately two hundred and twenty-five journals in social gerontology concerned with such social and psychological issues as housing, income, legal assistance, and the economics of aging. Health and biomedicine, and retirement and pensions are included. Newsletters that report on conferences, workshops, meetings, and legislative issues as well as government publications are listed. The final portion of the guide provides information on statistical and reference tools, including bibliographies, abstracting and indexing services. Four separate indexes access the main contents by geographical, subject, title, and publisher or sponsoring organization approaches. Each serial is numbered and provided with the information that typical users will need and in a consistent display arrangement. These data include an entry number, serial title, date the serial was founded, any title changes which have taken place in the interim, current frequency of publication and price, place of publication and publisher, editor's name, whether the serial is self-indexed and illustrated, whether advertising is accepted, circulation, manuscript selection method (e.g. whether it is a refereed journal), availability of microforms and reprints, whether book reviews and special issues are published, titles of indexing and abstracting services and on-line data bases which analyze its contents, target audiences (academic, for example), and availability of sample issues. A descriptive one- or two-paragraph annotation follows. Consider using this technique of numbering each unit (serial in this case) for the organization of any substantial bibliographic project, because it facilitates reorganization, indexing and cross-referencing, as well as accessing (retrieving) the data and information with which you provide the user. Detailed statements describing the potential users, the organization of the tool and each unit, and how to use the book should always precede the body of such a work.

Today, highly selective, subject-specialized bibliographies can be generated by skilled computer-assisted literature searching of hundreds of data bases which are also available for handsearching in print format, e.g. *America: History and Life, Historical Abstracts,* MLA *Bibliography, Medline,* and *Sociology Abstracts.* Messrs. Gilbert and Tatla relied on a computer-assisted keyword search of the dissertation titles stored in the *Comprehensive Dissertation Index* data base to generate their costly published compilation, *Women's Studies: A Bibliography of Dissertations, 1870–1982.* For the introduction to their "unique bibliography," they acknowledge material from Sally Graves's unpublished dissertation. Their qualifications are listed as experience in compilation of bibliographies of dissertations in fields other than women's studies. Their chief source was a computer search using sixty-four keywords in twenty-one conventional subject-areas, e.g. anthropology, education, history, and a "short list of widely influential women (mainly from Uglow's *Dictionary of Women's Biography*)."[50] There are no author and title indexes. Entries are numbered within each of twenty-three topics, e.g. criminology, employment, family, feminism, reproduction, sexuality, sport, and women in the Third World. Only the author's surname and initial, thesis title, degree awarded, and university are provided (i.e. transcribed from the data base printout). There are no *Dissertation Abstracts International* abstract numbers. Granted, women's studies are vast and interdisciplinary, but there are too many "missing" dissertations. A few which spring to mind are Bowles's *Suppression and Expression in Poetry by American Women: Louise Bogan, Denise Levertov and Adrienne Rich*, Feather's *Women Band Directors in Higher Education*, McLeod's *Sex Discrimination Complaints Against Florida Public Institutions of Higher Education: Perceived Effects on the Complainant and the Institution*, Nomura's *The Allied Occupation of Japan: Reform of Japanese Government Labor Policy on Women*, Pharr's *Sex and Politics: Women in Social and Political Movements in Japan*, Roberts's *The Female Image in the Caldecott Medal Award Books*, Shanor's *Social Variables of Women's Sexual Fantasies*, and Yaco's *Suffering Women: Feminine Masochism in Novels by American Women*. University Microfilms International distributes gratis lists which appear competitive and provide fuller data.

Annotating is a skill which you acquire by practicing it. Once it is yours, you will also be able to scan and to read more rapidly for meaning. The purpose of such an annotation is to provide useful information for the reader-user. Annotations can compare, describe, evaluate, relate (to each other), highlight, underscore, summarize. Sometimes they are written in cryptic style (incomplete sentences), but your annotations should consist of full sentences. They should also be consistent. Do not fill space with generalizations. Avoid such adjectives as "excellent" and "good"—rarely would you select a publication which was not "good," although it is conceivable, in which case your annotation should justify your having had to select it. Avoid the first person singular. It is not necessary to say, "This is included because. . . ." Do not begin with, "This book. . ." or "This article. . . ." Don't use contractions (such as "don't"). In short, there are some specific requirements connected with this type of publication work, but there are also numerous benefits which you can, if you wish to, learn from this experience.

The utility of any selective bibliography is enhanced by the provision of meaningful annotations which justify inclusion of the selections on the particular bibliography for its particular purpose, which you should clarify at the outset. These annotations are not simply summaries or descriptions—they are also your personal perception of each publication. This bibliography is an enabler tied to a specific purpose. Examine and evaluate it and decide whether to select (or deselect) it for inclusion. Include the publication's relevance to your topics, where and how you predict it would be supportive in research and writing. You might note some relationship to another publication, which might appear on the same bibliography. The annotation is derived from your reasons for including it on this bibliography. Thus, it is not simply a description.

You are preparing a selected bibliography to support someone's subsequent work which must accomplish a definite function. So your annotations communicate to the reader-user the publication's content, potential, special utility in the context of their subfield. Why you have selected it for this purpose is your recommendation.

How is it possible to select and annotate without reading an entire book cover-to-cover? In this case, it is not. The table of contents, introduction, appendices, and even the index can communicate a lot, however. As you look at these and other aspects of the volume ask yourself how they would fit into users' informational needs. You must read and use and examine the book. Exploit all of the information on the cataloging record even before you select the book, however. Get the information down to inspire your annotating. The series of which the book may be a part can influence your perception of it, but be cautious about assumptions. Consider whether there is significant bibliographic support in it; whether it is illustrated *and* these illustrations are crucial in utilizing the publication; what the added entries are in the cataloging records. Other sources of inspiration and confirmation for the neophyte bibliographer are reviews. Check out what others whose needs are similar to yours and your readers' have said. Rarely quote from annotations contained in a guide to the literature or from book reviews. It is, however, occasionally necessary to quote briefly within your annotation from the book or article itself. Include the page number of the quote.

• • •

"Of what a strange nature is knowledge! It clings to the mind, when it has once seized on it, like a lichen on the rock." Mary Wollstonecraft Godwin Shelley (1797–1851.) English author. *Letter 4, To Mrs. Saville, England.* Chapter 13. Frederick L. Jones, ed. Norman, Oklahoma: University of Oklahoma Press, 1944.

A textbook, particularly when an instructor assigns and follows it religiously, can become a powerful influence. The accoutrements of the traditional lecture-textbook method include a required purchase by each student in a course which is required or satisfies a requirement. Some instructors attempt to alleviate this situation by providing a list of supplementary readings usually available on library reserve from which students can choose. Where they have the option, instructors have turned to the contemporary cut-and-paste "course reader" of related readings they select and have duplicated, collated, and sold locally. Some instructors utilize this "course reader" as a trial phase in giving birth to their own textbook publication. Somewhere in between is the anthology approach to replacing the college textbook. When carefully and expertly compiled, edited, and revised, an anthology can be commercially and educationally successful, especially in lower division, interdisciplinary courses. Freeman's *Women: A Feminist Perspective,* now in its fourth edition, is an example of an anthology used as a textbook with and without supplementary reading in many undergraduate courses.[51]

Writing a textbook as your first book publication is not recommended, and relatively little space will be devoted to this topic here. Decide early whether you are writing a general nonfiction book for trade publication *or* you intend it to function as a textbook, because there are significant differences between the two in your approach to the publishers, the publication process itself, and marketing. The prospectus should provide considerable detail. Plan on providing much more of the work itself for the publisher's examination, including a table of contents, outlines of the chapters, and several sample chapters. You will need to defend your credentials as more than an expert — as an authority on the subject. Explain your intended users — students *and* teachers — in terms of courses, levels, institutions, and enrollments. How will your textbook be special and competitive? Perhaps provide a list of nations where it would sell well or a list of colleges outside the United States to be contacted. (Consult *The World of Learning* and the institutions' catalogs, which are available in microfiche form in university libraries.) In addition to the United States and Canada, markets for English-language college textbooks are the United Kingdom, Europe, Australia and New Zealand, the British Commonwealth, the Middle East, Scandinavia, Latin America, the Netherlands, Japan, Africa, and Southeast Asia, in that order. It is these nations with English as a first or second language that have courses resembling the collegiate structure of the United States.

Textbooks provide the source of 90 percent of instruction. They provide 80 percent of the information to which elementary and secondary school students are exposed. Government funding is provided more consistently for textbooks than for other instructional materials.[52,53,54] Textbook publishing is generally considered low-profit and very competitive, but it is nonetheless big business. Publishers of textbooks include some of the big names (Doubleday, McGraw-Hill, and Macmillan, for example) and some you may not have heard of yet (Enslow, Dellen, and Salem, for example). A list of "major" textbook publishers would include Prentice-Hall; McGraw-Hill; CBS Educational and Professional Publishing; Scott, Foresman; and Harper and Row. Other large publishers of significant numbers of textbook titles are Addison-Wesley, Random House, Academic Press, D.C. Heath, Houghton Mifflin, W.B. Saunders, J. Wiley and Sons, and Little, Brown. Small publishers with some textbook publication emphasis include Charles E. Merrill, C.V. Mosby, W.W. Norton, St. Martin's

Press, Wadsworth, and Bobbs-Merrill. Member-publishers of the influential Association of American Publishers include Cambridge, Oxford, and Harvard university presses, and the University Press of America. Conglomerate corporate interests and influences are represented among college textbook publishers: CBI Publishing Company, a division of Van Nostrand Reinhold, and CBS Educational and Professional Publishing, with textbook publication imprints of Holt, Saunders College, Dryden, and Praeger, are examples.

The best textbook returns in 1986 were in the elementary and high school markets. One study predicts 100 percent elementary–high school market growth by 1991, reaching four and one half billion dollars.[55] Unless one is on a college of education faculty, textbook-writing for this market is unlikely to be considered a major contribution to scholarship. Many school textbooks are written by two or more persons. One, a higher education faculty member, the pedagogue professor with academic credentials, is primary author. The other, an elementary grade or high school subject, classroom teacher with the experience in the trenches, is usually secondary.

To be adoptable by a school district, a textbook tends to be all things to all people, acknowledging current topics but not controversial in its evident commitments. When a textbook is adopted by an instructor for a course or by a department for a regularly offered course, it is purchased by a captive audience representing considerable potential sales. Textbook authorship can be more lucrative for the skilled writer than most types of book publication, although many experts contend that a trade book generates more money from its ongoing sales. Because they cost more to publish than general nonfiction tradebooks, publishers print many more copies of textbooks, which generate more royalties. On the other hand, a textbook can become outdated rapidly.

Textbook writing is so specialized and technical that one continuing education program offers seminars on preparation of the manuscript for social science and business textbooks. The time and effort required for a textbook's creation should be carefully considered in relationship to advancement in academe. Published textbooks are presumably written by authorities on the subject. A successful textbook can generate the admiration (or jealousy) of one's colleagues. We have all heard of Professor XYZ's great reputation, documented in part by his having authored *the* textbook on the subject. The rewards in academe of textbook publishing, then, are variable—the textbook which is widely adopted and financially successful may enhance one's reputation, which may contribute to professional advancement. Whether it will be judged a scholarly contribution or meritorious is unpredictable.

From the perspective of getting published for professional advancement, even a college textbook is not usually the result of specific scholarly research or endeavors as is a doctoral dissertation, research report, or theoretical treatise. Creation of a textbook for use in numerous institutions' Sociology 1 course, for example, requires skills and knowledge which will enable its author to take the discipline and to arrange it comprehensively and accurately in an appealing manner while focusing on selected aspects of it. All this must be accomplished at the easy-reading level of a group of students and provided with summaries, bibliographic and other supportive features, and accompanying instructor's materials. To sell your textbook to the publisher, you must be an authority who has already accomplished the opposite—specific detailed research and reportage of a relatively minute aspect of that field. Furthermore, your textbook must be a unique, competitive, commercial product. It is possible to write a great textbook for a subject or course in which one is not yet a great teacher. In fact, writing a textbook contributes to the instructor-author's teaching abilities.

When your textbook is published and marketed, the next step is to begin its revision, the second edition.

Notes

1. Astin, Helen S., and Diane E. Davis. "Research Productivity Across the Life and Career Cycles: Facilitators and Barriers for Women." In *Scholarly Writing & Publishing: Issues, Problems, and Solutions*, pp. 147–160. Edited by Mary Frank Fox. Boulder, Colorado: Westview, 1985.

2. Anderson, Dorothy J. "ALA's Hidden Agenda." *American Libraries* 16 (June 1985): 424, 426.

3. Bowles, Gloria. "'Feminist Scholarship' and 'Women's Studies': Implications for University Presses'." *Scholarly Publishing* 19 (April 1988): 163–168. p. 166.

4. *1987–1988 Books in Print, 40th edition*. Volume I: pp. xi, xii, xiv. There are also spinoff and related titles which list paperbound, children's, and forthcoming books.

5. "Letters of Support Needed for Dr. Sharon Leder." *NWSA Perspectives* 4 (Fall 1986): 17. Leder, Sharon, with Andrea Abbott. *The Language of Exclusion: The Poetry of Emily Dickinson and Christina Rossetti. (Contributions in Women's Studies #83.)* Westport, Connecticut: Greenwood, 1987. Positive prepublication reviews of the book by Professors Martha V. Vicinus, Mary Anne Ferguson, Moira Ferguson, and Berenice Fisher had been received. Leder also faced the gatekeeping aspect of academic judgment which seemingly depreciates women's publications that are not sole-authored or senior-authored books.". . . some feminist literary scholars, such as Lillian Robinson, have held that recent efforts to add women's names to core reading lists have been too strictly based on the standards already established in the canon. Expanding the canon on that basis, they argue, could lead to the promotion of only those female writers whose work most closely resembles that of accepted male authors." [Draine, Betsy. "Academic Feminists Must Make Sure Their Commitments Are Not Self-Serving". *Chronicle of Higher Education* 34 (August 10, 1988): A40]. Robinson is cited in the preface of *The Language of Exclusion* as having contributed part of the intellectual and ideological apparatus with which the authors

worked. She has evaluted the book as taking the words "spinster recluse poet," so often and uncritically applied to both Rossetti and Dickinson, and considering them as features to examine rather than cause for dismissal. "The study grasps each of those words and embraces them in all their historical and literary dimensions, while also turning them inside out and upside down. It's an exciting process for the reader to be part of." [July 14, 1988, letter from Dr. Robinson, Affiliated Scholar, Stanford University Institute for Research on Women and Gender, and author of *Sex, Class and Culture* and *Monstrous Regiment,* co-author of *Feminist Scholarship: Kindling in the Groves of Academe.*]

6. McMillen, Liz. "Legal Experts Eye 2 Sex-Bias Lawsuits Brought by Women's Studies Scholars; Plantiffs Hit Tenure Evaluation Process, Raise Questions About Status of Feminist Scholarship." *Chronicle of Higher Education* **32** (April 9, 1986): 23–26. p. 26.

7. Arnold, June. "Feminist Presses and Feminist Politics." *Quest: A Feminist Quarterly* **3** (1976): 18–26.

8. Stewart, Donald E. "Publishing, Book" pp. 249–54. *The ALA Yearbook of Library & Information Services: A Review of Library Events. Volume 12.* Chicago, Illinois: American Library Association, 1987. p. 249.

9. Kozol, Jonathan. *Illiterate America.* Garden City, New York: Anchor/Doubleday, 1985.

10. West, Celeste, and Valerie Wheat. "The Passionate Perils of Publishing." *Booklegger* **4** (Summer 1978): issue. p. 10.

11. The authors of the Council on Library Resources, Inc.'s *Scholarship in the Electronic Age* . . . refer to "a sizable, repetitive body of literature, reflecting in part the economic difficulties faced by scholarly publishers and the seemingly widespread dissatisfaction among authors with the prices of scholarly publications, time lags in the publishing process, etc." (page viii). Lowry, Anita, and Junko Stuveras. 1987.

12. Dessauer, John. "Book Publishing," pp. 292–294. *ALA Yearbook: A Review of Library Events. Volume 1.* Chicago, Illinois: American Library Association, 1976. p. 293.

13. West, Celeste, and Valerie Wheat. "The Passionate Perils of Publishing." *Booklegger* **4** (Summer 1978): issue. p. 5.

14. *Media Report to Women* **14** (March–April 1986): 6.

15. Bagdikian, Ben. *The Media Monopoly, 2nd edition.* Boston, Massachusetts: Beacon. 1987.

16. West, Celeste and Valerie Wheat. "The Passionate Perils of Publishing." *Booklegger* **4** (Summer 1978): issue. p. 7.

17. Abramson, Joan. *The Invisible Woman: Discrimination in the Academic Profession.* San Francisco, California: Jossey-Bass, 1976. Although this title is out of print, it is listed in *1987–1988 Books in Print* as obtainable through Books on Demand, a University Microfilms International imprint which reprints out-of-print books that are in demand.

18. Abramson, Joan. *Old Boys—New Women: The Politics of Sex Discrimination.* New York: Praeger, 1979.

19. Correspondence dated January 24, 1985.

20. Powell, Walter W. *Getting into Print: The Decision-Making Process in Scholarly Publishing.* Chicago, Illinois: University of Chicago Press, 1985. p. 209–10.

21. Correspondence dated May 11, 1988.

22. The American Library Association adopted in 1983 *Guidelines for Authors, Editors and Publishers of Literature in the Library and Information Field* which

declare that an author should submit the manuscript or query to only one publisher at a time, but that if this is done, the author should inform each publisher. "The publisher shall acknowledge receipt of a manuscript or query promptly, at least within two weeks, and indicate acceptance or rejection for publication within twelve weeks of receipt. If a publisher cannot meet this timetable, an approximate length of time needed for the decision on publishing should be disclosed to the author before the end of the twelve-week period."

23. Stewart, Donald E. "Publishing, Book," pp. 264–67. *The ALA Yearbook of Library & Information Services: A Review of Library Events. Volume 13. Chicago, Illinois: American Library Association, 1988.* p. 264.

24. *Chronicle of Higher Education* **34** (January 13, 1988): A4.

25. Bowles, Gloria. "'Feminist Scholarship' and 'Women's Studies': Implications for University Presses." *Scholarly Publishing* **19** (April 1988): 163–168. p. 163.

26. International Federation of Women Lawyers, 186 Fifth Avenue, New York, New York, USA 10010. In the United States, the National Association of Women Lawyers is located at 750 North Lake Shore Drive, Chicago, Illinois 60611. The *Encyclopedia of Associations* has information about both.

27. *Chronicle of Higher Education* **34** (January 13, 1988): A4. University of Nebraska Press Director and Editor-in-Chief Willis G. Regier, during the Modern Language Association 1988 conference session on the ethics of publishing.

28. The Authors Guild, Inc., 234 West 44th Street, New York, New York 10003. The *Encyclopedia of Associations* has information about the Guild and related organizations.

29. The National Writers Union, 13 Astor Place, 7th floor, New York, New York 10003.

30. Bunnin, Brad. *The Writer's Legal Companion, with a Chapter on the Author and the Business of Publishing, by Peter Beren.* Reading, Massachusetts: Addison-Wesley, 1988.

31. Searing, Susan. *Introduction to Library Research in Women's Studies.* Boulder, Colorado: Westview, 1985.

32. See for example, Proof Readers' Marks and Symbols, pages 116–17, with examples, page 118 of marginal and in-line marks, provided by the Council of Biology Editors, in Brock, Thomas D., *Successful Textbook Publishing: The Author's Guide.* Madison, Wisconsin: Science Tech, 1985.

33. Larsen, Michael. *Literary Agents: How to Get and Work with the Right One for You.* Cincinnati, Ohio: Writer's Digest, 1986. p. 81.

34. Henderson, Bill. *Rotten Reviews: A Literary Companion I and II.* Wainscott, New York: Pushcart, 1986 and 1987.

35. McMillen, Liz. "Legal Experts Eye 2 Sex-Bias Lawsuits Brought by Women's Studies Scholars; Plaintiffs Hit Tenure Evaluation Process, Raise Questions About Status of Feminist Scholarship." *Chronicle of Higher Education* **32** (April 9, 1986): 23–26. p. 24. "Says Annette Kolodny, a feminist scholar who was awarded more than $100,000 in an out-of-court settlement against the University of New Hampshire."

36. Gilbert, Victor Francis, and Darshan Singh Tatla. *Women's Studies: A Bibliography of Dissertations, 1870–1982.* New York: Blackwell, 1985.

37. University Microfilms International, 300 North Zeeb Road, Ann Arbor, Michigan 48107. Telephone 800-521-0600.

38. *1971 Current Biography.* New York: Wilson, 1971. p. 273.

39. Peyre, Henri. "Random Notes on a Misunderstanding." In *The Thesis and*

the Book. Edited by Eleanor Harmon and Ian Montagnes. Toronto: University of Toronto Press, 1976.

40. Larsen, Michael. *Literary Agents: How to Get and Work with the Right One for You.* Cincinnati, Ohio: Writer's Digest, 1986. pp. 37–38, 42–50.

41. Luey, Beth. *A Handbook for Academic Authors.* New York: Columbia University Press, 1987. Pages 75–79, "Subventions"; Chapter 5, "Working with Your Publisher."

42. Smith, John Hazel. "Subvention of Scholarly Publishing." *Scholarly Publishing* **9** (October 1977): 19–29.

43. Germano, William P. "Helping the Local Faculty with Publication Support." *Scholarly Publishing* **15** (October 1983): 11–16.

44. Sheehy, Eugene P. *Guide to Reference Books, 10th ed.* Chicago, Illinois: American Library Association, 1986. pp. 1–106.

45. Farley, Jennie. *Academic Women and Employment Discrimination: A Critical Annotated Bibliography. (Cornell Industrial and Labor Relations Bibliography Series #16.)* Ithaca, New York: New York State School of Industrial and Labor Relations, Cornell University, 1982. Franzosa, Susan Douglas, and Karen A. Mazza. *Integrating Women's Studies into the Curriculum: An Annotated Bibliography.* Westport, Connecticut: Greenwood, 1984.

46. Sontag, Susan. "The Double Standard of Aging." *Saturday Review* **55** (September 23, 1972): 29–38.

47. Doress, Paula Brown, and Diana Laskin Siegal and the Midlife and Older Women Book Project. *Ourselves, Growing Older: Women Aging with Knowledge and Power.* New York: Simon & Schuster in cooperation with the Boston Women's Health Book Collective, 1987.

48. *Women Studies Abstracts.* Rush, New York: Rush, 1972– .

49. *AgeLine* is a data base produced by the American Association of Retired Persons at the National Gerontology Resource Center, Washington, D.C., available on-line through BRS.

50. Gilbert, Victor Francis, and Darshan Singh Tatla. *Women's Studies: A Bibliography of Dissertations, 1870–1982.* New York: Blackwell, 1985. p. vii. Graves, Sally. *Library Provision Resources for Women's Studies Courses in the United Kingdom.* Presented to the Department of Information Studies, University of Sheffield, 1984. Uglow, Jennifer S. *The International Dictionary of Women's Biography.* New York: Continuum, 1982.

51. Freeman, Jo. *Women: A Feminist Perspective.* Mountain View, California: Mayfield. 1st edition, 1975; 2nd edition, 1979; 3rd edition, 1984; 4th edition, 1989.

52. Solomon, Margaret. "Textbook Selection Committees: What Teachers Can Do." *Learning* **6** (March 1978): 43.

53. English, Raymond. "The Politics of Textbook Adoption." *Phi Delta Kappan* **62** (December 1980): 275–78.

54. Benthul, Herman F. "Trends in Education: The Textbook Past and Future." *Curriculum Review* **17** (May 1978): 89–91. (ERIC EJ 184–426).

55. Stewart, Donald E. "Publishing, Book," pp. 249–54. *The ALA Yearbook of Library & Information Services: A Review of Library Events. Volume 12.* Chicago, Illinois: American Library Association, 1987. p. 249.

Bibliography

In addition to many of the titles cited in the Notes, the following publications should be consulted.

Bagdikian, Ben H. *The Media Monopoly, 2nd edition.* Boston, Massachusetts: Beacon, 1987.

Balkin, Richard. *How to Understand and Negotiate a Book Contract or Magazine Agreement.* Cincinnati, Ohio: Writer's Digest, 1985.

Bernstein, Harriet Tyson. "When More Is Less: The 'Mentioning' Problem in Textbooks." *American Educator* (American Federation of Teachers) 9 (Summer 1985): 26–29, 44.

Bridgewater, Carol Austin, et al. "Ethical Issues and the Assignment of Publication Credit." *American Psychologist* 36 (May 1981): 524–5.

Brock, Thomas D. *Successful Textbook Publishing: The Author's Guide.* Madison, Wisconsin: Science Tech, 1985.

Clardy, Andrea Fleck. ". . . Feminist Presses." *Ms.* 14 (August 1985): 65–8.

Cleaver, Diane. *The Literary Agent and the Writer: A Professional Guide.* Boston, Massachusetts: The Writer, 1984.

Cook, Beverly, et al. *Report on Twenty Textbooks Used in American Government* [an analysis of the coverage of women in politics and government, as presented in 20 texts used in American Government courses]. 1984. Available from Dr. Cook, Department of Political Science, University of Wisconsin, Box 413, 620 Bolton Hall, Milwaukee, Wisconsin 53201.

Denham, Alice, and Weldenn Broom. "The Role of the Author." *Scholarly Publishing* 12 (April 1981): 249–58.

Dorn, Fred J. "Do Scholarly Authors Need Literary Agents?" *Scholarly Publishing* 14 (October 1982): 79–86.

English, Raymond. "The Politics of Textbook Adoption." *Phi Delta Kappan* 62 (December 1980): 275–78.

Fox, Mary Frank. "The Transition from Dissertation Student to Publishing Scholar and Professional." In *Scholarly Writing & Publishing: Issues, Problems, and Solutions,* pp. 6–16. Edited by Mary Frank Fox. Boulder, Colorado: Westview, 1985.

Freeman, Jo. "Publishing a College Textbook." In *Scholarly Writing & Publishing: Issues, Problems, and Solutions,* pp. 51–72. Edited by Mary Frank Fox. Boulder, Colorado: Westview, 1985.

Harman, Eleanor, and Ian Montagnes. *The Thesis and the Book.* Toronto, Canada, and Buffalo, New York: University of Toronto Press, 1976.

Holmes, Olive. "Thesis to Book: What to Get Rid Of." *Scholarly Publishing* 5 (July 1974a): 339–49 [Part 1]; 6 (October 1974b): 40–50 [Part 2]. "Thesis to Book: What to Do with What Is Left." *Scholarly Publishing* 6 (January 1975): 165–76.

Jalongo, Mary Renck. "Faculty Productivity in Higher Education." *Educational Forum* 49 (Winter 1985): 171–82.

Larsen, Michael. *How to Write a Book Proposal.* Cincinnati, Ohio: Writer's Digest, 1985.

————. *Literary Agents: How to Get and Work with the Right One for You.* Cincinnati, Ohio: Writer's Digest, 1986.

Luey, Beth. "Revising a Dissertation," pp 23–35. In her *Handbook for Academic Authors.* New York: Columbia University Press, 1987.

McMillen, Liz. "A Doctoral Dissertation Is Not Yet a Book, Young Tenure-Seeking Scholars Are Told. More Revisions, Less Documentation, and Scrutiny of Presses Urged by Editorial Consultants." *Chronicle of Higher Education* 31 (February 5, 1986): 23–24.

Mallis, Ronald. "Textbook Publishing: Some Notes on Responsibility." In *Women in Print, Volume II: Opportunities for Women's Studies Publication in Language and Literature,* pp. 35–40. Edited by Joan E. Hartman and Ellen Messer-Davidow. New York: Modern Language Association of America. 1982.

Markland, Murray T. "Taking Criticism—and Using It." *Scholarly Publishing* **14** (February 1983): 139–47.

Mullins, Carolyn J.A. *Guide to Writing and Publishing in the Social and Behavioral Sciences.* New York: Wiley, 1977.

Norwick, Kenneth P., and Jerry Simon Chasen. *The Rights of Authors and Artists: The Basic ACLU Guide to the Legal Rights of Authors and Artists.* New York: Bantam, 1984.

O'Connor, Kathleen. "Why Don't Women Publish More Journal Articles?" *Chronicle of Higher Education* **21** (November 3, 1980): 25.

Orr, Carol. "Feminist Scholarship and the University Press." In *Women in Print, Volume II: Opportunities for Women's Studies Publication in Language and Literature,* pp. 13–22. Edited by Joan E. Hartman and Ellen Messer-Davidow. New York: Modern Language Association of America, 1982.

Persell, Caroline Hodges. "Scholars and Book Publishing." In *Scholarly Writing & Publishing: Issues, Problems, and Solutions,* pp. 33–50. Edited by Mary Frank Fox. Boulder, Colorado: Westview, 1985.

Rinzler, Carol E. "When Is a Manuscript Acceptable?" *Publishers Weekly* **224** (September 23, 1983): 26–28.

Scholarly Publishing: A Journal for Authors and Publishers. Society for Scholarly Publishing. University of Toronto Press. 1969–   .

Topkis, Gladys S. "Book Publishing: An Editor's-Eye View." In *Scholarly Writing & Publishing: Issues, Problems, and Solutions,* pp. 73–98. Edited by Mary Frank Fox. Boulder, Colorado: Westview, 1985.

United States Commission on Civil Rights. *Characters in Textbooks: A Review of the Literature. (Clearinghouse Publication #62.)* Washington, D.C., May 1980. 19pp.

Valian, Virginia. "Learning to Work." In *Working It Out,* pp. 163–78. Edited by Sara Ruddick and Pamela Daniels. New York: Pantheon, 1977.

Warming, Eloise O. "Textbooks." In *Encyclopedia of Educational Research,* 5th edition. Volume 4. New York: Macmillan, 1982.

Winkler, Karen J. "To Revise, or Not to Revise, the Textbook." *Chronicle of Higher Education* **20** (January 17, 1982): 17–18.

Chapter Four

A Liberal Education
in Twelve Volumes

"There; how d'ye like that, eh? A liberal education in twelve volumes, with an index." Dorothy M. Richardson (1873–1957). English novelist. *Pilgrimage*. Volume II, Chapter 24. New York: Knopf, 1938.

In addition to those basics of scholarly and professional publication — journal articles and monographic books — several other forms can take on the character of potential contribution to the promotion-tenure dossier, scholarship, and one's profession. Some of these other modes of publication which should be considered in this context are reviews of books and other creative works, essays and chapters "in" books, anthological books, translations and bilingual international works, and audiovisuals and their related printed materials. This chapter concludes with consideration of several matters closely related to most writing for publication. They include ways to facilitate getting the first academic publication; sources of ideas and ways of generating topics for research and publication in academe; some writing and work organization guidelines including application of aspects of the "new technology" to getting published; and the need to go beyond mere avoidance of stereotyped language, images, and concepts. Some recommendations regarding professional development of women in academe through their contributions as published authors and scholars are also in order.

Book and Other Reviews

"My book came out last week. I have prayed to be kept out of sight, and to be honored as an instrument in the hand of God. Who knows what good may be done. I have also prayed to be kept humble if it should meet with any approbation and am not sensible of any elation regarding it." Janet Sinclair Colquhoun (1781–1846). Scottish. *Diary* entry, March 2, 1823. Of her book, *Thoughts on the Religious Profession and Defective Practice in Scotland.* From *A Memoir of Lady Colquhoun* by James Hamilton, Chapter 2. J. Nesbet, 1849.

A review is generally considered to be an evaluation of a specific book, play, or motion picture, published in a periodical such as a newspaper or magazine shortly after its appearance. Publication of a review in a scholarly or professional journal is likely to be considerably delayed. A scholarly book may receive only one review in a specialized journal. If that review is inadequate or unfair, there may be no others to offset its effect on the author's career and the book's sales. Although book reviews may be acceptable to one's institution, department, or promotion committee as evidence of scholarly productivity or professional contribution, some types of reviews are regarded as more meritorious than others. The *review essay* is a bibliographical essay on the literature of a subject, and it is normally written by a recognized published expert. *Book reviews* are also sometimes confused with "criticism," which is usually concerned with some aspect of a writer's style, dominant themes, or critical reputation and may appear at any time.

Try to determine how your department values reviews as publications and professional service. These are usually reviews of individual creative works, mainly book reviews. Other possibilities include reviews of periodicals themselves — one of the numerous new journals perhaps — and especially in the humanities, motion pictures and theatrical productions. Most book reviews are now "signed," i.e., the author-reviewer and her or his institution are identified.

It is acceptable to volunteer to review a particular book for one of the many periodicals in academe which publish various types of book reviews. Start early and small, and make your offer to a periodical allied with an association or association task force or caucus of which you are an active member. Check the current issue for the name and address of the person who organizes and edits the book reviews section. Offer to review a specific newly published book which you have read in your mutual field. Reviewing foreign publications appears to increase chances of getting book reviews published. Later, you can offer to review regularly, which suggests that the book review editor will route to you review copies of newly published books. The journal book review person requests these, or they are sent spontaneously by book publishers to the journal. An increasing number of journals list "Books Received" (but not reviewed); you can offer to review one of these titles.

Remuneration for book reviewing typically consists of the book reviewed. If one is asked to prepare an extensive review, in a sense an article, for a journal which pays for articles, there may be the possibility of payment. Include with your offer to review a particular book or to be in the pool of reviewers for your specialized aspect of the journal's subject a brief biography highlighting your qualifications as a book reviewer. Your resume might not suffice to communicate the specific relevancies for this responsibility. They might derive from your education, dissertation topic, teaching and other experience, current appointment and institution, other publications and published reviews, honors, reputation, and commitments. Focus on specialized aspects of your field or discipline which are the journal's concerns that you uniquely can provide. Specify your strengths for this service. Within the *performing arts*, this might be expressed as string instruments, or nineteenth and twentieth century music history. Other examples are *science and technology:* agricultural plant science and agronomy; *history:* Pacific history; *anthropology:* European ethnology; *political science:* country studies, e.g. Turkey and Greece; *sports and physical education:* coaching "women's sports"; *women's studies:* theory, feminist perspectives of art; as well as *business management* and *nonprint media* areas.

Think in terms of five weeks turnaround, and indicate how often you would be able to schedule such a responsibility. Better still, ascertain the time limit and length and types of reviews normally published by the journal, and express your interest in these terms. Be sure you are able to commit yourself to whatever arrangement you volunteer.

If you offer to review books for a periodical sponsored by an association of which you are a current member, the journal or book review editor may respond with a form eliciting information considered relevant by the editorial board and the association. Approaching relatively new periodicals which have not yet set up a stable of on call reviewers can be productive. The new (1988) quarterly NWSA Journal asks whether you are a current National Women's Studies Association member and about your affiliation and position, Association caucuses and task forces participation, your "academic discipline," major area of interest, and books you have written. Whether you would like to review books with an interdisciplinary or multidisciplinary focus is a logical question for this journal. Areas in which you would like to review books and other materials reflect the structure of academe and scholarship as well as particular feminist concerns, e.g. government and politics, women and religion, women and work, Third World women, psychology, feminist literary criticism, music; poor and working class women, international feminism, lesbian issues, sexual harassment, and feminist pedagogy, aging and ageism, censorship and pornography, battering, and reproductive technology.

Although it is unwise for the author to attempt to influence a periodical's book review editor to route her or his book to a particular reviewer, it is less subject to criticism if one communicates to a book review editor interest in a book as potential reviewer of it. In this case, the implication is that the journal will receive the book from its publisher based on subject specialization of the book and the journal, and might route it to you as a regular reviewer.

Although book reviews which appear in "recognized journals" will be valued more than others, there are occasions when you might offer to review a particular book title for a periodical with small circulation which is neither indexed nor abstracted. *The Campus Troublemakers* is an important book deserving wide reception. When it was published, it appeared that the *Journal of Educational Equity and Leadership* had a feeble publishing record of articles on *gender* equity. Because I owned a copy of the book, I offered to provide a review for JEEL's occasional essay review section.[1]

The term "feminist criticism" can and should be applied to the study of literature. Kolodny explains that when applied to the study of literature, it is used in a variety of contexts to cover a variety of activities, including criticism by a woman, criticism from a feminist perspective by a woman of a "man's book," and criticism by a woman about a "woman's book" or about female authors.[2] Bibliographies of women in literature are conventionally organized in terms of literary criticism examining women characters in relation to their environments and as myth or symbol, essays viewing feminist criticism as simply an approach to literature, biographical studies and interviews of women writers, and *reviews* of their works.

The distinction between a *review* and a *critical study* is important for retrieval of both information and documents. When you need to locate critical studies, scholarly interpretations, or in-depth analyses, use bibliographies, guides to library research, subject catalogs, and periodical indexes for literature, history, and other disciplines. A citation index such as the *Arts and Humanities Citation Index* is particularly useful in providing leads to reviews and criticism.

The two basic types of book reviews are the lengthy essay and the short evaluation. The *essay review* should not be confused with the review or bibliographical essay of the literature. The essay review of a book cites other research or publications which support, refute, modify, or clarify what is presented in the reviewed book, and can be a lengthy critical study considering all major points. It goes into considerable detail about how the book compares with others in the same field. If it reports research, it answers the questions of where and how well this research fits into the whole body of research in the subject. The essay review writer provides both a critical review of the book *and* a reflection on its place in relationship to other publications. Related titles should be included and the book itself related to both recent publications and landmark books. Strengths and weaknesses may be spelled out, particularly for a periodical readership that may be considering purchase or use of the book in connection with a course, and especially if it is a costly reference book. Essay reviews are published primarily in subject-specialized journals. As essays, they may also be indexed as articles in standard periodical and essay indexes.

Another book review format is the consideration by one reviewer of several current books in the same discipline. A journal may connect several books having something in common with a reviewer who has broad experience and concern for the subject matter and is able to consider each in a relatively brief review. For example, Chambers reviewed one 1985 book and three 1986 books from three publishers together in four pages of the winter 1988 *Signs* journal issue: Birke's *Women, Feminism, and Biology,* Bleier's *Feminist Approaches to Science,* Rosser's *Teaching Science and Health From a Feminist Perspective,* and Sapiro's *Women, Biology, and Public Policy.*[3]

James Russell Lowell considered that "nature fits all her children with something to do; he who would write and can't write, can surely review." In addition to half the population, he also overlooked the expert, shorter review perceived by many of those who have not tried their hand at it to be little more than a 75–150 word annotation! This type of review is usually evaluative. Short reviews of this type are published by scholarly journals as well as periodicals functioning as reviewing media. The American Library Association's *Booklist* annotations are prepared by staff members, while the commercial *Library Journal* features a section of short reviews prepared by librarians employed in the field. Reviews for the Association of College and Research Libraries' review journal, *Choice*, are prepared by undergraduate "faculty members and librarians" representing almost nine hundred United States and Canadian colleges and universities. Approximately 77 percent of the reviewers are men, "paralleling the gender distribution in academe" explains away a *Choice* editorial. Five percent review nonprinted media. The typical *Choice* reviewer reviews 2.5 books a year. Reviews appear approximately six months after publication. "The subject strength of the reviews and reviewers, and the acceptance of *Choice* in the academic community aligns the journal closely with scholarly publications." [sic][4]

When allocating their time, even academic librarians concerned with the "equivalent tenure" afforded some should attempt to determine the relative credit that short reviews published in periodicals such as *Library Journal* and *Choice* will generate. Probably reviews published in *Choice* offer more potential for them, but one must be prepared to have what she may consider significant changes made in her copy and to defend her statements about books. I find that the best way to deal with a periodical's apparent fear of alienating book publishers or not remaining competitive with other review periodicals is to provide with my review a cover letter documenting everything in my review, a not unfamiliar situation when preparing forthright and utilitarian reviews on gender-related topics. For example, I accompanied my review of *Women's Studies: A Bibliography of Dissertations, 1870—1982* with a list to document my contentions that, although reference was made by the compilers to "12,000 unpublished dissertations," a fair number had been published, occasionally with the same title, e.g. Millett's *Sexual Politics*, and that although women's studies is vast, there were too many "missing" dissertations.[5] Each year members of the reviewers' pool are surveyed and may be dropped if they are no longer considered qualified. Their nominations of potential reviewers in areas for which reviewers are needed is usually part of the survey. In 1985, for example, these areas included nonprint media in biology, business management, and political science; books on coaching, and sociology areas of drug and alcohol use, statistics, theory and research methods.

When you accept a book for review there is a tacit agreement that you will not review the same book for another journal, and you may be required to sign such an agreement. You would usually be able to use a short review prepared for a review journal to write an expanded review of the same title for a scholarly discipline journal.

●   ●   ●

"Without an index a reference work is similar to a well-groomed woman without her left shoe—beautiful, but not good for mileage." William A. Katz. *Introduction to Reference Work. Volume I: Basic Information Sources.* Page 92. Standard textbook in use in accredited library school reference courses during the 1970s. New York: McGraw-Hill, 1969.

Choice provides a useful model for mastering the technique of the short evaluative review, which is difficult to construct in twenty lines or one hundred fifty words and a few weeks. Many people need to be able to rely on these reviews in their work. And the reviewer does not merely critique a title. Place the book in the context of the literature of its field by comparing it with similar titles and rank it with comparable titles. Normally the shorter review indicates *content* and possible *use.*

Begin with the complete bibliographical data: author, full title, place of publication, name of publisher, date of publication, pagination, and price. It is also helpful to mention illustrations, diagrams, and any distinctive features of the format. Your comments should cover the book's purpose, scope, audience, unusual arrangement (such as a reference work without an index *if* an index is clearly needed), as well as the authority, or qualifications of the author and reputation of the publisher. If it is a new edition, how much revision has taken place? Study *Choice* reviews of books with which you are familiar in your field for an idea of how all this is accomplished. Then consult the *Book Review Digest* or *Technical Book Review Index* for excerpts from others' reviews.

Most of the many indexes to published reviews list bibliographical citations locating reviews of books for subject fields and time periods, e.g. *Technical Book Review Index's* Volume 52 covers 1986, more or less. An understanding of *Book Review Digest's* provisions and mastery of its use can provide insights into several aspects of book reviewing as a specialized skill, art, and technique to be valued as an element of scholarly merit and achievement. *Book Review Digest* can provide a shortcut comparison of reactions of several reviewers representing varied perspectives to a book. Although it is a locator (an index) of general book reviews, it also provides excerpts from representative reviews and identifies each reviewer, the periodical in which the review was published, and its length. The list of magazines and scholarly journals from which book reviews are regularly derived is located in the front of each *Book Review Digest* issue. Criteria for inclusion of review information about a book require it to be published or distributed in the United States or Canada, fiction or nonfiction in English. At least one review must have appeared in a journal published in the United States, within eighteen months following publication of the book. Alphabetically arranged by authors, with a subject-title index in the back of each issue, *Book Review Digest* has listed and selectively excerpted reviews from (currently approximately ninety) periodicals since 1905. Its scope is humanities and social sciences rather than pure science. *Technical Book Review Index* is similar but provides only one review excerpt, which it derives from science, technology, and trade journals.

Tools such as *Book Review Index, Index to Book Reviews in the Humanities,* and *Combined Retrospective Index to Book Reviews in Scholarly Journals* function solely to locate published reviews of books which have appeared in numerous publications in their respective fields. Reviews of new books, periodicals, films, motion pictures, and plays are also cited in many of the general and subject-specialized periodical indexes, abstracting services, and citation indexes, e.g. *Applied Science and Technology Index, Women Studies Abstracts,* and *Social Science Citation Index.* Reviews of motion pictures can be accessed by using such specialized locators as the *Film Literature Index* and *International Index to Film Periodicals,* as well as such general periodical indexes as *Art Index, British Humanities Index,* and even *Readers' Guide.* Specialized review locators for theatrical productions include the *New York Times Critics' Reviews* and *New York Times Theater Reviews.* Drama reviews can also be accessed by use of the standard periodical indexes already mentioned for other genres, e.g. *Humanities Index* and *Readers' Guide.*

Keep in mind that reviews of highly specialized creative works may appear in journals many months after their appearance, e.g. publication of a book, making it necessary to consult index cumulations for the following year(s). The title of each review-locating tool in the following summary list is accompanied by the year in which indexing coverage began, rather than the initial date of publication, and by its code number for locating full information about it in the *Guide to Reference Books*.[6] Periodical indexes published by the H.W. Wilson Company (e.g. *Readers' Guide, Social Sciences Index, Art Index*) and some other companies, as well as abstracting tools, list citations to book reviews separately, in the back of periodical index issues and in a separate section of abstracting tools.

Applied Science and Technology Index, 1913–   . (EA66)
Art Index, 1929–   . (BE168)
Arts and Humanities Citation Index, 1977–   .
Book Review Digest, 1905–   . (AA513)
Book Review Index, 1965–   . (AA514)
Book Review Index to Social Science Periodicals, 1978–   . (CA43)
British Humanities Index, 1962–   . (AE238)
Canadian Book Review Annual, 1975–   . (AA515)
Catholic Periodical and Literature Index, 1967–   . (AE247)
Combined Retrospective Index to Book Reviews in Scholarly Journals,
*   1886–1974. (AA516)*
Current Book Review Citations, 1976–   . (AA517)
Film Literature Index, 1973–   . (BG186)
Film Review Annual, 1981–   . (BG193)
General Science Index, 1978–   . (EA68)
Guía a las Reseñas de Libros de y sobre Hispano-América, 1972–   . (AA518)
Humanities Index, 1974–   . (AE235)
Index to Australian Book Reviews, 1965–1981. (AE519)
Index to Book Reviews in the Humanities, 1960–   . (AA520)
International Index to Film Periodicals, 1972–   . (BG188)
New York Times *Film Reviews, 1913–   . (BG198)*
New York Times *Theater Reviews, 1920–   . (BG48)*
Readers' Guide . . . , 1905–   . (AE231)
Reviews in Anthropology, 1974–   . (CE31)
Science Citation Index, 1961–   . (EA72–73)
Social Sciences and Humanities Index, 1970–74. (AE235)
Social Sciences Citation Index, 1972–   . (CA36)
Social Sciences Index, 1974–   . (AE236 and CA39)
Sociological Abstracts, 1952–   . (CC16)
Technical Book Review Index, 1917–   . (EA74–75)
Times (London) Index, 1906–   . (AF93)
Women Studies Abstracts, 1972–   . (CC502)

● ● ●

"Pardon her bold Attempt who has reveal'd
Her thoughts to View, more fit to be Conceal'd
Since thus to do was urged Vehemntly.
Yet most no doubt will call it Vanity."
Martha Wadsworth Brewster (b 1710, fl 1741–1757). American poet. *Poems
on Divers Subjects*. From the Introduction. Boston, Massachusetts: Printed
and sold by Edes and Gill, 1757. (Facsimile reproduction: Delmar, New
York: Scholars' Facsimiles, 1979.)

The *review essay* or bibliographic essay, as a critical article on the
literature of a subject, usually requested by a journal of a recognized expert,
is especially useful in planning literature searches preliminary to research
and publication. The bibliographic reviews published in *Signs* journal are
an example par excellence. They cover both broad areas (e.g. religion,
economics, political science) and specialized concerns (e.g. women and
literature in France, sociology of feminist research in Canada, American
critics and Spanish women novelists 1942–1980, African women, women in
international development). Review essays are also published in such other
scholarly journals as the New Zealand-based *Women's Studies Journal.
Differences: A Journal of Feminist Cultural Studies*, and *NWSA Journal* which
began publication in 1988, plan to feature review articles.[7] These review,
or bibliographic, essays can bring the user up to date on the advances in
many fields as well as provide current awareness. Occasionally the term
"review of the literature" is heard here. The *Index to Scientific Reviews* identifies them in the sciences. One of the distinctive aspects of the review essay
is the acceptance of, indeed reliance on, the scholarship and expertise, and
thus to some extent, personal judgment and opinion, of the writer-compiler.
Given the tendency to apply higher expectation levels to women's scholarship and to gender-related manuscripts, nonfiction works which do not
eschew personal expression stand little chance of being a scholar's first
publication. They are particularly subject to labeling as unscholarly. *Choice*,
which regularly publishes bibliographic essays on timely and developing
topics, solicits nominations from its reviewers of both bibliographic topics
and writers. Standard length of these essays is about twenty-five typed
pages, involving comparison of no more than one hundred titles.[7]

Anthologies

Like textbook publication, responsibility for an anthological book is
not advised the first time out. Compilation of some articles or essays on the
same topic with an introduction is not an easy route to publication and
royalties, fame and fortune. Anthology editorship can be an enervating,
albeit worthwhile, experience, often without proportionate monetary or

professional reward. Freeman's *Women: A Feminist Perspective* is an example of a successful anthology functioning as a college textbook. It clearly communicates ongoing feminist attention to a perfected publication of its type. The first edition relied on nominated classics; recent editions have included original works created for this purpose. Freeman describes the book's creation as a labor of love and its publication by Mayfield, which specializes in college text classroom publications, as an act of faith. *Women: A Feminist Perspective* had its genesis at a conference gathering in 1968, when there were no books or anthologies presenting a feminist perspective on women's status, and "those books about women that were not written from a wholly traditional view discounted feminism as outmoded, extreme, or both." Freeman solicited nominations and contributions for that edition and has continued to do so openly for subsequent editions. The book was from the first "to contain pieces that were comprehensive, lucidly written, and well grounded in scholarly research." By the time she began work on the second edition, she was able to "draw upon a network of feminist scholars who were engaged in the kind of substantive research" she was looking for, and who moreover "were committed to researching a wide audience. Thus in many ways the compilation of the second edition reflected the maturation of the scholarly side of the women's movement."[8]

Anthologies, or multi-authored books, are generally collections of original "pieces" or essays, already-published material, including periodical articles, or a combination of these. Strictly speaking, some festschrifts, symposium proceedings, and commissioned "books" on current topics are anthological because they are collections of several authors. A woman scholar may be more concerned with publicaton of an anthology like the many collections indexed in the *Essay and General Literature Index* (1900–   ), which are often literary anthologies.

Many important writings are published in the form of essays, only to be buried in collections. The *Essay and General Literature Index* indexes collections of essays on all subjects, although it is particularly strong in the humanities and social sciences, providing access by subjects and authors of essays and of anthologies. Examination of the list of anthologies indexed, inserted at the end of each issue, can provide an idea of currently publishable and commercial compilers, editors, essay writers, anthology topics and themes, and essay writers. The 1987 cumulation analyzed anthologies published mainly in 1986 and 1987, including a significant number and variety of titles clearly communicating concern for or focus on women writers of a variety of characteristics, locales, and times. This indexing uses subject-headings structured like those derived from the Library of Congress *Subject Headings* for the contents of books. (See Resources section and later in this chapter.) Geographical and chronological *sub*-subject-headings can be assumed for the following examples appearing in the 1987

Essay and General Literature Index in order to access relevant anthologies and essays within these collections:

AFRO-AMERICAN WOMEN
FEMINISM
MEXICAN AMERICAN WOMEN
MOTHERS
ITALIAN-AMERICAN WOMEN
PLATH, SYLVIA—ABOUT [INDIVIDUAL WORKS BY TITLE]
RAPE
WOMEN, BLACK
WOMEN AND LITERATURE
WOMEN ARTISTS
WOMEN IN LITERATURE

Publishers may initiate collections of original essays which function like chapters and are coordinated by an editor. Invited scholars who contribute papers on designated topics to symposia or conferences *may* find their work published as part of an anthology or proceedings. Probably the most frequently published type of collection is the project initiated by the textbook publisher for use as a required or supplementary text for a course. Faculty members who create "readers" may be violating the law and creating potential liability for themselves and possibly for their institutions.[9]

The main question with which to deal in order to propose publication of an anthology to a publishing house is its purpose, true of any book which is to be published commercially, but crucial in this endeavor. And as usual, ask yourself—and be able to respond clearly—how will this anthology compete with other compilations? The function of yours should demonstrate that the anthological format is essential to its fulfillment. You must then select the essays or articles, which you will organize to fulfill this function. If they are classics or landmark titles, they have probably already been reprinted. That an article is published or reprinted for the first time in your book can be a positive factor. An extended introduction should communicate the purpose of the book, for whom it is designed, how you selected the essays. If it is to be a collection whose primary function is as college-level reading, consider providing related further-reading titles for each essay or for each section of related pieces, and possibly commentary. Most books need indexes.

The publisher to whom you propose your anthology will want to know whether it is a collection of previously published articles, and if so, whether you have obtained permissions. You must get permissions from all the authors and/or the publications in which the essays were originally published. I advise against abridging or editing others' texts which you reprint. When you serve as the editor of a collection of other people's creations, you have an obligation to respect their communications. You do not have to agree with their ideas when you function as editor. Your scholarship and authorship are important in providing the background, balancing the overall book, and supplying the reader with perspective and a way about the collection. There is also the collection of original articles by the compiler-author or others published for the first time.

International Publications: Translations, Foreign Language and Bilingual

> "I will write under my own name
> I am a woman
> I will write only under my own name
> myself."

Akiko Otori Yosano (1878–1942). Japanese essayist, novelist, poet. Part of "Sozoro-goto." In *Seitō*, no. 1, 1911, founded and edited by Raichō Hiratsuka. Yoko Hasegawa, transl.

While a visiting scholar in Japan I noticed copies of *Our Bodies, Ourselves* available for students in the Kyoto Seika College office of feminist educator Mioko Fujieda. She had just returned from the Berkshire History Conference at Smith College. In 1987 she served on the International Advisory board of the Third International Interdisciplinary Congress on Women, held in Ireland. While in England I saw a copy of the British edition of *Our Bodies, Ourselves* in SisterWrite Bookstore. International translations and editions of feminist theoretical and literary works and of women writers exist but lack adequate distribution. Many women's studies standards can be located by using the books-in-print type publications of various languages. Beauvoir's *The Second Sex*, Firestone's *Dialectic of Sex*, Horney's *New Ways in Psychoanalysis*, Mead's *Male and Female* and *Coming of Age in Samoa*, Millett's *Sexual Politics*, and Woolf's *A Room of One's Own* are just a few examples of English-language standard nonfiction books which have been translated into other languages, including Japanese and Spanish and are read in other nations today. Other best-sellers originating in English-speaking nations which have been translated and published in many languages include Friedan's *Feminine Mystique*, Wollstonecraft's *A Vindication of the Rights of Women*, Jong's *Fear of Flying*, and Nin's *Diary*.

Recently the work of such black American writers as Toni Morrison, Alice Walker, Ntozake Shange, Nora Neale Hurston, and Michele Wallace have become available in translation in Japan. Watanabe and Naka edited a 1983 collection of Japanese women scholars' essays on such American women writers as Joan Didion, Ellen Glasgow, Mary McCarthy, Susan

Sontag, Alice Walker, and Eudora Welty, who "seem to influence Japanese women writers."[10] Of women's studies texts used in Japan, 13 percent are translated copies of foreign materials, and another 13 percent are foreign materials studied in the original language.[11] Tomii has translated a contemporary feminist work into English: Higuchi's *Bringing Up Girls*. Sociologist Junko Wada Kuninobu, member of the Women's Studies Association of Japan board and founding member of the Women's Studies Society, has prepared women's studies bibliographies.[12] Translating classic works of women writers and feminist perspective can be a major contribution to education and the status of females of one's nation. For many women throughout the world, it is also a labor of love. Resnick and de Courtivron found that, as in most areas of women's studies, translating is yet another volunteer activity, dependent on the good will of those committed to retrieving creative women from historical silence and absence — the *herstory* concept. Their experience confirmed that although women are interested in the field of translation, their work is not respected or encouraged, economically or professionally. "In universities, little is done to encourage translations as thesis work or as valid scholarly research with a view to promotion."[13] Their *Women Writers in Translation* is an annotated bibliography covering 1945 through 1982 and focusing in the humanities. Organized by language groups, descriptions of each author precede annotations of individual works. Comparable book resources in university library collections can be located by use of the subject-heading LITERATURE — WOMEN AUTHORS — TRANSLATIONS INTO [ENGLISH] — BIBLIOGRAPHY.

If translations are to "count" as publications, one should also note in advance the aspects which relate to receiving positive reviews from the right reviewers. One criterion involves qualitative comparison with other translations as well as with the original work. Provision by the translator of useful notes and commentary and bibliographic support which supplement the translation intended for academic use is a plus. For her Stanford University Ph.D. dissertation (copyrighted 1970), Sievers translated a work by Kotoku Shusui (1871–1911), *The Essence of Socialism*, and provided with it a bibliographic essay. Mulhern's *Koda Rohan* (1867–1947), published in 1977 by Twayne, was based on her 1973 Columbia University thesis. She has translated into English some *Selections* of Rohan Koda's short stories.[14]

Translations and international distribution and sales are important contractual considerations. They include direct sales internationally of already-published books as well as the rights for foreign translation. Obtain permission to translate *and* publish from the original author or book publisher currently holding rights. Working as a women's studies or feminist team to translate a lengthy text can sometimes be successful, and hastens the availability of sources while limiting the pressure and isolation of this type of scholarly work.

During 1986 the largest amounts (in dollars) of books exported by the United States continued to go to Canada, the United Kingdom, Australia, Japan, and the Netherlands.[15] Since 1980, the Feminist Press has been producing in its International Series "highly course adoptable" bilingual volumes of feminist poetry and translations of fiction and autobiography from Europe, Asia, and Latin America. Opening the classroom to the lost and distorted literary history of females throughout the world is a major element in *herstory*. Seal Press's *Women in Translation* Series was introduced in 1984 and features works by contemporary and classic women writers of fiction and nonfiction which might otherwise not appear in English, translated from Arabic, Catalan, Danish, Japanese, and Norwegian. *Signs* journal welcomes new English translations of material published in other languages and has international correspondents throughout the world.

The First International Feminist Book Fair was held in 1984 in England, the second in Norway in 1986, and the third in 1988 in Canada. The goal of this biennial gathering of women writers and people in the book trade from throughout the world is to pool experiences in building national and international markets for women's writing. The first three days are reserved for professionals in the book trade — agents, authors, booksellers, distributors, publishers, and translators — who meet to negotiate translation and distribution rights and copublishing options.

The *Literary Market Place* lists publishers from abroad with United States representatives. The *International Literary Market Place* covers one hundred sixty nations. Information is similar to that in the *Literary Market Place* (both are published by the R.R. Bowker Company), although there are no subject indexes. United Kingdom entries include many publishers which are familiar names throughout English-speaking nations. Information about copyright conventions and translation agencies and associations for each country are useful provisions. The *Encyclopedia of Associations* has an *International Organizations* volume, as does *Association Periodicals*.

Audiovisuals and Related Printed Materials

A faculty member in the field of professional education *may* be able to offer nonprint media work for consideration along with research and scholarly journal publications. But acceptable writing for publication is not usually equated with nonprint media creation at any level. One of the surest ways to get the attention of an experienced reviewer of audiovisual media intended for instructional use is the provision of quality related printed materials. A skilled reviewer will underscore them as well as the presence of representative and nonsexist narrative in an audiovisual which is not about sex, gender, females or women's studies.

Teachers' manuals and study guides accompanying audiovisual instructional media are the main types of written programming beyond scripting and related involvement with production of audiovisual multimedia. Teachers of elementary grades and of high school subjects need to be able to rely on keyed examination and test questions, discussion outlines and exercises, paper and report topics, and related student activities. Well-selected, further reading–type bibliographies at appropriate grade–age range levels should be included. Book titles should be in print and provided and with publishers' addresses, full titles and authors' names, edition numbers, years of publication, and standard book numbers (ISBN's). Selections should clearly be based on knowledge of the titles rather than the result of a dip into the *Subject Guide to Books in Print*. Most writers are now aware in scripting K-12 media products that the authoritative narrator's voice does not need to be masculine. But alternating female and male voice narration and carefully attending to the content of her lines not being stereotypically supportive or endorsement are also important.

The *Literary Market Place* identifies book publishers which also produce audio cassettes (spoken word) and audiovisual materials. The *Audio Video Market Place* does not provide in the same way as LMP for the scholar's publishing needs. It is geared more to acquisitions. The main section, listing products, services, and companies, is not annotated, and there is no subject-indexing. One can consult a general Products and Services Index (pages A1–A12 of the 1988 edition), however. Be sure to read the How To Use AVMP (pages ix-xi of the 1988 edition) first. Related associations, periodicals, and reference books are identified in three useful sections. *Booklist* and *Library Journal* reviews include audiovisuals. Nonprint materials reviewed by *Choice* for undergraduate level use include computer software.

Letters to the Editor
Or Can a Woman Get Away with Criticizing
and Being Criticized in Print?

"The press treated women's liberation much as society treats women — as entertainment not to be taken seriously." Jo Freeman. Contemporary United States writer, political scientist, educator. *The Politics of Women's Liberation*. McKay, 1975.

Casual perusal of the letters to the editor of a major periodical in your field, profession, or discipline can be enlightening if you keep in mind that you have no way of knowing how many letters on any given point of view are received or how those published are selected. Whether a scholarly journal, an association serial, or a commercial periodical, this reading can be time well spent in relationship to getting published by women scholars and women studies personnel. Are unsigned letters published, and if so, who and which topics are selected to receive the publisher's protective anonymity? Which persons, institutions, and topics are chosen to receive attention?

The conventional guide to getting published does not consider letters to periodical editors, and the intent of this brief discussion is not to convey them as a means to acceptable publishing. Becuase they can serve writers as well as readers, it should be noted that letters which do get published tend to:

- support or endorse the periodical, a recent article, or an institution
- comment on an article which appeared recently in the periodical and to provide related response or suggestions
- defend or correct, possibly include provision of further information which sometimes provides a fuller picture

There are several questions people have asked during my Getting Published workshop breaks . . . as if they were really not important or apply only to themselves. One is, "How can I get *XYZ Periodical* to publish my letters?" They may assume the reasons relate to something defective in their letters' construction or content. Letters which get published, but which are not entirely blessings-on-thee-little-man, usually have several characteristics in common. These letters:

- are clearly identified responses to an interview, article, news, editorial, review, cartoon, or reportage published in recent issues of the periodical.
- do not respond to another, previously published letter or address something about an advertisement.
- do not consist of solely personal messages. Exceptions appear occasionally, e.g. the *Chronicle of Higher Education* publishes in the Letters section requests such as Freeman's call for input for a new edition of her *Women: A Feminist Perspective,* and mine for *Getting Published.*
- are written by subscribers or sponsoring association members, or better still, officers in it.
- are written by "affiliated" persons, whose institutions and titles are identified.
- are on acceptable sides of gender-related topics. "There are two sides to every story" is often insinuated, sustaining devisive manipulation of a complex human concern. This attitude has been utilized by the media to

introduce and sustain adversarial situations. The thoughtless use of the word "story" (as in fiction) in this context adds insult to injury.

- often slide into it with praise, endorsement, or at least acknowledgment, easing into the point they are trying to communicate — the medium is the massage.

- do not exceed the number of words or any other parameters designated by the periodical for publication in this forum. The shorter the letter, the less likely the possibility of its being condensed (edited), which may also alter meaning. A statement declaring these instructions may appear in the vicinity of the Letters "page." A maximum of five hundred words is typical. When shorter letters are given preference, it is attributed to the competition for space, although lengthy letters get published.

The headings for the examples of publishable letters, Figures 4:1–3, were created by the periodical. Presumably they reveal its perception of each letter's main concern or of what will attract its readers. Some editors utilize a keywords phrase derived from the letter itself for the heading. It is worth the effort to attempt to provide your own heading by concluding your letter with a brief final paragraph, "I hope that it will be possible to publish this brief contribution in an early issue of XYZ *Periodical*. For it, I suggest the heading _____."

Some professional periodicals commission opinions. The *Chronicle of Higher Education* Opinion section precedes the Letters to the Editor. Professor Carl Bode's opinion's catchy title and what it might portend for better education and employment (which are concomitants to one another in academe) attracted me. But "Saint Paul Started It All, But Now It's Time to Abolish Letters of Recommendation" was a ranting, irresponsible piece which concluded, "I'm going to restrict myself to making judgments over the telephone."[16] Such an article from a woman evidencing unprofessionalism would run the risk of being labeled Opinion*ated*. My inquiry as to whether opinion pieces are commissioned and their authors paid by the *Chronicle of Higher Education* was unanswered. The Guidelines for Contributors (April 1987) refer to "articles expressing the opinions of outside contributors for publication in its Opinion pages and on its back page, called Point of View. All news stories, however, are written by members of *The Chronicle's* staff and by its regular part-time correspondents. . . . Opinion pieces . . . should be written in a clear, informal expository style that is free of jargon. We welcome unsolicited manuscripts. However, we do not accept commentary pieces that respond to Opinions or Points of View that we have just published. . . . We pay between $200. and $300. for unsolicited articles that are accepted for publication."

• • •

Research methodology on women in academe

Diana Paul's nine years' work at Stanford University "was discounted because it focused on women" ("Legal Experts Eye 2 Sex-Bias Lawsuits Brought by Women's-Studies Scholars" and "Suing a College Can Be a Long, Expensive, Draining Ordeal," April 9). Annette Kolodny observes that "most faculty members are not acquainted with the scholarship in women's studies. They don't read it, so they don't know what it is or even how to evaluate it."

I believe that most of the women who have been involved in systematic response to sexism in academe will agree that this reportage, while welcome, is not overdue.

Reading it reminded me of something recently noted in *The Chronicle of Higher Education:* Sociologist and Women Studies Pioneer Athena Theodore's new book, *The Campus Troublemakers: Academic Women in Protest* (Houston: Cap and Gown Press, Inc., 1986) was on the New Books on Higher Education list (March 12, 1986). As a feminist scholar with some knowledge of this research's history, I had hoped to see it reviewed, but failing that, certainly listed (characterized, evaluated, communicated) among New Scholarly Books, for, as a demonstration of excellence in research methodology, readable organization of a vast amount of significant material, and anecdotal writing, it is a model.

HELEN RIPPIER WHEELER
School of Library and Information Sciences
University of California
Berkeley, Cal.

Letters of reference for academic jobs

Paul B. Hamel's plea that letters of reference not be stipulated in the initial phase of a search process (Letters, April 18) is related by *The Chronicle* to "the burden of writing letters of reference." I suggest that this requirement should also be related by academicians to implementation of nondiscriminatory "affirmative action."

The job seeker may hesitate to request her/his referee to write again and again and to relay the requirement that the letter be written quickly in order to make the deadline. Beyond this are the time and money involved in the initial requirement of transcripts, often stipulated "official."

It is not unusual to find advertisements that stipulate impossible closing dates in these contexts.

Costly placement files involve time, prepayment, and authorization. I know of only one professional periodical that requires employers to include some level of salary information.

The concept of salary negotiability has been shown to be potentially discriminatory, especially with regard to qualified mature women. (I am not now referring to commitment or even to a specific salary.) Notably, in the last year or two, the proportion of advertisements providing no level of salary information whatsoever appears to be increasing; likewise, the significant "chairman" is back and spreading.

HELEN R. WHEELER
Berkeley, Cal.

Figure 4:1 *Chronicle of Higher Education* 32, no. 11 (May 14, 1986):41. Figure 4:2. *Chronicle of Higher Education* 28, no. 12 (May 16, 1984):33.

'New women's' network: sexist methodology

TO THE EDITOR:

How do the women quoted by Liz McMillen ("Women's Groups: Going the Old Boys' Network One Better," December 3) justify modeling even a "new women's" network on the old boys' sexist methodology?

They appear to be practicing the old fraternal manipulative, feminine getting around the problem. Non-discriminatory affirmative action recruitment, fully understood by all, would involve merely good management. If these persons with power who are advised to phone around, seek nominations, etc., merely advertised, posted, and shared news of all jobs in a timely, non-disparate fashion — with minimum and desirable qualifications, some level of salary information, and reasonable application methodology — they would likely find themselves in (1) compliance and (2) possession of good pools. The question Can a woman be one of the boys? is asked elsewhere in the same issue. Do they actually *want* to be?

HELEN R. WHEELER
Womanhood Media
Berkeley, Cal.

Figure 4:3. *Chronicle of Higher Education* 33, no. 18 (January 14, 1987): 49.

In addition to the basic procedures previously suggested for publication of journal articles and books, there are ways of facilitating getting published in academe.

As soon as you receive them, carefully scan current issues of journals to which you subscribe and periodicals published by associations of which you are a member. They may publish "calls" for papers and presentation proposals. The *American Studies International*'s newsletter, with its calls for papers, calendar of upcoming conferences, and information requested sections is a good example. Significant numbers of the opportunities it shares relate to women in academe. Regularly check the *Chronicle of Higher Education*. Such periodicals announce conferences and gatherings at which papers are presented and for which submissions are invited. The submission guidelines may require an abstract, with a copy of a paper selected for presentation at a later date well before the meeting. You *may* also be required to provide a copy for each member of the audience, but these papers are sometimes published as proceedings. If they are not published, conference presentations can lead to publication through the feedback, productive revision suggestions, etc., which you receive. Announcements may be reprinted in newsletters of women's centers, women's studies programs, task forces, and caucuses, but they are often relayed too late for adequate preparation and the deadlines.

Women's centers in academe, women's studies programs, association feminist task forces and caucus newsletters publish compilers' requests for original contributions to anthologies. Their design is usually intended to support women's studies curricula and to be appropriate for courses examining gender-related topics and issues. The compiler-editor may not have a book publication contract yet, because the system requires her to line up the contents of her anthology in order to propose her book in order to get a contract! Thus, you should assume neither financial remuneration nor assured publication, although one or both may ultimately be forthcoming. The system places her in this position of making you literally a contributor. But at least consider responding with an offer of an unpublished essay which you have in your files, and describe its scope, perspective, length, and coverage.

Active participation in association task forces, divisions, caucuses, and regional groups, and elective and appointive offices provide the visibility and contacts which may lead to invitations to write for publication and to coordinate special thematic issues of journals. Despite printed calls for contributions, the work of unknown or notorious persons is less likely to be published than that of known safe quantities who are also competitively qualified, capable, diligent, reliable workers. I am not advocating joining the system; rather, I suggest being aware of how it operates. Some journals are in a sense more honest when they express forthrightly "manuscripts by invitation only," e.g. Haworth Press' "The Publishing and Review of References Sources" issue of the *Reference Librarian*.[17]

If you must be employed for wages while working on a graduate degree, try to identify a faculty member who is a journal editor in your field and approach her or him regarding the possibility of employment as a journal editorial assistant. This work is typically part-time and clerical, but has the potential for professional contacts and insights. An appointment as Professor Editor's teaching or research assistant might also doubly serve your need. The principle applies to employment on the staff of a journal, review, university press, or yearbook located on a university campus where you are a student. Some women may testify to this being as foolish as serving as a secretary or typist in order to get a foot in the door, but note that I have tied this to the necessity of employment while a graduate student.

Publishers' calls for manuscripts are worth watching for in the media; look for Pergamon Press's Athene Series, for example. Some publishers offer awards for the best unpublished, book-length manuscript in their field, e.g. Fairleigh Dickinson University Press's award in women's studies in any discipline. These arrangements usually reward the publishers with publishable manuscripts, because a contract is generally part of the process and may constitute the touted award. And be cautious with the "publishing opportunities..." publication, preconference workshop, or conference

session. The title is often a misnomer and come-on. *Publishing Oppor-*
tunities for Energy Research is actually a guide to serials in the social and
technical sciences, for example.

Some members of the academy consider documents stored in and
retrievable from ERIC as publications. In addition to functioning as another
mode of publication without payment, the Educational Resources Information Center (ERIC) provides the scholar with information related to getting
published. Because ERIC is a well-organized information system within
American academe sponsored by the federal government, it is useful to consult as a reflection of the status quo. Documents are indexed and accessible
since 1966 by means of the ERIC thesaurus and two indexes, *Resources in*
Education (RIE) and *Current Index to Journals in Education (*CIJE). Also,
ERIC can provide a means of sharing information and documents which
have not yet been and may never be conventionally published. It is
therefore of interest to scholars and writers with something worthy of sharing as well as reading.

The Educational Resources Information Center is part of the National
Institute of Education, a nationwide information system acquiring,
abstracting, indexing, storing, and disseminating significant reports and
projects. It defines education so broadly as to make these tools and
documents relevant to social and behavioral scientists. Specialized clearinghouses evaluate, index, and abstract publications and documents which
are then accessible through the two ERIC printed indexes and the ERIC on-
line data base. Many of the indexed publications are themselves available
in microform in most academic libraries and many large public libraries, as
well as for sale in microform or hard copy.

The locations in academe of the various clearinghouses and descriptions
of their scope are provided in the back of the *Thesaurus of ERIC Descrip-*
tors, a controlled vocabulary listing established subject-headings used in indexing and retrieving ERIC documents. (Their current addresses are also
listed in the back of RIE and CIJE issues.) The clearinghouses span the
following areas: adult, career and vocational education; counseling and personnel services; educational management; elementary and early childhood
education; handicapped and gifted children; higher education; information
resources; junior colleges; languages and linguistics; reading and communication skills; rural education and small schools; science, mathematics,
and environmental education; social studies; social science; teacher education; tests, measurement, and evaluation; and urban education.

To enhance the possibility of acceptance of your publication and its ac-
cessibility (indexing and reproduction) and availability via the ERIC network, the following steps are recommended:

- Determine the appropriate clearinghouse for your paper, report, article, or other type of document by referring to the current list and the indexing of its publications' titles.

- Mail two legible copies of the document to that clearinghouse, with a cover letter, preferably on an academic institution's (including schools and school districts) letterhead, conveying your creation.

- Identify in your letter several relevant descriptors derived from the latest edition of the ERIC thesaurus, which is usually located near ERIC indexes in the library. Star (*) two or three of the strongest ones, following the style of the display samples in Step 3 of Figures 4:4–6.

- Enclose a signed copy of the reproduction release form, which can be duplicated from the copy provided in the back of RIE issues.

- Enclose two copies of an abstract of the contents of your document. See the ERIC abstract portions in Step 3 of the samples, Figures 4:4–6.

When you browse the ERIC RIE index, you will notice references to all types of publications. Types of documents stored in ERIC include monographs, position papers, feasibility studies, syllabi, manuals, conference papers, proceedings, project descriptions, and dissertations. Many are indexed and made available in both microform and hard (paper) copy. Book titles are indexed only. Some established ERIC descriptors which may be particularly useful in storing one's document and in retrieving information related to getting published in academe are provided in the Resources section.

Some ERIC clearinghouses publish monographs. The Clearinghouse on Higher Education, for example, invites individuals to submit proposals for writing monographs for the Higher Education Report series. A detailed manuscript proposal should consist of not more than five pages, a seventy-five word summary to be used by several review committees for the initial screening and rating, a vita, and a writing sample. (See Chapter One, Note 29.)

It is also possible to retrieve lengthy abstracts when searching either the printed RIE index by hand or the ERIC data base on-line. Using most printed abstracting tools involves two steps: (1) In the index locate the abstracted publication's abstract number, which ERIC refers to as a document number; and (2) Move to the volume (or section) which contains the abstracts arranged by abstract, or document, numbers.

This two-step sequence would apply to using *America: History & Life, Historical Abstracts, Psychological Abstracts, Sociological Abstracts. Women Studies Abstracts,* and any indexing tool which provides abstracts—unlike *Readers' Guide,* for example.

While searching for subject information, use the ERIC thesaurus descriptors for productive, well-focused results. You can, however, also take the keyword approach when searching, *if* you assume that all writers include in their titles and abstracts the word *you* are thinking about! Suppose you need current information about *getting published, gaining tenure in academe*, and related considerations. Start by consulting the ERIC thesaurus, which generates all of the following relevant established subject-headings (descriptors):

ACADEMIC RANK (PROFESSIONAL)	PROMOTION (OCCUPATIONAL)
AGING IN ACADEMIA	PUBLICATIONS
CONTRACTS	PUBLISH OR PERISH ISSUE
EMPLOYMENT PRACTICES	SENIORITY
EMPLOYMENT QUALIFICATIONS	TEACHER EMPLOYMENT BENEFITS
FACULTY PROMOTION	TEACHER RIGHTS
FACULTY PUBLISHING	TENURE
NONTENURED FACULTY	TENURED FACULTY
PROBATIONARY PERIOD	WRITING FOR PUBLICATION

TENURE and TENURED FACULTY attract you. See Figure 4:4, Step 1. UF (Use For) instructs you to search under TENURE, rather than Job Tenure; it says that Job Tenure is not an established descriptor in the ERIC system. BT (Broader Term) communicates that in this thesaurus, EMPLOYMENT LEVEL is another established descriptor, but that TENURE is more specific. RT (Related Term) designates a list of additional established terms related to TENURE which you may want to check out. Using these two established subject-headings, TENURE and TENURED FACULTY, you can turn directly to the index portion of RIE volumes. Figure 4:4, Step 2. On page 520 of the RIE 1985 annual cumulation index, for example, under TENURE, titles of ten documents for this period are alphabetically listed by the first regarded word of the document titles; five are about TENURED FACULTY. The fact that there is no overlap among the two sets of titles is not surprising when we study the Scope Notes (SN) provided for these two descriptors in their thesaurus displays. "A Study of Male and Female Faculty Promotion Tenure Rates. AIR 1985 Annual Forum Paper" appears in the index under TENURE. Note the "ED Number" — ED 259 685 — and turn to the counterpart volume for this time period (Figure 4:4, Step 3), the annual cumulation for 1985: *Abstracts*, pages 1966–67, where the document resume for this publication appears. The abstract is the final portion of the entry, or display, of each.

Documents of interest are usually available in microform in the library, arranged by document numbers in filing cabinets. Many are also available for purchase in microform and paper copy according to the EDRS Price Line in the Document Resume. An NT (for Narrower Term) is a thesaurus searching option not included in these sample searches.

Documents about FACULTY DEVELOPMENT are going to be accessible under that wording because it is, according to the ERIC thesaurus, an established descriptor. See Figure 4:5, Step 1. In the 1986 annual RIE cumulation, on page 191 (Step 2), under FACULTY DEVELOPMENT are references to numerous publications on this subject, defined in the thesaurus scope note (SN) as activities to encourage and enhance faculty professional growth. Of interest is "The Elimination of Sexism in University Environments" ED 267 348. Turning to the Document Resumes arranged by number, first (Step 3) we find 267 348 on page 1142: "The Elimination of Sexism . . ." is by Linda Forrest and others. The list of descriptors assigned to this document includes our FACULTY DEVELOPMENT. Other strong descriptors (marked with asterisks in the entry) are COLLEGE ENVIRONMENT, FEMALES, SEX DIFFERENCES, SEX DISCRIMINATION, and STUDENT DEVELOPMENT.

Suppose you need information about WRITING FOR PUBLICATION. You know that it is an established subject-heading in the ERIC system because it is listed in the thesaurus, Figure 4:6, Step 1. You can then look directly under this wording in the subject index portion of the RIE for 1986, for example, Figure 4:6, Step 2. On page 538, several such publications are listed, including "Perceptions of Women and Men in Counselor Education About Writing for Publication," ED 265 445. In the counterpart volume, the annual cumulation for 1986 Document Resumes, on page 838, sequentially arranged is 265 445, by Arden White and Nelda Hernandez, Figure 4:6, Step 3.

• • •

"When you choose your fields of labor go where nobody else is willing to go." Mary Lyon (1797–1849). United States educator, missionary. Quoted in *Eminent Missionary Women* by Mrs. J.T. Tracey. New York and Cincinnati, Ohio: Eaton and Mains, 1898.

Ideas for research and publication and ways to generate acceptable and feasible topics for theses and journal articles and other professional publication just seem to evolve for some scholars. Others struggle. Some sources of ideas involve efficient use of abstracting services, review literature, "current contents" services, special and thematic journal issues, dissertations, and catalogs of specialized collections. Ways to publication include conversion of speeches, bibliographic and collation work, historical walks, "action research," and extrapolating, updating, and replicating others' work. Occasionally, prominent scholars' recommendations of needed research appear in journals and elsewhere.

TENURE   *Jul. 1966*
    CIJE: 750   RIE: 989   GC: 630
SN   Status of a person in a position or
     occupation (i.e., length of service, terms
     of employment, or permanence of posi-
     tion)
UF   Job Tenure (1967 1978)
BT   Employment Level
RT   Academic Rank (Professional)
     Aging In Academia
     Contracts
     Contract Salaries
     Employees
     Employer Employee Relationship
     Employment
     Employment Experience
     Employment Practices
     Employment Qualifications
     Faculty Promotion
     Job Layoff
     Labor Problems
     Labor Turnover
     Nontenured Faculty
     Occupational Mobility
     Personnel Data
     Personnel Policy
     Probationary Period
     Promotion (Occupational)
     Reduction In Force
     Seniority
     Teacher Employment
     Teacher Employment Benefits
     Teacher Promotion
     Teacher Rights
     Teaching (Occupation)
     Tenured Faculty
     Work Life Expectancy

TENURED FACULTY   *Oct. 1983*
    CIJE: 27   RIE: 21   GC: 360
SN   Academic staff who have been granted
     tenure (permanence of position) by their
     school or institution
UF   Tenured Teachers
BT   Faculty
RT   Academic Rank (Professional)
     College Faculty
     Full Time Faculty
     Nontenured Faculty
     Professors
     Teachers
     Tenure

Tenured Teachers
USE TENURED FACULTY

Tenure
Career Plateaus of Public Sector Managers.   ED 259 238
Characteristics of Instructional Faculty at Maryland's Pub-
   lic Colleges and Universities. Postsecondary Education
   Research Reports.   ED 253 174
A Computer Model for Prediction of Tenure Ratios in
   Higher Education.   ED 248 799
Full-Time Humanities Faculty, Fall 1982. Higher Educa-
   tion Panel Report Number 61.   ED 248 771
Managing Resource Uncertainty through Academic Staff-
   ing in Four-Year Colleges and Universities. ASHE 1985
   Annual Meeting Paper.   ED 259 621
The Project on Reallocation. An Executive Summary.
                                             ED 257 344
Structural Reform in Higher Education Collective Bargain-
   ing. Proceedings of the Annual Conference of the Na-
   tional Center for the Study of Collective Bargaining in
   Higher Education and the Professions (12th, New York,
   New York, April 1984).   ED 255 143
A Study of Male and Female Faculty Promotion and
   Tenure Rates. AIR 1985 Annual Forum Paper.
                                             ED 259 685
A Study of the Status of Tenure in the Nation's Public
   Two-Year Colleges.   ED 250 029
Tenure Policies. SPEC Kit 9.   ED 251 069

Tenured Faculty
Age Discrimination on Campus.   ED 250 999
Current Appointment & Tenure Practices: Their Impact
   on New Faculty Careers. ASHE 1985 Annual Meeting
   Paper.   ED 259 648
An Investigation of the Status of Post-Tenure Faculty
   Evaluation in Selected Community Colleges. ASHE
   1985 Annual Meeting Paper.   ED 259 635
Is Concession Bargaining a Threat to Stability in Higher
   Education Collective Bargaining?   ED 252 166
Post-Tenure Faculty Evaluation in Community Colleges:
   Anomaly or Reality? Innovation Abstracts, Volume VI,
   Number 29.   ED 251 152

Figure 4:4. (Left) Step 1: *Thesaurus of ERIC Descriptors.* **(Right) Step 2:** *RIE 1985 Index,* **Page 520.**

ED 259 685   HE 018 613
Ochsner, Nancy L.   And Others
A Study of Male and Female Faculty Promotion
and Tenure Rates. AIR 1985 Annual Forum
Paper.
Pub Date—May 85
Note—27p.; Paper presented at the Annual Forum
of the Association for Institutional Research
(25th, Portland, OR, April 28-May 1, 1985).
Pub Type— Reports - Research (143) — Speeches/-
Meeting Papers (150)
EDRS Price - MF01/PC02 Plus Postage.
Descriptors—*Employment Practices, *Faculty
Promotion, Higher Education, Institutional Re-
search, Longitudinal Studies, Males, *Sex Differ-
ences, State Universities, Teacher Employment,
*Tenure, Women Faculty
Identifiers—*AIR Forum, *University of Maryland
College Park
Sex differences in tenure and promotion rates and
time to tenure and promotion at the University of
Maryland, College Park, were studied longitudi-
nally. The study population consisted of tenure-
tract assistant and associate professors appointed or
promoted in 1973, 1975, and 1977, excluding
part-time and visiting faculty. Campus-wide, 42 percent of the female and 43 percent of the male faculty
in the assistant professor class of 1973 were tenured,
and 25 percent of the females versus 27 percent of
the men in 1977 were tenured. Promotion rates for
the assistant professors were very similar to their
tenure rates. Because of the small number of faculty
who were hired as associate professors, statistical
analyses could not be conducted. Results indicated
no statistically significant sex differences in promotion and tenure rates and in time to promotion and
tenure for all classes of assistant and associate professors studied. The proportions of faculty promoted and tenured, however, had declined
substantially from the assistant and associate professor classes of 1973 to the classes appointed in 1977.
Problems are noted of doing a study of this type
(e.g., small sample sizes, lack of data on important
variables, political pressures and sensitivity, con-
founding effects of policy changes, and market
changes). (SW)

Figure 4:4, continued. Step 3: *RIE 1985 Abstracts*, pages 1966–7.

Abstracting services in one's field aid in focusing topical ideas and publications. Both hand searching of the printed format (necessary for *Women Studies Abstracts*) and on-line computer-assisted searching of the data base counterparts available for many printed abstracting services (e.g. *Sociological Abstracts*) are now possible.

Review literature and recent work can be identified and the search for topics consolidated by means of the abstracts. REVIEW can be used as a data base document format as well as a title keyword in some abstract searching. The review essay, sometimes referred to as the bibliographic essay, can function as a source of topical and timely publication ideas. The two major sources of reviews of developments are review serials and primary journals. Review serials are mainly published annuals with such titles as

FACULTY DEVELOPMENT   *Oct. 1977*
  CIJE: 773   RIE: 1092   GC: 320
SN Activities to encourage and enhance fac-
    ulty professional growth
UF Faculty Growth
    Faculty Improvement
BT Professional Development
    Staff Development
RT College Faculty
    Faculty
    Faculty Evaluation
    Faculty Fellowships
    Faculty Handbooks
    Faculty Promotion
    Faculty Publishing
    Individual Development
    Inservice Education
    Inservice Teacher Education
    Organizational Development
    Professional Continuing Education
    Professional Training
    Sabbatical Leaves
    Teacher Evaluation
    Teacher Exchange Programs
    Teacher Improvement
    Teacher Promotion

Faculty Development

Academic Computing Projects at Six Liberal Arts Colleges. Final Report to the Exxon Education Foundation.
                                    ED 266 762
Academic Renewal: Advancing Higher Education toward the Nineties. A Collection of Essays Based upon Presentations at the Conference on Academic Renewal Held at the University of Michigan (Ann Arbor, MI, June 1983).   ED 267 680
ADAPT: A Developmental Activity Program for Teachers.
                                    ED 271 923
Advising and Faculty Development: The Institution's View.   ED 261 614
Analysis of Professional Development Activities of Iowa Community College Faculty.   ED 260 756
The Application of Computers in Liberal Arts Instruction. A Computer Literacy Faculty Development Project.
                                    ED 263 875
Approaches to Staff Development for Part-Time Faculty. ERIC Digest.   ED 270 180
ASHE Reader on Faculty and Faculty Issues in Colleges and Universities.   ED 265 780//
The Bush Foundation and the University of South Dakota: A Case Study of Public and Private Sector Collaboration in Faculty Development.   ED 264 200
The Career Ladder Program in Tennessee.   ED 268 073
Communication Studies in Australia: Achievements and Prospects.   ED 271 042
The Community College Professor: Teacher and Scholar. ERIC Digest.   ED 272 248
Compiling Instructors' Perceptions of Learners' Deficiencies: A Problem-Centered Approach to In-Service Training and Language Program Development.   ED 264 722
The Complex Challenge of Professional Development: Current Trends and Future Opportunities. ED 265 911
A Comprehensive Program of Evaluation and Professional Development: A Working Model.   ED 270 866
Curriculum Implementation, Classroom Change and Professional Development: The Challenge for Supervision.
                                    ED 269 853
Determinants of Teacher Preparation: A Study of Departments of Special Education. Technical Report.
                                    ED 269 939
Development as the Aim of Instructional Supervision.
                                    ED 263 655
Diversified Inservice Staff Development Using Models of Teaching.   ED 270 852
The Effects of Teacher Sex Equity and Effectiveness Training on Classroom Interaction at the University Level.   ED 270 005
Effects on Teacher Practice of a Staff Development Program for Integrating Teaching and Testing in High School Courses. Final Report.   ED 267 501
The Elimination of Sexism in University Environments.
                                    ED 267 348
Encouraging Scholarly Investigation, Striving for Expertness, Collegial Exchanges.   ED 260 454
Evaluation of Extension In-Service Education: Ritual or Precursor of Program Excellence?   ED 266 149
Everyday Acts: Staff Development as Continuous and Informal Routine. Draft Copy.   ED 264 645

Figure 4:5. (Left) Step 1: *Thesaurus of ERIC Descriptors.* (Right) Step 2: RIE 1986 [Subject] Index, page 191. "Faculty Development.

Figure 4:5, continued. Step 3: *RIE 1986 Document Resumes*, page 1142.

"Advances In _____," "_____ Annual," "Progress In _____," and
"Review of _____." Annual reviews of the research and publication activity of a field or discipline may suggest aspects needing further research
and thus publication. Underrepresented considerations, questions raised
by recent work, and types of books, journal articles, and dissertations which
have appeared during the review period may be identified. For example,
from 1980–1985, subject specialists reviewed for the *Women's Annual* series
the year's scholarship in education, health, the humanities, politics and law,
psychology, and work, as well as such other concerns as international issues,
lesbians, mass media, and the Third World. G.K. Hall discontinued this
series with Volume Five, published in 1985. Write the publisher [a letter
of protest and include] an offer to prepare a chapter in your specialization,
which will also serve to belie the claim that qualified people are not
available to prepare such articles. The *Annual Review of Anthropology*

WRITING FOR PUBLICATION　　*Oct. 1983*
　　CIJE: 197　　RIE: 105　　GC: 720
SN　Writing intended for acceptance by a
　　　publisher
BT　Writing (Composition)
RT　Authors
　　　Editors
　　　Faculty Publishing
　　　Journalism
　　　News Writing
　　　Periodicals
　　　Professional Development
　　　Publications
　　　Publishing Industry
　　　Publish Or Perish Issue
　　　Scholarly Journals
　　　School Publications
　　　Student Publications
　　　Technical Writing

Writing for Publication
Children as Authors Handbook.　　　　　ED 262 429
Money, Money, Money.　　　　　　　　ED 264 594
New Routes to Writing K-8. [Revised].　　ED 260 452
On Revising Noun Compounds: Four Test . CDC Tech-
　　nical Report No. 5.　　　　　　　　ED 261 388
Perceptions of Women and Men in Counselor Education
　　About Writing for Publication.　　　ED 265 445
Publishing an Anthology of Adult Student Writing: A
　　Partnership for Literacy.　　　　　ED 260 184
The Research on Higher Education Program: An Over-
　　view. Swedish Research on Higher Education, 1985:8.
　　　　　　　　　　　　　　　　　　ED 265 792
Teaching and Research: Independent, Parallel, Unequal.
　　　　　　　　　　　　　　　　　　ED 268 150
Teaching Audience.　　　　　　　　　ED 260 458

ED 265 445　　　　　　　　　　CG 018 769
White, Arden   Hernandez, Nelda
Perceptions of Women and Men in Counselor
　Education About Writing for Publication.
Pub Date—[85]
Note—15p.
Pub Type— Reports - Research (143)
EDRS Price - MF01/PC01 Plus Postage.
Descriptors—*College Faculty, *Counselor Educa-
　tors, Faculty Development, Higher Education,
　Professors, *Sex Differences, *Work Environ-
　ment, *Writing for Publication
　　Women in academic appointments have published less frequently than men. Since this difference is only partially explainable on the basis of
fewer years in higher education, a study was conducted to determine men's and women's perceptions and experiences of writing for publication in
the field of counselor education. A sample of 82
counselor educators balanced by sex, academic
rank, and appearance or non-appearance as authors
in the Social Sciences Citation Index (SSCI) between 1966 and 1983 was drawn from the fifth edition of a national directory of counselor education
programs. Subjects completed a questionnaire on
job activities, professional memberships, journal
subscriptions, and recollection about having had
mentor experiences. In addition, SSCI respondents
were asked to recall perceptions, impressions, and
judgments of variables that might bear differently
on women's circumstances in scholarly work compared to those of men. Comparison group subjects
were asked their views about writing for publication
and any barriers or difficulties bearing on research
and writing they perceived as present in their work
or personal situations. The results indicated that
more SSCI members had assigned time for research,
engaged in fewer non-job professional activities, and
had more statistics courses in their training than did
non-SSCI subjects. Comparisons between women
and men revealed two significant differences: the
number of statistics courses taken in training, and
perceptions of institutional emphases on writing for
publication. Women reported less access/entry to
writing possibilities within departments than did
their male colleagues. They also noted lack of confi-
dence and training, and the pressure of family responsibilities and commitments as conditions
affecting publishing opportunities. Overall, women
perceived a lower institutional emphasis on publishing than did men. (Author/ABB)

(1973–   , CE27) is only one example of the many annual reviews providing chapters by specialists, with bibliographies of works discussed.

Review articles are an especially good source for people in science fields. The *Index to Scientific Reviews* cites the current review literature from both review serials and primary journals of the environmental sciences and engineering, technical, and applied sciences. In addition to its basic purpose of keeping the user up to date, each review article in one's field has the potential for suggesting timely topics and ideas for further, or other, research and publication, and it will have many citations which can function as further access points. Indexing provided by the United States–based *Women Studies Abstracts* refers one *from* reviews *to* (See) LITERATURE REVIEWS. *Studies on Women Abstracts* is an international abstracting service based in England.

Thematic or special issues of journals tend to include discussion of needed changes and provisions in research methodology and publication, e.g. issues of *Resources for Feminist Research/Documentation sur la Réecherche Féministe,* a bilingual serial publication which is also notable here for its summaries of research in progress outside the United States.

Current Contents is the title of a weekly compilation of the tables of contents of recent journal issues in all fields, published in seven sections. The social and behavioral sciences section, for example, reproduces the tables of contents of more than a thousand journals, and indexes the articles by author, subject, and title keywords. "Current contents" is also a technique or approach to awareness which has been applied to many subject fields by various providers. *Feminist Periodicals: A Current Listing of Contents* is a quarterly reproduction of the tables of contents of more than eighty major feminist periodicals, which aims to provide representation of all English-language feminist periodicals with substantial national or regional readerships and to include emphases on scholarly journals and small presses.

Comprehensive Dissertation Index and the related *Dissertation Abstracts International* are particularly good sources of inspiration, ideas, and current interests in relationship to getting published as well as generating dissertation topics. Selected dissertations are also indexed and abstracted in appropriate disciplinary tools such as *Psychological Abstracts.* Kuehl's *Dissertations in History* is an example of numerous subject-selective indexes to these dissertations in specific disciplines. Not simply a CDI subset, such a tool provides the standard data plus information from institutions not covered by DAI and subdivides geographically and chronologically, with author and subject indexing. For your dissertation, it

Figure 4:6. (Clockwise from top left) Step 1: *Thesaurus of ERIC Descriptors.* Step 2: *RIE 1985 [Subject] Index*, page 538: "Writing for Publication." Step 3: *RIE 1986 Document Resumes*, page 838.

is practical to identify a topic about which relatively little has been published in book form — so that yours will be among the first — but on which some work has been done and appeared in the periodical literature (the so-called cutting edge), so that you can get some support for your endeavors and demonstrate that it exists as a recognized concern. Later, the dissertation may be your source of ideas or material for several journal articles or the basis for a book publication. Dissertations completed recently in one's field should be gleaned for suggestions of topics appropriate for further exploration. Less recent dissertations and reactions to them can be taking-off points for additional perspectives and other points of view.

An approach to publication and research consists of maintaining records of aspects of research which need to be enhanced and publications which could be improved. Hypothesize: "What if. . .?" Consider what is needed, what needs redoing, and what is selling and will be selling in two years.

Some concerns and methodologies deserve to be extrapolated to other fields and disciplines. Bart and Frankel's *Student Sociologist's Handbook* could serve as a model for other disciplines.[18] Some work should be updated, supplemented, or replicated. If the author is deceased, the publisher might be interested. If the copyright is in the writer's name, approach her or him; encouragement as well as permission might be forthcoming. Basow and Silber's "Student Evaluations of College Professors: Are Female and Male Professors Rated Differently?" published in the *Journal of Educational Psychology* might suggest disseminating the results of studies of the effects of age and age-sex variables on students' evaluations of college teachers in multi-section courses utilizing the same syllabi.[19]

The survey of research as reported in a recently revised edition of the encyclopedic publication of one's field is a useful first step approach to research and publication for the professionally young scholar. The *Encyclopedia of Educational Research, 5th edition,* for example, includes survey articles with bibliographic support by specialists about women's education, equity issues in education, racism and sexism in research and in children's literature, and textbooks.

Consider *reading* parts of a compilation such as *Women's History Sources: A Guide to Archives and Manuscript Collections in the United States,* especially when focus on regional and state history primary sources is required or when you are already involved in oral or public history. Research libraries usually have the book catalogs of such collections as the Arthur and Elizabeth Schlesinger Library of the History of Women in America, which serve doubly because they also identify actual sources that are accessible for on-site reading, research, and scholarship. The ten-volume catalog of the Schlesinger collection of manuscripts, books, pictures, and periodicals describes materials processed through October 1983.

These holdings concentrate on the period 1820 to the present and contain manuscripts and microfiches, oral history tapes and transcripts, and photographs documenting most aspects of the history of women in the United States.[20] The seven-volume book catalog of the Sophia Smith Collection Women's History Archive is more internationally oriented and includes national and international organizations' files.[21] Descriptions of these and other research-and publications-related collections and catalogs can be found in such tools as the "Women's Collections" issue of *Special Collections*.[22] A brief list of catalogs of accessible collections is included as part of this chapter's bibliography. For a search leading to such collections and their catalogs, use the Library of Congress subject-headings WOMEN — BIBLIOGRAPHIES — CATALOGS and WOMEN — U.S. HISTORY — BIBLIOGRAPHIES — CATALOGS. Scholarly book publications which are also of interest to general readers have evolved from these approaches, e.g. Hampsten's *Read This Only to Yourself: The Private Writings of Midwestern Women, 1880–1910*, Luchetti and Olwell's *Women of the West*, Rosen's *The Maimie Papers*, Schlissel's *Women's Diaries of the Westward Journey*, and Stratton's *Pioneer Women*.[23]

Conversion of a speech can occasionally be a way to recycle both ideas and work. If you are not reading a formal preparation, tape your talk or seminar preparation. Transcribe it, and use this draft to reorganize and make your first revision. Repetition and shorter sentences will need to be curtailed. A talk will probably be longer on paper than the article and cover less material.

One of the publishing activities in which several persons can engage and which has potential for an infusion of funds is the Women's History Tour, or walk, of a neighborhood, community, or section *(barrio, chiiki-shakai, quartier, vicinato . . .)*. Such a project aims to present a taste of the experiences and major involvement of girls and women in their community's early settlement and development. It should not attempt to be a comprehensive history of female residents of a very small area, but rather a portrayal of buildings, business enterprises, and other visible features which serve as physical reminders of the accomplishments of some of these women. Nor should the "walk" itself cover too much territory! A script for an actual historical tour should be a part of the document for publication. In book form, interesting facts, statistics, and photographs can be utilized to set off the historical settings surrounding them. The females to be met on a Women's History Tour or walk may be from the recent or dim past — prominent social leaders, literary figures, immigrant servants, laborers in the canneries and mills, caretakers of the sick and needy, as well as women associated with well-known men, the anonymous women whose stories are largely unchronicled, and the occasional women who achieved autonomy or notoriety. Glimpses of women's lives and work in a defined locale will broaden appreciation of their varied experiences and provide insight into the people and forces that shaped development of the area. Many communities are rich resources in women's history with potential for organization into walks, self-guided tours, and commercial and even scholarly publication.

The research is not difficult. Consult *Women's History Sources...*; Tinling's *Women Remembered: A Guide to Landmarks of Women's History in the United States; Historical Abstracts; America: History and Life* and Harrison's related tool, *Women in American History.*[24] Check library catalogs under title entries beginning *Literary Landmarks of...* and *Historical Landmarks of....* Planning, small grant proposal preparation, reading, interviewing, testing, evaluating, coordinating, publicizing, photographing, writing, editing, etc., make this an ideal group project, although an individual could certainly write such a book. She or he might also propose it in connection with a requirement in a women's studies, public history, or other degree program. Published examples of women's history "walks" include Clarke's *In Our Grandmothers' Footsteps* and Mason and Lacey's *Women's History Tour of the Twin Cities.*[25]

For people in degree programs and jobs which accept bibliographic and collation work as publication, there are gaps in most disciplines' indexing, comprehensive and selective bibliographic support, union lists, and directories. Compilations, supplements, and updates are always needed. Work comparable to Harrison's *Women in American History,*[24] drawn from *America: History and Life,* might be attempted for history of other nations via the complementary abstracting service, *Historical Abstracts.*

Action research is a process by which practitioners attempt to study their problems scientifically in order to guide, correct, and evaluate their discussions and actions. It is often associated with the field of professional education, but can apply to professions generally and to all of the social and behavioral sciences. Action research is designed to yield practical results immediately applicable to specific situations and problems, which can make it conducive to change and to publication. Some consider it nontraditional research methodology and therefore do not regard it highly.

Identification and discussions of currently needed research and publication concerns in all disciplines are serviceable, and they too are needed. Daniels' 1975 survey of women's issues–related research concerns was an early approach to this type of publication, which can involve going out on a limb. Palmer and Grant's 1979 analysis of the status of clerical workers included forty-five key topics on which research was needed. Shakeshaft's *Dissertation Research on Women in Academic Administration: A Synthesis of Findings and Paradigm for Future Research* is another related example. Updates of these compilations and creation of others need to be encouraged and disseminated. In 1987 Josephine and Bloom suggested areas in women's studies needing new reference works by analyzing ten such reference works said to be representative of the seventy-four published in 1984 and 1985; their analysis was based on criteria provided by Katz in his library school text, *Introduction to Reference Work* (but see earlier in this chapter). Hartman and Messer-Davidow's *Women in Print, Volume II: Opportunities for Women's Studies Publication in Language and Literature* was prepared for the Commission on the Status of Women in the Profession in 1983. They included discussions of publication opportunities abroad, particularly in France, opportunities for research in lesbian literature, and women's studies opportunities for research and publication in Russian literature.[26]

Roberts' 1975 doctoral dissertation on the prestigious Caldecott Medal Award books (for the most distinguished picture book for children published in the United States during the previous year; the Newbery Medal is the counterpart for children's literature) and other such studies should be updated. Attention to her recommendations continues to be needed. Representation of females and feminists in "best books" and award winners as well as in "banned books" is a vast area for potential research and publication.[27]

McLeod utilized a limited population for her 1980 doctoral dissertation, *Sex Discrimination Complaints Against Florida Public Institutions of Higher Education*. Such work should be extended to a large number of states, institutions, and persons. Controversial, activist, and energizing topics and "hard approaches" to them are, however, unacceptable to many journals and book publishers. Frequently they must be delicately and conventionally [re-]written even for women's studies periodicals.[28]

Studies which control for sex *and* other characteristics are needed. Social science research methodology as applied to the subject of aging and aging females has typically been based on assumptions which include male elderly as the norm, and research populations have not been representative. Aging and aged women are an underresearched and thus relatively unpublished area. Publications about the aging of females and about old women (usually referred to euphemistically as "older" women) have begun to be of interest in the literary marketplace, provided they do not dwell on stressful topics such as rape and old women, age and sex discrimination in employment of women, etc. Diaries and oral histories are other innovative approaches to viewing women as they really were and are and could be.

Correcting the record as recorded by mostly male historians is necessary. Alas, the new market for what many publishers misleadingly refer to as their women's studies books, in combination with women academics' inordinate need to get published, sometimes results in marketing titles whose flamboyant style appeals to some, but which are patronizing in tone and lean toward the sensational. "Ladies of easy virtue," "petticoat pioneers," and "feminine daintiness" are too frequently incorporated and accepted by the gatekeepers, women writers, and readers.[29]

As singular as the need to correct and complete women's history is, and although the need for unity among women is strategic (I have referred in earlier writing to the delay-divide-discredit syndrome to which they are particularly subject), I must also focus on recording current *herstory*.[30] Contemporary and recent women's history can be overlooked, and it can be structured. In permitting a bit of feminist history to be introduced into curricula, courses, theory, and publications, the authorizing body may perceive dead women as acceptable because they are relatively safe. Certainly they cannot speak for themselves, compete, sue, or even file a charge! Questions to ask oneself and in teaching in order to bring women into view have been suggested by Lerner, for example. They also provide excellent topics for further study, writing, and all types of publications.[31]

An impression of the subjects, topics, and concerns which are and have been emphasized, neglected, or distorted in the periodical literature of your discipline can be derived from its specialized abstracting service(s), which are often searchable on-line as well as by hand in hard copy. When initiating a computer-assisted literature search of periodical indexes, abstracts, and citation indexes in your behalf, you must communicate to the searcher exactly what your subject interests are, what their scope is and is not. Your search together can initially also function to determine the relative number of documents on an aspect of your topic present in a particular data base file. The more specific you are, the more direct the path and usable the information that can be provided. For example, if you are concerned with television violence, do you mean covert or overt? in educational, public, or commercial TV? in plot, action, dialog, or advertising perhaps? Or suppose you refer to discrimination. Are you using this word negatively, and if so, on what basis does the disparity you have in mind take place? Be complete, nonjudgmental. Do not refer to sex discrimination if you really have in mind discrimination in education of contemporary high school females in the United States based on their gender!

You can consult the on-line or card catalog of a large research library system or of a specialized library for information about the subjects and titles represented in its book (and sometimes periodical) collections. Access to subject information (as opposed to author-title combinations) contained in the collections of most United States and some other nations' college and university libraries is based mainly on the Library of Congress *Subject Headings* (LCSH) thesaurus, a controlled vocabulary. Subdivisions of the many established subject headings provide a way to focus on a topic. An awareness of changes in existing, and reaction to new, subject headings is especially productive for research and publication by scholars in all disciplines and fields.

LC subject-headings can be systematically subdivided several times in order to access specific information and types of documents, e.g. WOMEN – U.S. – HISTORY – ARCHIVAL RESOURCES – U.S. describes and accesses *Women's History Resources: A Guide to Archives and Manuscript Collections in the United States.* Although a book usually has several subject-headings assigned to it in order to communicate its contents fully, examples here related to each work's primary, encompassing subject-heading, listed first in the Arabic-numeraled tracings which appear at the bottom of a printed catalog card and on some other types of records.

Some standard *sub*divisions can be added to most basic subject-heading stems. These are used to subdivide topics (subject-headings) *geographically, chronologically,* and in terms of whatever physical or other *form* (format) the publication itself takes. A geographical location subdivision consists of the name of a country or other political entity, region, or geographical feature. A geographic subdivision is added to a subject-heading when it is needed to describe a publication's contents fully and accurately. The LCSH indicates whether a subject-heading can be subdivided geographically. The LC subject-heading COPYRIGHT – U.S. has been assigned to Johnson's *Copyright Handbook, 2nd edition* because it describes the book's contents in terms of copyright applicable specifically to the United States better than just COPYRIGHT would. COPYRIGHT is a separate subject-heading in the LCSH thesaurus; there is the possibility of numerous other COPYRIGHT dash NATION subject-headings in terms of other books' scope and contents.

Chronological, time-period *sub*divisions are often utilized following countries or nations to subdivide their history or literature. In the following example, the subject-headings are listed as they would be filed in an "alphabetical" catalog, demonstrating the chronological arrangement following the UNITED STATES – HISTORY portion, which may or may not be the case in a computer-generated file:

U.S. – HISTORY
U.S. – HISTORY – QUEEN ANNE'S WAR, 1702–1713
U.S. – HISTORY – KING GEORGE'S WAR, 1744–1748
U.S. – HISTORY – FRENCH AND INDIAN WAR, 1755–1763
U.S. – HISTORY – REVOLUTION

Time can also be expressed in an open-ended way (ENGLISH LANGUAGE – GRAMMAR – 1950–   , for example) and in terms of centuries, e.g. WOMEN AUTHORS, AMERICAN – 20th CENTURY, which describes and accesses Yalom's *Women Writers of the West Coast; Speaking of Their Lives and Their Careers.*

Form subdivisions are provided to identify the particular format in which the document is published. They can be added as the *final* subdivision of any heading. They do not describe what the book is about, but, rather, of what it consists. Subdivisions by form which are most useful in research and publication work include:

SUBJECT—ABSTRACTS
   WOMEN AND RELIGION—ABSTRACTS accesses Anne Carson's *Feminist Spirituality and the Feminine Divine* (Crossing, 1986).
SUBJECT—ADDRESSES, ESSAYS AND LECTURES
   SCHOLARLY PUBLISHING—ADDRESSES, ESSAYS AND LEC-TURES accesses Mary Frank Fox's *Scholarly Writing & Publishing: Issues, Problems and Solutions* (Westview, 1985).
SUBJECT—BIBLIOGRAPHY
   REFERENCE BOOKS—WOMEN—BIBLIOGRAPHY accesses Susan Searing's *Introduction to Library Research in Women's Studies* (Westview, 1985).
SUBJECT—YEARBOOKS
   FEMINISM—U.S.—YEARBOOKS accesses *The Women's Annual. . .; The Year In Review* (G.K. Hall, 1980–1985). *The Women's Annual* was about feminism in the United States, not about yearbooks; it *is* a year-book on the subject of feminism in the United States. Especially at the beginning of a literature search, selective bibliographies and surveys of the status quo, which specialized yearbooks often provide, are useful.
SUBJECT—CATALOGS
   VENEZUELAN LITERATURE—WOMEN AUTHORS—BIBLIOG-RAPHY—CATALOGS accesses *La Mujer en las Letras Venezolanas: Homenaje a Teresa de la Parra en el Año Internacional de la Mujer: Cátalogo . . .* (Caracas, 1976).
SUBJECT—DICTIONARIES
   INTELLECTUAL PROPERTY—U.S.—DICTIONARIES accesses Elias' *Intellectual Property Law Dictionary.*
SUBJECT—DIGESTS
   WOMEN—LEGAL STATUS, LAWS, ETC.—CALIFORNIA—DI-GESTS accesses *Summary of New Laws Affecting Women* (California Commission on the Status of Women, 1987).
SUBJECT—DIRECTORIES
   FEMINIST LITERATURE—PUBLISHING—DIRECTORIES ac-cesses Clardy's *Words To The Wise* (Firebrand Books, 1986).
SUBJECT—ENCYCLOPEDIAS
   WOMEN'S ENCYCLOPEDIAS AND DICTIONARIES accesses *Lex-ikon der Frau* (Zurich: Encyclios Verlag: 1953–54).
SUBJECT—INDEXES
   DISSERTATIONS, ACADEMIC—U.S.—INDEXES accesses *Com-prehensive Dissertation Index.*

SUBJECT—PERIODICALS
  WOMEN—GREAT BRITAIN—PERIODICALS accesses *Radical and Reforming Periodicals For and By Women* (Brighton, Sussex, England, 1983–   ).
SUBJECT—SOURCES
  WOMEN—U.S.—HISTORY—COLONIAL PERIOD ca 1600–1775—SOURCES accesses Norton's *Liberty's Daughters: The Revolutionary Experience of American Women, 1750–1800* (Little, Brown, 1980).

Standard topical subdivisions of established subject-headings or of other subdivisions limit the concept expressed to a specific *sub*topic, e.g. WOMEN—EMPLOYMENT. Some useful ones for getting-published work include:

SUBJECT—ECONOMIC ASPECTS (or ECONOMIC CONDITIONS)
  WOMEN IN POLITICS—U.S.—ECONOMIC ASPECTS accesses Uhlaner's *Candidate Gender and Congressional Campaign Receipts* (1986).
SUBJECT—SOCIAL LIFE AND CUSTOMS
  WOMEN—NEW GUINEA—SOCIAL LIFE AND CUSTOMS accesses Conton's *Women's Roles in a Man's World: Appearance and Reality in a Lowland New Guinea Village.*

Free-floating *sub*divisions may be used as needed under subject headings. They too can be combined with each other and with form, geographical, and chronological subdivisions. They are rarely spelled out in the LCSH thesaurus. Some examples which are particularly useful in locating specific information supportive of publication and research include:

SUBJECT—HISTORY AND CRITICISM
  ENGLISH PROSE LITERATURE—HISTORY AND CRITICISM accesses Graves' *The Reader Over Your Shoulder: A Handbook for Writers of English Prose, 2nd edition.*
SUBJECT-LEGAL STATUTES, LAWS, ETC.
  AUTHORS—LEGAL STATUTES, LAWS, ETC.—U.S. accesses Bunnin's *Author Law and Strategies: A Legal Guide for the Working Author* (Nolo 1983).
SUBJECT—RESEARCH
  FEMINISM—RESEARCH—GERMANY (WEST) accesses *Frauenforschung oder Feministiche Forschung* (1984).
SUBJECT—TRANSLATIONS INTO [LANGUAGE]

ENGLISH POETRY—TRANSLATIONS FROM HEBREW and
ISRAELI POETRY (HEBREW)—WOMEN AUTHORS—TRANS-
LATIONS INTO ENGLISH access Glazer's *Burning Air and a Clear
Mind: Contemporary Israeli Women Poets* (Ohio University Press,
1981).

• • •

"I learned three important things in college—to use a library, to memorize
quickly and visually, to drop asleep at any time given a horizontal surface
and fifteen minutes. What I could not learn was to think creatively on
schedule." Agnes DeMille (c1905–   ). American dancer, choreographer,
author. *Dance to the Piper.* Boston, Massachusetts: Little, Brown, 1952.

There's no panacea for Mary Shelley's dull Nothing, or ye olde writing
block. Outline. Write without ceasing for sixty minutes a day or whatever
amount of time beyond sixty minutes you want to set for yourself. Write.
Write for that amount of time every day, or Monday–Friday, without exception. Need to go to the library, to discuss something with someone else, to
do something for someone else, ad infinitum are delaying tactics. While going to the library or consulting someone may be a relevant activity at the
appropriate time, neither is acceptable in this context. Write without ceasing. Stop going to conferences and workshops. Having gotten beyond a personal writing block, another routine involves getting the work accomplished within a time requirement. Make a general schedule and keep to
it. Keep a library shopping list, and schedule a day and time at the library.

Break the work down in terms of your outline. Whether you initially
handwrite or use a word processor, do not move to revision until you have
the equivalent of ten typed pages. When a deadline is imminent or you have
lost time to illness or supporting another person's writing perhaps, you must
double up. One way to tackle a work orgy is to write, type, or revise for no
less than sixty minutes (when you get going, don't stop, of course), and then
spend ten doing something in-house and essential to the maintenance of
daily life (yours), e.g. open mail, peel potatoes, scrape carrots.

It is standard operating procedure to commend a "readable style" to
writers. Easier said than done. If *it* is a problem, ask for your colleague
reader's frank reaction particularly in this area. Strunk and White's classic
Elements of Style provides "an approach to style" with a discussion of
twenty-one "reminders." The entire small volume is basic reading or review
and consists of five parts: elementary rules of usage, elementary principles
of composition, a few matters of form, words and expressions commonly
used, and the approach to style.[32]

Some of the things to avoid include:

- clichés
- dating your manuscript in content and references
- contractions, e.g. "don't," which are for speaking, not writing
- words which may be part of professional vocabularies but which a reviewer may consider jargon, e.g. linkages, interface
- recently coined words ending in "ize," e.g. prioritize
- assigning priorities as a technique of divisiveness
- the "there are two sides to every story" concept
- thoughtless phrases like working woman, working wife, working mother
- stereotypes
- exclamation points
- dangling and misplaced modifiers
- unclear antecedents
- incorrect or inconsistent abbreviations

Take care with:

- languages which are used in several nations, e.g. American and British spellings and meanings (catalog/catalogue, honor/honour, center/centre, motion picture/cinema)
- potential stumbling blocks in spelling and meaning, e.g. infer/imply, principle/principal, capitol/capital, effect/affect
- evolving language and technical vocabulary, e.g. on on-line data base, descriptors
- words which are currently misused, misunderstood, or overused, e.g. mentor, networking, hopefully, problematic, or the verb "to feel." Regarding this last: Women are, commendably, feeling persons, but they may tend to use this verb inappropriately without thought or from habit, when other verbs are more meaningful and precise, e.g. to judge, to evaluate, to know, to sense.
- data is one example of a plural form often mistaken for a singular. "These data *are* . . ." is correct. The care with which such words should be used relates to the way one's "peer" reviewer or evaluator deems acceptable.

Allow time to revise. Make a schedule, organize, outline, and revise. Do not over-cogitate. When in doubt, the first word or phrase that comes to mind is usually the best way of expressing it. Keep quotations requiring costly permission fees to a minimum. Limit quotations to three hundred words and you will usually not need permission, unless you arequoting something in its entirety or very nearly. Publications of the United States government are in the public domain, and permission to quote them need not be obtained.

The importance of the title has been mentioned in connection with conversion of the doctoral dissertation to trade book. Whether structuring the title of a journal article or a nonfiction book, its construction is important in attracting editors, publishers, and readers. Journal article titles like Bacchi's "'First Wave' Feminism in Canada: The Ideas of the English-Canadian Suffragists, 1877–1918" and Borish's "The Robust Woman and the Muscular Christian: Catharine Beecher, Thomas Higginson, and Their Vision of American Society, Health and Physical Activities" illustrate the formulation of an initial attraction amplified by a description replete with keywords communicating scope and perspective.[33]

Guides to publication routinely include instructions for preparation of the manuscript. Some of these guides and related handbooks are pointed out within Chapters Two and Three and included in the Resources section. Details of manuscript preparation vary with the type of publication and among disciplines and authorities whose style manuals are prescribed by publishers and journals. I will use this space to focus on some refinements and skills which may ease the transition to requirements usually stressed in academe and scholarly publication. They might be termed tips ("inside information given as a guide to action"—*Random House Dictionary*). To omit or overlook some of them often will not be tolerated. Readers' experiences and skills vary greatly, but their goals and commitments are no less worthy and needy. In defining "tip," Webster provides the demonstration, "Take my tip and do not venture in there without a guide!" *(Webster's Third New International Dictionary.)*

In preparing the manuscript, use subheadings generously, particularly in journal articles. Place one table to a page. Proofread carefully. Allow time for preparation of your manuscript which permits time to lapse between its completion and parting with it. Proofread several times. Do not hyphenate at the end of a line, begin a sentence with a numeral, or use cockle bond or erasable paper. Do follow these standard operating procedures:

- Spell out acronyms the first time you use them, e.g. "National Organization for Women (NOW)"
- Beware that *ibid.* and *op. cit.* are becoming things of the past. Use them only when instructions and style manuals specify their use.
- Be consistent; stick to one form throughout your work, e.g. women studies, women's studies, Women Studies, *or* Women's Studies.
- Use two typewriter hyphens with no space between to create a dash.
- Include a credits statement at the beginning of your papers, manuscripts, and publications. For example, "Portions of this work were presented at the meeting of the Oom Pah Pah Association, place, date. I would like to express my gratitude to the participants in this study as well as to the anonymous and other reviewers of this paper for their helpful comments."

If the article is published based on changes suggested by anonymous reviewers, by all means include this message.

- Use 12 pitch type, i.e. 12 strokes or letters to an inch. Typewriters are 10, 12, and 15.
- Use a new or film-type typewriter ribbon. Be aware that carbon copies are a thing of the past. Use high quality photoreproduction processes.
- Keep in mind that there are approximately two hundred fifty words per double-spaced, typed manuscript page, and that currently the manuscript for a book generally consists of at least two hundred fifty double-spaced typed pages, preferably three hundred.

· · ·

"How shall I ever find the grains of truth embedded in all this mass of paper." Virginia Woolf (1882–1941). English novelist. *A Room of One's Own.* Chapter 2. London:Hogarth, 1929.

For each publishing project, whether or not publication results, structure a simple tax-related recordkeeping system. I suggest a Finances & Records folder into which you put receipts and related memoranda. You will have to itemize for tax purposes. Include a record of expenses covered by your department or institution's professional development program. These might include all, part or none of your postage, duplicating, stationery, preparation of illustrations, and subventions costs, and submission, processing, and page fees. In addition to the basic expenses—duplicating and postage—which you may not be able to cover completely at your place of employment, other professional development, publications-related categories of expense may ultimately include:

Accounting services	Postage
Attorney fees	Processing fees
Computer searches	Professional conferences and
Consultant fees	seminars
Duplicating	Publicity
Freight charges, shipping	Stationery
Illustrations preparation	Subscriptions
Indexing	Submission fees
Insurance	Subventions
Membership fees	Supplies
Messenger service	Travel
Page fees	Word-processing

If you do not use a word processor, an electric typewriter—some would say an electronic typewriter—is essential. If you use a word processor for your book or other manuscripts, use a letter-quality printer. If you have a continuous sheet printer, use twenty-pound paper and separate the pages before mailing the manuscript. Proofread the printout.

One publisher asks that you submit the final approved journal article version both on printed format ("hard copy") and floppy diskette (one original diskette and one duplicate needed). Due to "the volatility of electronic media, authors are encouraged to include a printout of the file. Floppy disks are not returned unless requested." Some book publishers respond to book proposals with forms that include a production-related question regarding the possibility of your rendering the manuscript in disk or cassette form. In your proposal conveyance letter, mention your computer model, disks, and word processing program.

If you are approaching the computer as well as word processing for the first time, you do not need to be intimidated. The things to consider here are ease in learning and operation, useful features, speed, and the way you, the user, must interact with the program. For example, some of the programs on the market are better than others at doing footnotes. You will hear references to one program which probably does everything most writers and editors need, but some consider it difficult to learn and object to the fact that what appears on the screen does not necessarily reflect how your text will appear on the page. This is particularly true if one uses a so-called mainframe text formatter; these are full of weird symbols, but worth learning. Writers who often need to use tables and figures should consider what graphic facilities are incorporated into or supported by a particular word processing program. Disciplines requiring extensive use of statistics include anthropology, business and management, economics, forestry, and linguistics. The Modern Language Association of America has adopted, endorses, and sells Nota Bene, a word processing program specifically for academic writers. *Consumer Reports* and *Buyers' Guide* can be consulted for information about the many brands, models, and features of word processors and programs. If you continue to have some relationship with the university where you received the doctorate or if you are on a university faculty, check with the computer services department. It is possible to use very powerful computers with less cost than purchasing one. Buying an entire system is not ideal, because they are being improved on a daily basis.

Affirmative management of professional and staff development programming enables publishing-related activities expected of women doctoral students, faculty, and professional staff, and it can also provide college and universities with uniquely cost-effective benefits. Because women must take the initiative and follow through on provision of such programs and compliance with legal requirements relating to their well-being, the suggestions which follow are directed to college and universities through the members of this "protected class."

Provision of campus women's centers, recognition of women reentry students' special needs, and authorization of surveys and reports have demonstrated-potential for contributing to qualified women's getting published and thereby fulfilling their goals. Some specific provisions related to their getting published should include:

- Budget for their computer-assisted literature searches.
- A feminist bibliographer on the libraries' professional staff who has specific responsibility for supervision of women's studies collection development, reference service, and computer-assisted literature searches.
- Training sessions for searchers on data bases with greatest potential for gender-related research and publication and in behalf of women doctoral candidates' and faculty members' current specializations and interests and of gender-related topics.
- Training for candidates in use of personal computer and word processing early in the doctoral program.
- Encouragement of women graduate students' and faculty's involvement in colloquia on campus and in city, state, and region.
- Enabling for their sharing of drafts, papers, and manuscripts for comments, including development of a network and duplicating and postage for off-campus communication.
- Dissemination of unpublished papers presented by doctoral students and faculty who are tenure track aspirants.
- Provision of getting-published training among various forms of professional development technical assistance as well as faculty tenure dossier preparation assistance.
- Encouragement of and support for attendance at and participation in disciplinary and professional conferences, congresses, and colloquia.
- Compilation, revision, and distribution of directories of current research and publication interests *and* recent publications and presentations of women scholars.
- Scheduling work-support groups, to include space and facilities.
- Communication networks of women on campus who are certified doctoral candidates and tenure-track faculty.
- More advisors' office hours and advisors who meet posted office hours.
- Women advisors, faculty, graduate students in departments and throughout campus in proportions reflecting populations. Women are 52.9 percent of higher education enrollment at United States institutions, approximately 28 percent of faculty. Women were 35 percent of 1986 recipients of doctorates in the United States.[34]
- Workshops which consider problems associated with selection of topics and completion of doctoral dissertations.

- Lounge-type facility for drop-in and meeting rooms for scheduling in women's center and/or in each department.
- Arrangements with the (nearest) university press to provide a tour, and subsequent meetings with (1) the acquisitions editor involved with women's studies or gender-related books and journals, (2) a manuscript editor who has recently completed work on such a book (and possibly the author), and (3) journals personnel.
- Liaison among area small colleges which can work together on implementing many of these suggestions.
- Initiative among community colleges, which generally place less value on publication but do utilize tenure systems, to recognize the potential in implementing some of these provisions, perhaps in cooperation with tenure- or doctoral-granting public colleges which they feed.
- Clear and accessible policy statements declaring and defining publication requirements and their relative value among other requirements for faculty employment, retention, promotion, and tenure, to be included in the affirmative action program and the faculty handbook, as well as departmental faculty documents.
- Selective and regularly updated getting-published resources lists, to include titles of publications which are in the collections of campus libraries, including but not limited to the women's center library.
- Feminist affirmative action and professional development personnel with ability, time, and staff to manage such a program.

Universities with commitments to affirmative management practices affecting education and employment (which are concomitants) *can* sponsor professional development training for doctoral students and professionally young faculty who need to get acceptably published. The emphasis on prestigious journals which they constantly hear *can* be accompanied by guidance; e.g., compilations of journals in which tenured faculty have recently published, as well as journal titles and book publishers which the department considers prestigious, acceptable, and recommended should be created and regularly updated. Recognition for a doctoral candidate who has already published a journal article as well as her insights and information for other graduate students might be provided by having her discuss her experience and to provide suggestions and answer questions. Presentations can be videotaped and reused. Meetings can be arranged on campus following conferences and professional gatherings. Doctoral students, recent doctoral recipients, and professionally young faculty who have attended and presented papers can discuss with leadership the relationship to the next step — getting their papers published. Often these women invest considerably more in time, effort, and money in such trips and presentations than men, and the comparable worth of their resources puts them at a disadvantage.

Colleges and universities which are endeavoring to increase international enrollments in doctoral and professional programs would likely find these simple provisions to be synergistic. Foreign enrollment at United States institutions of higher education constitutes 2.7 percent of the 12,500,798 students; mose are from Asia.[35]

Mentorship has received attention from feminists, women, and the academic press. Mentoring is a two-person relationship involving the mentor's empathetic commitment and the mentoree's trust, so that by definition there could never be enough mentors on a graduate faculty to provide for everyone's needs. Universities and even some women fail to realize that mentorship is not yet another assignment to be juggled among responsibilities, and that a role model does not necessarily a mentor make.

Plan your career in academe while you are still a graduate student, and don't spread yourself too thin, especially during your early career. Successful women in academe advise publishing articles rather than books early in one's career and concentrating on research activities. What about good teaching? Neither they nor I have satisfactory responses. After you have completed your first manuscript and when it has ultimately been accepted for publication in a specific journal issue, include it on your resume as "In Press." If you are in the humanities, contact the Modern Language Association regarding the possibility of your work being recorded in the Research-in-Progress Database (RIPD) of humanities papers that have been submitted for publication but have not yet been published and of research that is underway but not has yet been reported.

• • •

"Truth burns up error." Sojourner Truth (c1797–1885). American social reformer, feminist. Comment c1882.

Linguistic patterns which limit perception and experience can also restrict choices and rights. The use of euphemisms and rhetoric — semantic whitewash — to meet political ends is common practice by government. The coverup of the concentration camps in which Japanese Americans were held during World War II, for example, was managed through euphemistic terminology, and other parts of American society entered into this detention of citizens. The practice continues to be considered necessary to meet political ends.[36] When the old boys of Louisiana State University declared they would "never conciliate on women," they were enabled to say publicly what they meant because there was little likelihood of repercussions resulting from such boastful forthrightness. When an educational institution or organization advertises for a "chairman," the easily-observable record demonstrates this is generally their intent. Insistence on using feminine language and sexist nomenclature damages everyone. Morgan referred in 1977 to sexism as "the root oppression, the one which, until and unless we uproot it, will continue to put forth the branches of racism, class hatred, ageism, competition, ecological disaster, and economic exploitation."[37] A decade later Vellela writes that "More than racism, more than homophobia, more than economic pressures levelled directly at students, sexism affects the greatest number of people on college campuses. However unfocused or diffuse the concerns, strategies, and constituencies may be, women's issues have the potential to generate a renewed round of feminist activity on college campuses."[38] There has been little real progress in the academic or literary marketplaces in attempting to understand what is involved in the sociolinguistics of gender. Changes are made in images of and reference to race, ethnicity, and national origin according to pressure. Maintenance of the gender status quo involves only occasional avoidance of troublesome situations . . . getting around it, dealing with it.

Getting-published training programs and publications usually allude to "considerations of language." Their message is, don't offend anyone by letting your biases show in the way you use words and illustrations. Some publishers provide authors with insights on the technique of masking ageist, racist, sexist, and other assumptions. Stainton wearily describes "feminist pressures" which have brought the situation about.[39] In her getting-published handbook for academic authors, Luey identifies several types of "pitfalls" to avoid because they "can detract from the authority you should be able to convey." They are exaggeration, "obvious bias, especially if it is unacknowledged," representation of schools of thought in economics and psychology in textbooks, and "dogmatic and arbitrary statements . . . largely a matter of tone." "A little imagination makes the problem go away," refers to "the fuss [which] has been raised about sexist language." For people who "feel [note the emotional verb] that making these elements sex-neutral renders them too vague or even inaccurate, you can divide them roughly equally by gender."[40] Her way around the problem which sexist language and images imposes on the writer-reader is to divide by gender, which is likely to be unrealistic in a textbook illustration intended to reflect life on a building site or in a shipyard.

Society reflects and shapes language. But it is not sufficient to recognize and acknowledge that reference to Mary Smith as chairman is technically inaccurate. To refer to John Smith thusly excludes all females from chairing or chairperson status, responsibility, influence, and rewards. To refer to them as chairpersons says that the job can be done equally well by and is open to both sexes. "Mr., Miss, Ms., or Mrs." on a form is not an equitable choice. ("Mr.-Married, Mr.-Not Married, Miss, or Mrs." would provide a technically equitable determination of sex and marital status!) The message that gender is irrelevant must be clear before females can reach their potential. The structure of thesauri can influence writers and publishers to maintain the status quo *or* to expand opportunities leading to equity. Going beyond the present reluctant avoidance of the alleged awkwardness and not going around all things which tend to permit change are necessary.

This has been an attempt to incorporate some of the mechanics of scholarly publication with the facts of academic life as they relate, often uniquely, to women graduate students and faculty and professional staff without security of employment. Progress has taken place and opportunities have been introduced because of the strength and struggles of some women to accomplish enforcement of existing laws. The need for watchfulness and ongoing activism is evident in both the subtle and the obvious losses of the 1980s. Courage is required to reject stereotyped, socially sanctioned ways of perceiving, thinking, and living.

Notes

1. Theodore, Athena. *The Campus Troublemakers: Academic Women in Protest.* Houston, Texas: Cap and Gown, 1986. Wheeler, Helen Rippier. "Essay review" in *Journal of Educational Equity and Leadership* 6 (Winter 1986): 335–6.

2. Kolodny, Annette. "Some Notes On Defining a 'Feminist Literary Criticism.'" *Critical Inquiry* 2 (Autumn 1975): 75–92.

3. Chambers, Nancy Goddard. "Book Reviews." *Signs* 13 (Winter 1988): 340–43. Birke, Lynda Sue. *Women, Feminism, and Biology.* New York: Methuen, 1986. Blair, Ruth. *Feminist Approaches to Science.* Elmsford, New York: Pergamon, 1986. Rosser, Sue V. *Teaching Science and Health from a Feminist Perspective.* Elmsford, New York: Pergamon, 1986. Sapiro, Virginia. *Women, Biology, and Public Policy.* Newbury Park, California: Sage, 1985.

4. Editorial. *Choice* 24 (January 1987): 723.

5. Gilbert, Victor Francis, and Darshan Singh Tatla. *Women's Studies: A Bibliography of Dissertations, 1870–1982.* New York: Blackwell, 1985. Reviewed in *Choice* 23 (April 1986): 1194.

6. Sheehy, Eugene. *Guide to Reference Books, 10th edition.* Chicago, Illinois: American Library Association, 1986.

7. *Signs* subject index to its volumes 1–10 lists its review essays on pages S85–S88 under REVIEW ESSAYS. Searing has a list of those which appeared in *Signs* volumes 1–9 in her *Introduction to Library Research in Women's Studies* (Appendix C, pp. 229–33); the balance are:

Vol. 11, no. 1, Autumn 1985
  Henley, Nancy M. "Psychology and Gender." pp. 101–119.
  Mayne, Judith. "Feminist Film Theory and Criticism." pp. 81–101.
Vol. 11, no. 2, Winter 1986
  Geiger, Susan N.G. "Women's Life Histories: Method and Content." pp. 334-51.
Vol. II, no. 3, Spring 1986
  Jordan, Rosan A., and F.A. deCaro. "Women and the Study of Folklore." pp. 500–518.

Vol. 12, no. 1, Autumn 1986
  Basch, Norma. "The Emerging Legal History of Women in the United States:
    Property, Divorce, and the Constitution." pp. 97–117.
  Chesney-Lind, Meda. "Women and Crime: The Female Offender." pp. 78–96.
  Shanley, Mary Lyndon. "Suffrage, Protective Labor Legislation, and Married
    Women's Property Laws in England." pp. 52–77.
Vol. 12, no. 3, Spring 1987
  Fox-Genovese, Elizabeth. "Culture and Consciousness in the Intellectual History
    of European Women." pp. 529–547.
Vol. 12, no. 4, Summer 1987
  Haney, Wave, and Jane B. Knowles. "Women and Farming: Changing Roles,
    Changing Structures." pp. 797–800.
Vol. 13, no. 3, Spring 1988
  Blum, Linda, and Vicki Smith. "Women's Mobility in the Corporation: A Critique
    of the Politics of Optimism." pp. 528–545.
Vol. 13, no. 4, Summer 1988
  Jameson, Elizabeth. "Toward a Multicultural History of Women in the Western
    United States." pp. 761–791.

See, for good examples of bibliographic essays appearing in *Choice:*

Abbott, Linda M.C. "Women, Work and Self-Esteem." **25** (October 1987): 265–74.
Rosenthal, Naomi Braun. "Nineteenth Century Women." **25** (September 1987):
67–77.

    8. Freeman, Jo. *Women; A Feminist Perspective, 2nd edition.* Mountain View,
California: Mayfield, 1979. pp. xvii, xviii, xix.
    9. Steinbach, Sheldon Elliott. "Have Professors Forgotten the Copyright Law
on Photocopies?" *Chronicle of Higher Education* **34** (June 22, 1988): A40. The
American Association of Publishers' International Copyright Protection Group
estimates that pirates located in the Dominican Republic and other countries bilk
United States authors and publishers of at least $400 million a year; during 1986,
Payment for Public Use was formally established in Canada to pay authors for library
use of their books.
    10. Watanabe, Kazuko, and Michiko Naka. *Contemporary American Women
Writers* [in Japanese]. Kyoto: Minerva, 1983.
    11. *NWEC Newsletter* [A serial publication of the National Women's Education
Centre of Japan, edited by Ms. Hiroko Hashimoto] **5** (May 1988): 7.
    12. Higuchi, Keiko. *Bringing Up Girls,* translated by Aniko Tomii. Kyoto,
Japan: Shoukadoh Booksellers, 1985. Junko Wada Kuninobu teaches women's
studies and comparative culture at Meijyo University.
    13. Resnick, Margery, and Isabelle de Courtivron. *Women Writers in Transla-
tion: An Annotated Bibliography, 1945–1982. (Garland Reference Library of the
Humanities, v. 288.)* New York: Garland, 1984. p. vii.
    14. Sievers, Sharon Lee. *Kotoku Shusui: The Essence of Socialism: A Translation
and Bibliographic Essay.* Stanford University Ph.D. dissertation, c1970. Mulhern,
Chieko Irie. *Koda Rohan: A Study of Idealism.* Columbia University Ph.D. thesis,
1973.
    15. Stewart, Donald E. "Publishing, Book." In *The ALA Yearbook of Library
and Information Services: A Review of Library Events, 1988, Volume 13.* pp. 264–67.
Chicago, Illinois: American Library Association, 1988. p. 264.

16. Bode, Carl N. "Saint Paul Started It All, But Now It's Time to Abolish Letters of Recommendation." *Chronicle of Higher Education* **30** (May 29, 1985): 31. A Point of View article by Professor Carl N. Degler titled "The Legitimacy of Scholarship By and About Women" (**25** [September 15, 1982]: 56) drew many letters of protest and resentment, three of which were published about a month later (**25** [October 13, 1982]: 225–26). These four documents are important reading for feminists associated with academe. A Point of View article by Professor Eric Zencey titled "Extinct Enterprise: The 2-Person Career on College Campuses" (**33** [April 1, 1987]: 104), illustrated by Robert Alan Soule, drew at least two letters, which were published three weeks later: a woman's explanation of her "outrage" and a self-serving letter (**33** [April 22, 1987]: 47).

17. *The Reference Librarian* published by Haworth Press, "The Publishing and Review of Reference Sources," issue #15, Fall 1986. "Manuscripts are by invitation only and should not be submitted unless requested by the editors or by guest editors." The Reviews and Evaluation of Reference Works section consists of seven articles, one of which is by a woman: Sharon Quist's "Book Reviewing in Sociology" (pp. 75–85). She considers influential factors, prestige, location of reviews, scholarly *vs.* popular social science, comparison of reviewing sources, indexing practices.

18. Bart, Pauline, and Linda Frankel. *Student Sociologist's Handbook, 4th edition.* New York: Random, 1986.

19. Basow, Susan, and Nancy T. Silber. "Student Evaluations of College Professors: Are Female and Male Professors Rated Differently?" *Journal of Educational Psychology* **79** (September 1987): 308–14.

20. Radcliffe College. Arthur and Elizabeth Schlesinger Library. *The Arthur and Elizabeth Schlesinger Library of the History of Women in America: The Manuscripts, Books, and Periodicals, 2nd edition.* Boston, Massachusetts: Hall, 1983. 10 volumes. The Radcliffe Research Support Program of small grants to support postdoctoral research in the humanities and the social and behavioral sciences enables eligible projects to draw upon the resources of these collections and the Henry A. Murray Research Center at Radcliffe College. Contact the Director of the Library or of the Murray Center, Radcliffe College, 10 Garden, Cambridge, Massachusetts 02138.

21. Smith College. the Sophia Smith Collection. *The Author, Subject, and Manuscript Catalogs of the Sophia Smith Collection. (Women's History Archive).* Boston, Massachusetts: Hall, 1975. 7 volumes.

22. Hildenbrand, Suzanne, Guest Editor. "Women's Collections: Libraries, Archives, and Consciousness." *Special Collections* [issue] **3** (Spring/Summer 1986): issue. Jackson-Brown, Grace. *Libraries and Information Centers Within Women's Studies Research Centers. SLA Research Series No. 3.* Washington, D.C.: Special Libraries Assoc., 1988.

23. Hampsten, Elizabeth. *Read This Only to Yourself: The Private Writings of Midwestern Women, 1880–1910.* Bloomington, Indiana: Indiana University Press, 1982. Luchetti, Cathy, and Carol Olwell. *Women of the West.* Berkeley, California: Antelope Island, 1982. Rosen, Ruth, and Sue Davidson. *The Maimie Papers.* New York: Feminist, in cooperation with the Schlesinger Library of Radcliffe College, 1977. Stratton, Joanna. *Pioneer Women.* New York: Simon & Schuster, 1981.

24. Harrison, Cynthia. *Women in American History: A Bibliography.* 2 vols. Santa Barbara, California: ABC-Clio, 1979, 1988. See also ABC-Clio's *Women in the Third World: A Historical Bibliography* (1986), prepared by Pamela R. Byrne and Suzanne Robitaille Ontiveros.

25. Clarke, Jennifer. *In Our Grandmothers' Footsteps: A Walking Tour of London.* London, England: Virago, 1984. New York: Atheneum, 1984. Mason, Karen, and Carol Lacey. *Women's History Tour of the Twin Cities.* Edited and illustrated by Deborah Carlson. Minneapolis, Minnesota: Nodin, 1982. Tinling, Marion. *Women Remembered: A Guide to Landmarks of Women's History in the United States.* Westport, Connecticut: Greenwood, 1986.

26. Daniels, Arlene Kaplan. *A Survey of Research Concerns on Women's Issues.* Washington, D.C.: Project on the Status and Education of Women, 1975. Palmer, Phyllis M., and Sharon L. Grant. *The Status of Clerical Workers.* Washington, D.C.: Business and Professional Women's Foundation, 1979. 50 pp. Shakeshaft, Carol. *Dissertation Research on Women in Academic Administration: A Synthesis of Findings and Paradigm for Future Research.* Doctoral dissertation, Texas A & M University, 1979. See also Shakeshaft's *Women in Educational Administration*, Newbury Park, California: Sage, 1986. Hartman, Joan E. and Ellen Messer-Davidow. *Women in Print, Volume II: Opportunities for Women's Studies Publication in Language and Literature.* New York: Modern Language Association of America, 1982.

27. Roberts, Patricia Lee Brighton. *The Female Image in the Caldecott Medal Award Books.* Ed.D. dissertation, University of the Pacific, 1975. See abstract 36/06A:3392. This is in the collections of some university education and library science libraries. Related useful tools are Delores Blythe Jones' *Children's Literary Awards and Winners: A Directory of Prizes, Authors, and Illustrators* (Detroit, Michigan: Neal-Schuman, Gale, 1983) and *Children's Prize Books: An International Listing of 193 Children's Literary Prizes, 2nd Revision* edited by Jess R. Moransee (Munick and New York: Saur, 1982).

28. McLeod, Katie Patricia. *Sex Discrimination Complaints Against Florida Public Institutions of Higher Education: Perceived Effects on the Complainant and the Institution.* Ed.D. dissertation, Florida State University, 1980. Notably, the abstract (41/03A:962) is a nonabstract.

29. See for example, Dee Brown's *The Gentle Tamers: Women of the Old Wild West.* Lincoln, Nebraska: University of Nebraska Press, 1981.

30. Wheeler, Helen R. "Delay, Divide, Discredit: How Uppity Women Are Kept Down, Apart and Out of Academe." In *Alternative Library Literature, 1982/1983; A Biennial Anthology.* Edited by Sanford Berman and James Danky. Phoenix, Arizona: Oryx, 1984.

31. Lerner, Gerda. *Teaching Women's History.* Washington, D.C.: American Historical Association, 1981.

32. Strunk, William, and E.B. White. *Elements of Style, 3rd edition.* New York: Macmillan, 1979.

33. Bacchi, Carol L. "'First Wave' Feminism in Canada: The Ideas of the English-Canadian Suffragists, 1877–1918." *Women's Studies International Forum* 5 (1982): 575 ff. Borish, Linda J. "The Robust Woman and the Muscular Christian: Catharine Beecher, Thomas Higginson, and Their Vision of American Society, Health and Physical Activities." *International Journal of History of Sport* 4 (September 1987): 139–154.

34. U.S. Department of Education, 1986–87 (students) and 1985–86 (faculty). As reported in "Almanac," *Chronicle of Higher Education*, September 1, 1988, p. 3; **34** (February 3, 1988): A33.

35. U.S. Department of Education, 1986–87. Institute of International Education, 1986–87. As reported in "Almanac," *Chronicle of Higher Education*, September 1, 1988, pp. 3, 14.

36. "The complicity of the press, the Supreme Court, the civilians employed

by the camps, the American public, and even the Japanese detainees themselves, then and now, in the actions of the government and the military and their semantic whitewash . . . kept the historical record in the government's favor." Okamura, Raymond Y. "The American Concentration Camps: A Cover-Up Through Euphemistic Terminology." *Journal of Ethnic Studies* **10** (Fall 1982): 95–110.

37. Morgan, Robin. *Going Too Far: The Personal Chronicle of a Feminist.* New York: Random House, 1977. p. 9.

38. Vellela, Tony. "Food Co-ops for Small Groups." In *New Voices: Student Activism in the '80s and '90s.* Edited by Tony Vellela. Boston, Massachusetts: South End, 1988.

39. Stainton, Elsie Myers. *Author and Editor at Work.* Toronto: University of Toronto Press, 1983. pp. 37–38.

40. Luey, Beth. *A Handbook for Academic Authors.* New York: Cambridge University Press, 1987. pp. 116, 117.

Bibliography

In addition to many of the titles cited in the Notes, the following publications and mentioned tools within the Resources section should be consulted.

Some catalogs of accessible collections are available in book and microforms. These catalogs and bibliographies are in many university library reference collections:

American Journal of Nursing. Sophia F. Palmer Memorial Library. New York. *Catalog of the Sophia F. Palmer Memorial Library.* 1973. 2 vols.

Bibliofem: A Guide to the Joint Library Catalogues of the Fawcett Library and the Equal Opportunities Commission, Together with a Continuing Bibliography on Women. (Fawcett Library, City of London Polytechnic, Calcutta House, Old Castle Street, London El 7NT England.)

The Gerritsen Collection of Women's History, 1543–1945. 1983. 3 vols. (Guide from Microfilming Corp. of America.)

Indiana University. Institute for Sex Research Library. *Sex Studies Index:* 1980. 1982. 1 vol.

International Archives for the Women's Movement. Amsterdam. *Catalog of the Library of the International Archives for the Women's Movement. [International Archief voor de Vrouwenbeweging.]* 1980.

The Joint Bank-Fund Library, Washington, D.C. *Women and Devlopment: An Index to Articles, Books and Research Papers.* 1987. 1 vol.

Lady Aberdeen Library on the History of Women in the University of Waterloo Library Catalogue. Donated by the National Council of Women of Canada. 1982. 1 vol.

Papers of the Women's Trade Union League and its Principal Leaders: Guide to the Microform Edition. 1981.

Population Council. New York. *Catalogue of the Population Council Library.* 1979.

Princeton University. Office of Population Research. *Population Index Bibliography. Cumulated 1935–1968 by Authors and Geographical Areas.* 1971.

Radcliffe College. Arthur and Elizabeth Schlesinger Library. *The Arthur and Elizabeth Schlesinger Library of the History of Women in America: The Manuscripts, Books, and Periodicals, 2nd edition.* 1983. 10 vols.

Smith College. The Sophia Smith Collection. *The Author, Subject, and Manuscript Catalogs of the Sophia Smith Collection. (Women's History Archives.)* 1975. 7 vols.
Women's International League for Peace and Freedom Papers, 1915–1978: A Guide to the Microfilm Edition. 1983.
Women's Music Collection. University of Michigan Music Library Catalog. 1983.

Altbach, Philip G., et al. *Publishing in the Third World: Knowledge and Development.* Portsmouth, New Hampshire: Heinemann, 1985.
Appelbaum, Judith, and Nancy Evans. *How to Get Happily Published: A Complete and Candid Guide,* Rev. edition. New York: New American Library, 1982.
Barnes, Gregory A. *Communication Skills for the Foreign-Born Professional.* Philadelphia, Pennsylvania: ISI, 1982.
"Be An ERIC Author" and "Submitting Documents to ERIC." Brochures from ERIC Processing & Reference Facility, 4833 Rugby Avenue, #301, Bethesda, Maryland 20814.
Bernard, Jessie. *The Female World from a Global Perspective.* Bloomington, Indiana: Indiana University Press, 1987.
Budd, John. "Book Reviewing Practices of Journals in the Humanities." *Scholarly Publishing* 13 (July 1982): 363–71.
Council on Interracial Books for Children. *Guidelines for Selecting Bias-Free Textbooks and Storybooks.* New York, New York (10023): The Council, 1841 Broadway.
A Dictionary of British and American Women Writers, 1660–1800. Totowa, New Jersey: Rowman & Allanheld, 1985.
Encyclopedia of Educational Research, 5th edition. New York: Macmillan, 1982.
Germano, William P. "Helping the Local Faculty With Publication Support." *Scholarly Publishing* 15 (October 1983): 11–16.
Greene, Gayle, and Coppelia Kahn. *Making a Difference: Feminist Literary Criticism.* New York: Methuen, 1986.
Griffin, Susan, and J.J. Wilson. "Making Choices: Can Two Small-Town Feminists Publish with a Big-City Trade House and Remain Pure?" In *Women in Print, Volume II: Opportunities for Women's Studies Publication,* pp. 79–88. Edited by Joan E. Hartman and Ellen Messer-Davidow. New York, New York: Modern Language Association of America, 1982.
Heldt, Barbara. "Women's Studies in Russian Literature: Opportunities for Research and Publications; With a selective Bibliography by Sandra M. Thomson." In *Women in Print, Volume I: Opportunities for Women's Studies Research in Language and Literature,* pp. 149–58. Edited by Joan E. Hartman and Ellen Messer-Davidow. New York, New York: Modern Language Association of America, 1982.
Humm, Maggie. *An Annotated Critical Bibliography of Feminist Criticism.* Boston, Massachusetts: Hall, 1987.
_____. *Feminist Criticism — Women as Contemporary Critics.* New York: St. Martin's, 1986.
Jacobus, Mary. *Reading Woman: Essays in Feminist Criticism.* New York: Columbia University Press, 1986.
Klemp, P.J. "Reviewing Academic Books: Some Ideas for Beginners." *Scholarly Publishing* 12 (January 1981): 135–39.
Krathwohl, David R. *How to Prepare a Research Proposal: Guidelines for*

Funding and Dissertations in the Social and Behavioral Sciences, Rev. 3rd edition. Syracuse, New York: Syracuse University Press, 1988.

Laubacher, Marilyn R. *How to Prepare for a Computer Search of* ERIC: *A Non-Technical Approach, Revised and Updated.* Syracuse, New York: Syracuse University School of Education, Clearinghouse on Information Resources, Syracuse, New York 13210. 1983.

Lanham, Carol D. "Help on the Path to Word Processing." *Scholarly Publishing* **15** (October 1983): 82–90.

Long, Thomas J., John J. Convey, and Adele R. Chwalek. *Completing Dissertations in the Behavioral Sciences and Education: A Systematic Guide for Graduate Students.* San Francisco, California: Jossey-Bass, 1985.

Meese, Elizabeth A. *Crossing the Double Cross: The Practice of Feminist Criticism.* Chapel Hill, North Carolina: University of North Carolina Press, 1986.

Morgan, Robin. *Sisterhood Is Global: The International Women's Movement Anthology.* New York: Anchor/Doubleday, 1984.

Moi, Toril. *Sexual/Textual Politics: Feminist Literary Theory.* New York: Methuen, 1985.

Perkins, Jean A. "Publishing Opportunities Abroad (Particularly in France)." In *Women in Print, Volume II: Opportunities for Women's Studies Publication,* pp. 23–28. Edited by Joan E. Hartman and Ellen Messer-Davidow. New York, New York: Modern Language Association of America, 1982.

Pool, Gail. "Too Many Reviews of Scholarly Books Are Puffy, Nasty, or Poorly Written." *Chronicle of Higher Education* **34** (July 20, 1988): A36.

Rossi, Alice S. *The Feminist Papers: From Adams to De Beauvoir.* New York: Columbia University Press, 1973. Preface, pp. ix–xix.

Sadker, Myra, and Karen M. Harbeck. "Women's Education" In *Encyclopedia of Educational Research,* 5th edition, Volume 4, 2013–2021. New York: Macmillan, 1982.

Wheeler, Helen R. ERIC *and Equity: Using* ERIC *Products for Information and Publications Affirming Gender Equity.* ERIC ED 219–076, 1982, 24 pp.

Women's History Sources: A Guide to Archives and Manuscript Collections in the United States. New York: Bowker, 1980. 2 vols.

Women's Studies International Forum, 1978– . (Serial.) Oxford, England, and Elmsford Park, New York: Pergamon.

Zinsser, William. *Writing with a Word Processor.* New York: Harper & Row, 1983.

When I Step into This Library...

"When I step into this library, I cannot understand why I ever step out of it." Marie de Sévigné (1626–1696). French letter writer, salonist. *Letters of Madame de Sévigné to Her Daughters and Friends.* London, England: J. Walker, 1811.

A. Glossary
B. General Reference Tools
   English-Language Dictionaries and Word Books
   Style and Usage Manuals—General
   Style and Usage Manuals—Specialized
   Handbooks and Guides to Writing and Publishing—General
   Handbooks and Guides to Writing and Publishing—Specialized Journal and Periodical Directories Information by Disciplines
   Miscellaneous Resources: Abstracting, Proofreading, Indexing, etc.
   Gender–Equity Related Titles
C. Some Useful Library of Congress Subject-Headings
D. Some Related ERIC Descriptors

Information about many of the following reference works can be found in the *Guide to Reference Books.* An attempt has been made to list useful titles which are in print; in a few cases, where they are not in print, they are available for use in many libraries.

Glossary

abridged edition   An edition shortened by rewriting, condensing, omitting from the original, but retaining the general sense (as in an abridged dictionary).

abstract   A brief summary that gives the essential points of an article, dissertation, book, etc. It is not, or should not be, evaluative. *See* Chapter Two.

academic standards   Criteria established by an educational institution to determine levels of student achievement.

access point   A name, word, or phrase under which a bibliographic record can be found. *See also* **entry**.

accountability   Being held responsible and answerable for specified results of an activity over which one has authority.

action research   As opposed to traditional research, action research is designed to yield practical results that are immediately applicable to a specific situation or problem. It is the process by which practitioners attempt to study their problems scientifically in order to guide, correct, and evaluate their decisions and actions. See Stephen M. Corey, *Action Research to Improve School Practices* (New York: Teachers College Press, 1953) and Chris Argyris et al., *Concepts, Methods, and Skills for Research and Intervention* (San Francisco, California: Jossey-Bass, 1988). *See* Chapter Four.

added entry   A catalog entry other than the main (author) or subject entries by which an item is represented in a catalog. There may be added entries for such things as titles, series, translators, illustrators, authors of an introduction, corporate authors, secondary authors, etc.

administration evaluation   The evaluation or appraisal of administrators or managers.

advance   Money paid to an author after a contract has been signed and before the author has earned it through sales of the author's work. Advances are almost always recoverable as they are returned to the publisher out of the author's earned royalties. Some authors consider advances on their royalties deserved and automatic; some publishers may associate them with expenses incurred by the author in preparing the manuscript. *See* Chapter Three.

affirmative action   Positive action taken to overcome underrepresentation of women and minority group members in employment (including career advancement and professional development programs) and in the makeup of post-secondary student bodies as compared to the composition of the area population. As contrasted with mere passive "equal opportunity." Often referred to as "non-discriminatory affirmative action." Women in academe generally do not expect or receive special consideration.

aging in academia   The gradual aging of a particular academic staff or of the general community due to demographics and work-life extensions, with implications for hiring, tenure, salary costs, etc.

analytic entry   An entry for some part of a work or article in a collection with reference to the work containing it. For example, analytic entries may be made for each of the parts of a monographic series, or for each of the essays which make up an anthology, or for each of the stories constituting a collection of short stories.

annotation   A note describing, explaining, or evaluating an item (usually but not always a book) in a bibliography. *See* Chapter Four.

anthology   A collection of literary pieces usually by more than one author, as in *Future Females: A Criticcal Anthology,* edited by Marleen S. Barr (Bowling Green, Ohio: Bowling Green University Popular Press, 1981). Collections of selected writings or other materials, usually in one form, or from one periodical, or on one subject. Components may be original or reprinted. *Essay and General Literature Index* indexes the contents of numerous collections and anthologies. *See* Chapter Four.

appendix   Supplementary information pertaining to, but not essential to the completeness of, a book, usually following the text and preceding the index.

archives   A place where records and historical documents are kept. The term usually suggests primary source material that has not yet been codified.

article   *See* **journal article** and **paper.**

assessment centers (personnel)   Personnel evaluation centers using multiple assessment techniques for staff selection, promotion, or development. Typically included are simulated work experiences and the use of multiple observers to appraise job-related behaviors.

author   The person chiefly responsible for the intellectual or artistic content of a work under whose name that work appears in an index, catalog, bibliography, etc. A personal author may be distinguished from a corporate author—a body, such as a government or governmental department, learned society, or an institution which authorizes the publication of materials, and under the name of which, as the author, the publication may be entered in a catalog and credited. The principal author of a publication is listed first on the basis of importance rather than alphabetization, making "joint authorship" and secondary and tertiary authorship less significant.

author's questionnaire   A request from a potential publisher to the author for specific items of personal information (e.g. education, other publications, experiences in the field of the proposed book) as well as information about the book itself. At a later stage, author's questionnaire can also refer to information requested about a contracted book for use in marketing and packaging it. *See* Chapter Three.

bibliographic citation   A note of reference to a book, periodical, article, etc., which includes information required to locate that same item again. Each published form has its own standardized format of necessary information, which is available by use of the appropriate style manual. *See also* **citation** and **style manual**.

bibliographic essay   *See* **review essay**.

bibliography   An organized list of books or other formats which are related in some way, e.g. subject-matter, authorship, time period, location, function. *See* Chapter Three.

big budget books   The titles on a publisher's list that will receive the most advertising, promotion, etc. Generally no more than 10 percent of a publisher's list receives this kind of financial push.

blind judging (or double blind, or double refereed)   These tend to be used as elitist and redundant terms, with little special significance. Double blind implies that the author does not know the identities of the referees (judges, reviewers), assuming there is more than one, *and* (of more importance) that the referees do not know the identity of the submitting author.

book catalog   A catalog in book form, created by photocopying catalog cards or by computer printout. Example: *The Manuscript Inventories and the Catalogs of Manuscripts, Books, and Periodicals, 2nd revised and enlarged edition* is the ten-volume book catalog of the Arthur and Elizabeth Schlesinger Library on the History of Women in America. (Boston, Massachusetts: Hall, 1984).

career ladders   Hierarchies of occupational progression, with training, from entry level position to higher levels in the same occupation.

catalog   An arrangement of bibliographic items accessible by author, title, subject, etc. Formats of catalogs include microfiche, cards, on-line, and printed book catalogs. Library catalogs do not usually analyze or list parts of a whole, such as periodical articles (for which a periodical index would be used) or essays (for which a tool such as *Essay and General Literature Index* would be utilized). In a *dictionary catalog,* all entries (author, title, subject, added, etc.) are arranged alphabetically in one sequence, regardless of the type of catalog; in a *divided catalog,* author, title and other added entries are interfiled in one separate section of the catalog, and the balance—the subject entries—are filed alphabetically in the other.

citation   The listing of a book in a bibliography, footnote, or index. Citation is synonomous with "reference" and has sufficient bibliographic data to enable one to locate the same work again. *See also* **bibliographic citation** and **style manual**.

classification   The system by which a collection of material is organized for the purpose of retrieval of both documents and information. The two major classifications used for organization of subject matter and documents in United States library collections are the Library of Congress and the Dewey Decimal systems. Most college and university and many public libraries use the Library of Congress (LC) classification, which should be distinguished from Library of Congress *Subject Headings* (LCSH).

collection   *See* **anthology**.

comprehensive   All-inclusive; the opposite of selective, as in a comprehensive bibliography such as *Books in Print*.

continuing education   Educational programs and services, usually on the post-secondary level, designed to serve adults who seek particular learning experiences on a part-time or short-term basis for personal, academic, or occupational development.

contract(s)   Formal agreements between two or more parties in which, for a benefit or to avoid a penalty, one or more of the parties agree to do a certain thing.

copyright date   The year in which the author's application to the United States Library of Congress for copyright on a book is granted. A copyright, like a patent, insures the author against intellectual theft of a book and the ideas in it. The copyright date is usually on the **verso** of the title page. A copyright date is "better" than a simple year of publication. Exclusive privileges to publish, sell, or otherwise control works that can be reproduced, granted by governments to authors, composers, artists, publishers, etc., for a specified number of years.

cover price   The suggested retail price. To figure royalties under some trade and mass market contracts, multiply the number of copies of the book sold by the cover price. Then multiply this amount by the author's royalty percentage, e.g. 8 percent, to determine the dollar amount the author receives. For textbooks, normally the royalty is based on the price the publisher receives, either from distributor or retailer, or from retail customer if sold directly by the publisher (possibly through the mail), referred to as publisher's gross receipts. Most often it is the wholesale price the publisher gets from a bookstore or distributor. To figure royalty, multiply the aggregate amount the bookseller receives by the royalty rate, e.g. 10 percent. *See* Chapter Three.

cross-reference   In a catalog, index, bibliography, glossary, thesaurus, etc., a direction *from* one heading *to* another. Cross-references are usually either *see* or *see also*. A *see* reference directs the user from a term or name under which no entries are listed to a term or name under which entries are consistently listed and consolidated—e.g. de Beauvoir, Simone *See* Beauvoir, Simone de. A *see also* reference directs the user from a term or name under which entries are listed to another term(s) or name(s) under which additional or closely related information may be found—e.g. **tenure**. *See also* **seniority, teacher employment benefits**.

cumulation   To keep up-to-date systematically with new serial articles, a periodical index cumulates. It keeps coming out, just as the issues of the periodicals it indexes keep coming out. It interfiles—rather than supplements—the basic index volume's contents. This means that *Readers' Guide*, for example, is first published in the form of supplementary, temporary paper issues. At the end of the indexing period all of the entries appearing in all of the cumulations are interfiled into one "big," permanent, bound volume which replaces all of the interim coverage. In a card catalog, the cards and the entries for new books are interfiled right in among those already filed, which is one of the features of this type of tool. Many of the subject-specialized periodical indexes, abstracts, and citation indexes relating to journals cumulate. *See* Chapter Two.

current awareness　　Continuing search of current literature at regular intervals to provide the latest material reflecting the user's interest. SDI is an acronym for selective dissemination of information, a method of alerting perople to reports or articles of potential interest, sometimes used synonymously with current awareness.

curriculum enrichment　　In providing educational marketing ideas to your publisher, use this term in referring to courses where your book might be used as supplementary reading, enriching the curriculum.

descriptor　　An indexing term (subject-heading) describing the subject content · a document. The *Thesaurus of ERIC Descriptors* is an example of one controlled vocabulary; the United States Library of Congress *Subject Headings* is another. Both are available in book form. *See* Chapter Four.

dictionary catalog　　*See under* **catalog**.

dissertation　　Dissertations and theses are undertaken in partial fulfillment of a graduate degree and have become almost synonymous terms. A dissertation is a lengthy, formal treatise or discourse, especially when written by the candidate for a university doctoral degree. The term "thesis" (plural *theses*) may apply to both masters' and doctoral papers. In the United States one hears mainly "doctoral dissertation" and "master's thesis." The primary usage of "thesis" is as a proposition advanced by a candidate for an academic degree maintained by argument. *See* Chapter Three.

divided catalog　　*See under* **catalog**.

double blind refereeing　　*See* **blind judging**.

edition　　The total number of copies of a book printed from the same setting of type, as in "an edition of 1,500 copies was printed." The term "revised" or "new" edition indicates that the text has been changed or new material added. The new edition will have a new date. There are also numbered editions.

editor　　One who prepares for publication a text written by another. This may involve compiling, revising, or adding notes or other critical matter. A neophyte, unpublished author may be expected to do considerable editorial work on her or his own book. The editor of a journal or other serial is "the" decision-maker. In general, editors are persons who prepare materials, usually the works of others, for publication or public presentation.

entry　　The record of an item (book, periodical, etc.) in a catalog or bibliography, usually referring to bibliographic information in a catalog. *See also* **access point**.

equal opportunity　　*See* **affirmative action**.

essay review　　*See* Chapter Four.

exhibits　　Trade shows, conventions, conferences, etc., wherein publishers and others display their wares or information about their services and products. "Exhibits" often create opportunities for direct sales of books, for potential purchasers to examine books, and for potential authors and publishers to meet.

faculty development   Activities to encourage and enhance faculty professional growth, e.g. technical assistance, workshops, funding.

faculty evaluation   Judging the value or competence of administrative, instructional, or other academic staff in schools, colleges, or universities based on established criteria.

faculty promotion   Advancement in position or rank of administrative, instructional, or other academic staff in schools, colleges, or universities.

faculty publishing   The production and issuance of scholarly writings by academia.

festschrift   A complimentary or memorial publication in the form of a collection of essays, addresses, or other combinations issued in honor of a person, an institution, or a society, usually on the occasion of an anniversary celebration. *See* Chapter Four.

galleys   Galley proof in printing is a printer's proof taken from composed type before page composition to allow for the detection and correction of errors.

gatekeepers   "...in the academic community. These are the people who set the standards, produce the social knowledge, monitor what is admitted to the systems of distribution, and decree the innovations in thought, or knowledge, or values." (Dorothy Smith. "A Peculiar Eclipsing: Women's Exclusion From Man's Culture." Page 287.) "Many of these people are to be found as editors of journals, as referees or reviewers, or as advisors to publishers. They are in a position to determine what gets published and what does not, and most of them are men." (Dale Spender. *The Gatekeepers: A Feminist Critique of Academic Publishing*.) *See* Chapter One.

gross receipts   *See under* **cover price**.

herstory   Until very recently, history has been recorded mainly by members of one gender, whose records omit much by and about the other. The history of females is incomplete as well as inaccurate. This recognition and attempts to rectify the situation constitute the *herstory* concept. *See* Chapter Four.

imprint   A collective term which refers to a book's place of publication, publisher, and date of publication. These three elements are usually expressed in that order. (Also used to refer to a particular line of a publisher.) *See* Chapter Three.

in press   Books and articles which have been completed and accepted for publication, but which have not yet been printed and distributed.

in-print   Books available for purchase from the publisher. Out of print books (OP) may be available from a secondhand book dealer. Most in-print books are listed in the current edition of *Books in Print*. *See* Chapter Three.

individual development   Growth or maturation in the individuals of a species due to aging, learning, or experience.

in-service education   Courses or programs designed to provide employee or staff growth in job-related competencies or skills, often sponsored by employers, usually at the professional level.

instructional materials   Print or nonprint materials used in instruction.

ISBN   *See* **standard number**.

ISSB   *See* **standard number**.

joint author   A person who collaborates with one or more associates to produce a work in which the contribution of each is not separable from that of the other. (But *see also* **author**.)

journal   Scholarly periodicals are usually referred to as "journals." This word is usually but not always in their titles. Few scholarly journals utilize their own salaried staff-writers; many solicit articles and select persons with whom they make arrangements to write some of the articles. *See* Chapter Two. (A newspaper which has the word journal in its name reflects the original meaning of the word "jour"—French for "day.")

journal article A nonfiction composition that forms an independent part of a periodical which is a journal. It can also be a report or essay in form, but differs in academe from a "paper," which is an essay, treatise, or scholarly dissertation often delivered in person, sometimes evolving into a published journal article. *See* Chapter Two.

keyword(s) The keyword concept is important for all types of research and publication because it relates to storage and retrieval of both information and documents. Keywords are not the same as subject-headings or descriptors. Some library catalogs and reference tools today utilize keywording and may refer to Keyword in Context (KWIC). See for example the *Encyclopedia of Associations'* indexing. A book or article titled *Sign Language for the Deaf* would be listed alphabetically three times in such an index or catalog—under DEAF, under LANGUAGE, and under SIGN.

Library of Congress classification system A system to organize knowledge, developed for use by the Library of Congress and adapted by most university and other libraries with large collections to their needs. Because it uses both letters and numbers to classify, it is broader and more flexible than the Dewey Decimal system.

literature review(s) Surveys of the materials published on a topic. *See also* **research methodology, state of the art review, essay review,** and **review essay.** *See* Chapter Four.

magazine A periodical for general or popular reading, containing articles on various subjects by different authors, such as indexed in *Readers' Guide.* A magazine differs from a scholarly journal, although both are under the "serials" umbrella. Commercial "mass media" magazines published by large companies generally pay writers of the articles they publish, whereas scholarly journals published by professional associations generally do not pay the writers of the articles they publish. *See* Chapter Two.

manuscript (1) A work written by hand. (2) A handwritten or typed—nowadays usually typed—copy of an author's work before it is published.

mass market books 4″ x 7″ paperbacks sold in such places as drugstores, newsstands, airports, etc., usually from wire racks. *See also* **trade books.** *See* Chapter Three.

mentors Trusted and experienced supervisors or advisers who have personal and direct interest in the development or education of younger or less experienced persons. In the past, "mentor" and "mentoring" have been used in professional education and occupations. Recently mentoring has been recognized as having great potential as a feminist concept and methodology, especially in academe and including publishing-related activities. It is sometimes misused in the sense that it is assumed to be an "automatic" skill. *See* Chapters One and Four.

monograph A scholarly book on a specific and usually limited subject.

monographic series A series of monographic works issued in a uniform style under a collective title by an academy, association, learned society or institution. The monographs may or may not be bibliographically independent, but they are usually related in subject or interest; they may also be numbered.

newspaper A daily or weekly serial publication containing news and opinion of current events, feature articles, and usually advertising.

nonprint media Materials used in communication that are not in the print medium nor textual or booklike in nature.

nontenured faculty Academic staff who have not received tenure (permanence of position) at their school or institution. Includes those awaiting tenured appointments (who may or may not be on tenure track) and those who or whose appointments are ineligible for tenure. *See also* **tenure.**

offprint A reproduction or excerpt of a printed article that was originally contained in a larger publication. *See also* **preprint** and **reprint.**

on-line catalog A "computerized catalog" in which entries are stored in a computer by a numbered system and are accessible through local terminals by such fields as author, title, subject, series, date of publication, publisher, language, etc.

out of print Not obtainable through the regular publishing market or channels because the publisher's stock is exhausted. *See also* **in-print.** A book can be out of print (OP) and still be found on the market. *See* Chapter Three.

pamphlet A publication usually dealing with one current subject and consisting of a few pages stapled together in paper covers. The maximum number of pages constituting a pamphlet varies according to definition.

paper An essay, treatise, or scholarly dissertation often delivered in person by the writer, sometimes evolving into a published journal article.

peer evaluation Appraisal by one's peers; sometimes referred to as peer review.

periodical A publication such as a newspaper, magazine, or journal that has a distinctive title and is intended to appear in successive numbers or parts at stated or regular intervals, and as a rule for an indefinite period of time. It is usually issued with paper covers and later bound by libraries into "volumes." Often periodicals, especially newspapers, are microfilmed. *See also* **serial.** *See* Chapter Two.

preprint Copy of a book or section of a book or periodical [article] issued in a limited paperbound quantity for some special purpose before publication date. *See also* **reprint.**

primary source Original material which has not been interpreted by another person, e.g. letters, diaries, manuscripts, memoirs, interviews. *See also* **secondary source.**

probationary period Period in which a person might prove her or his ability to fulfill certain conditions as to achievement, behavior, or job assignment.

professional continuing education Education of adults in professional fields for occupational updating and improvement, usually consisting of short-term, intensive, specialized learning experiences often categorized by general field of specialization.

professional development Activities to enhance professional career growth. *See* Chapter Four.

professional recognition Expressed or implied acknowledgment of one's professional efforts, qualities, or training.

professional training Special instruction to develop skills needed to improve job performance of professional personnel—usually short-term and job-specific.

publication date The year a book or another publication comes off the press and is offered for sale. For a book, it is usually the same date as the coyright date, although the latter could be earlier. A book's publication date is usually shown on its title page or on the **verso.** A periodical issue's date of publication usually consists of month(s) and year or month, day, and year. The official date of book publication is commonly six weeks after bound books arrive at the warehouse, a historical convention of trade book publishing which coordinates the availability of the product with advertising and promotion.

publish or perish issue Controversial practice in some professions and in academe of linking scholarly writing and publishing to career advancement, remuneration, and security. *See* Chapter One.

publisher   The company or agency responsible for issuing a publication.

publisher's series   *See* **series**.

recto   The right-hand page of a book. *See also* **verso**.

refereed journal   A journal whose submissions (articles by authors) are reviewed by evaluators in addition to the journal editor. Evaluators may be paid or unpaid, and outside readers or the author's peers. *See* Chapter Two.

reference book   A book designed to be consulted for specific facts rather than to be read in its entirety. Easily consulted reference works, designed to provide information readily and often kept in a separate reference section, are often referred to as "ready reference."

remaindering   The publisher's last-resort effort to salvage something from an inventory of books that has not sold by disposing of the books for a pittance to specialists in such books, called *remainders.*

reprint   As a noun often used to refer to an offprint: an article, chapter, or other excerpt from a larger work printed from the original type or plates and issued as a separate unit. As a verb: to print a work a second or subsequent time without significant changes. *See also* **preprint**.

research   Systematic investigation, collection, and analysis of data to reach conclusions, establish effects, or test hypotheses.

research methodology   Procedures used in making systematic observations or otherwise obtaining data, evidence, or information as part of a research project or study.

review article   An historical survey of a subject up to the present state of the art, with reference to each significant step along the way. Presumably prepared by a subject-expert. Review articles may be used much like selective bibliographies; they are particularly important in the sciences, where there is a tool for locating them: *Index to Scientific Reviews*, published by the Institute for Scientific Information. But they exist in all fields, and can usually be identified by use of the abstracting service of one's discipline. They are a great starting point for ideas which can lead to publication. *See* Chapter Four.

review essay (or **bibliographic essay**)   A critical article on the literature of a subject which is usually written by a recognized expert and is especially useful in planning literature searches preliminary to research and publication. A review of the literature is similar. (*See* **literature review.**) There can be a focus on an aspect of the subject or publications during a defined period of time, etc.; criticism is an important part. *See* Chapter Four.

royalty   Payment based on the sale of the book, the rights to which you have licensed to your publisher by a contract. Put slightly differently, in exchange for your granting the publisher the right to publish your work, you are given certain payments. Occasionally (almost always in the case of a poem or magazine article), an author sells rights to a work for a one-time payment, in which case there is no continuing right to receive royalties. *See also* **cover price**.

Sapir-Whorf theory   *See* **Whorf-Sapir hypothesis**.

scholarship   Comprehensive mastery of an area of knowledge; also, the methods and attainments of scholars.

secondary source   Material based on primary sources which has been reported, analyzed, or interpreted by other persons. Encyclopedias and nonbook materials are typically considered secondary sources. The *World Almanac* frequently amounts to a tertiary source.

seniority   Priority in status or rank derived from age or length of service.

serial   A regularly issued publication which comprises newspapers, annual reports, yearbooks, periodicals, monographic series, and other irregular publications. This is a more inclusive term than "periodical." (*See also* **journal, magazines, newspaper**.) Materials issued in successive parts, usually at regular intervals and intended to be continued indefinitely. *See* Chapter Two.

series   A number of separate works, usually related to one another, issued in succession, normally by the same publisher, with a uniform style. Each item in the series has, in addition to its own individual title, a collective or series title. Parts of a series are usually numbered. A publisher's series refers usually to a subspeciality, usually not numbered, e.g. Westview Press' *Westview Guides to Library Research.*

simultaneous revision   *See* Chapter Three.

small press   Companies with sales of less than approximately one million dollars do not have their own salespeople or commissioned representatives. They rely on wholesalers and sell most of their books at a large discount. It is with small publishing houses that authors should most carefully review their royalty provisions. *See also* **royalty, trade book**.

sociolinguistics   The study of language in society, more specifically, the study of language varieties, their functions, and their speakers. See also **Whorf-Sapir hypothesis**. *See* Chapter Four.

sponsored book   *See under* subsidy.

staff development   Employer-sponsored activities, or provisions such as release time and tuition grants, through which existing personnel renew or acquire skills, knowledge, and attitudes related to job or personal development.

standard number   Standard book numbering was developed in Great Britain in 1967 and adopted by the United States the following year. Worldwide coordination is located in West Germany. As of 1982, forty-two nations participated in standard numbering, an internationally used number that uniquely identifies a book (ISBN) or serial (ISSN) publication. This information is usually included on the **verso** of the book's title page and is useful in distinguishing similar-sounding titles, particularly in ordering but also in bibliographic research. Consists of nine digits in three parts: the first part of the ISBN is the group identified (e.g. 5 refers to the U.S.S.R.); the second part consists of the publisher's prefix (e.g. McFarland's is 0-89950-   ); and the third part is the title identifier. A fourth part is a check digit.

state of the art review   Exhaustive, systematic and often critical review of the published or unpublished material on a topic.

style manual   A manual or book which gives directions for typing, quoting, footnoting, writing bibliographies, etc. Used in preparation of manuscripts for both books and journal articles. Typically the publisher or journal adheres to a specific style manual, of which there are many.

subsidiary rights   Rights to a literary property other than original publication rights; e.g. the right to reprint an already published hardcover book as a paperback.

subsidy (subsidy rights, subsidy publishing)   A subsidy (or subvention) is a grant or payment that funds an enterprise. Subsidy publishing is another designation for vanity publishing (*See also* **vanity press**), in which a book is produced with little or no regard to the merit of the work, at the author's expense, and at no risk to the publisher. Publishing of works of specialized interest to a small group, e.g. a corporation or local historians for which a grant or fund is provided, may also be called a "sponsored book," especially if the sponsoring organization or person guarantees to purchase a significant number of copies.

subtitle   A secondary and usually explanatory title which follows the main title and is generally indicated by a colon, semicolon, comma, or dash. In *Publicity for Books and Authors: A Do-It-Yourself Handbook for Small Publishing Firms and Enterprising Authors,* the subtitle is *A Do-It-Yourself Handbook for Small Publishing Firms and Enterprising Authors.*

subvention   *See* **subsidy (subsidy rights, subsidy publishing).**

teacher evaluation   Judging teachers' performance based on established criteria.

teacher promotion   Advancement in rank or position of a teacher; may be accompanied by salary increment.

teacher rights   Legal, procedural, and human rights of teachers.

tenure   Status of a person in a position or occupation, i.e., length of service, terms of employment, or permanence of position. "Security of employment" is not synonymous with tenure; it is often associated with nonfaculty academic or professional appointments in academe (and has also served as a bone tossed to women in discrimination settlements). "Equivalent faculty status" of professional librarians often leads to an "equivalent tenure" form which can be security of employment or not.

text   1. The main body of a work, as opposed to notes, appendix, index, preliminaries, introduction, etc.   2. The words of a song, song cycle, or a collection of songs.

textbook evaluation   Determining the efficacy, value, etc., of textbooks with respect to stated objectives or criteria.

textbook research   Systematic investigation of the design, content, biases, impact, etc., of textbooks.

thematic issue (of a journal)   Many journals publish "thematic," or special, issues devoted to a topic or consideration, rather than regular features and "departments." They often appoint an Issue Editor who solicits specialist-authors; she or he may receive a stipend or other remuneration within the profession.

thesaurus   An authority file or list of subject-headings (or **descriptors**), usually with **cross-references,** used in indexing a collection of documents. Subject-headings assigned to a book for cataloging a library's collection are derived from a thesaurus which provides a controlled vocabulary for this purpose. Most university libraries in the United States use the Library of Congress *Subject-Headings;* the latest edition may be available for the public to consult. Any thesaurus inter-relates by means of such things as two types of cross-references: *See* and *See Also.* A data base with index terms (**descriptors**) assigned from an authority list such as a thesaurus is referred to as a controlled vocabulary data base, although some data bases may also employ "natural language." A thesaurus is characterized by designation of broader and narrower terms and synonyms. *See* Chapter Four.

thesis   *See* **dissertation**.

Title IX.   Title IX refers to a federal law passed by Congress in 1972, which includes the statement that "no person shall, on the basis of sex, be excluded from participation in, be denied the benefits of, or be subjected to discrimination under any education program or activity receiving federal financial assistance." Thus, it forbids education programs receiving financial assistance from the federal government to discriminate against females and males in employment and education. Most United States colleges and universities and all public and some private schools receive some federal financial assistance. On paper the law covers all employees as well as all students of educational institutions. It guarantees equality of treatment to all persons regardless of gender, meaning that faculty, staff, and administrators are to be hired through an equitable process, and paid an equal wage for equal work. Academicians like the University of California Title IX coordinator who declared, "Title IX doesn't have anything to do with employment," should check out *North Haven Board of Education vs. Bell*, 102 S. Ct. 1912 (1982). Title IX of the Education Amendments of 1972 prohibiting sex discrimination in education repeats much of the same language as the Civil Rights Act, which prohibited race, color, or national origin discrimination in programs or activities receiving federal financial assistance. Sexual harassment is a form of discrimination. Some states have their own "Title IX's."

title page   A page at the beginning of a book which includes title, edition, and imprint (place of publication, publisher, and date). The back of the title page has the copyright date or date of publication, and usually considerable other useful information.

tracings   A list, located at the end of a catalog main entry (along the bottom of a catalog card), which traces all the subject and added entries for a particular book in that catalog.

trade book   A book of some production quality, sold through traditional retail book outlets such as bookstores. Trade books may be hardbound or softbound. Softbound trade books are referred to as "trade paperbacks" or "quality paperbacks" and are trimmed to a larger size than **mass market** paperbacks. Trade publishers are concerned with publishing books aimed at a general audience (as opposed to textbook publishers, for example). Of the various types of book publishers which include women's studies books among their concentrations (as listed in the *Literary Market Place*), the following are *trade publishers:* Beacon Press, Cherry Valley Editions, Duke University Press, Holmes and Meier, Ohio University Press, Persea Books, Praeger Publishers, Q E D Press, Rice University Press, Syracuse University Press, University of Oklahoma Press, and Markus Wiener.

trade publisher   *See* **trade book**.

trade revision   Usually used in reference to the restructuring and revision of a doctoral dissertation for subsequent publication as a **trade book**.

union catalog (union list)   A union catalog is an author or subject catalog of all materials, or a selection of materials, in a group of libraries or collections, covering material in all fields, or limited by subject or type of material. Such a catalog is generally established by a cooperative effort. The *National Union Catalog* is available in most university libraries. A union list is a complete record of the holdings for a specific group of libraries of material of a given type in a certain field, or on a particular topic, e.g. a union list of serials in the collections of the libraries of a state university system or of all the libraries in a metropolitan area.

union list   *See* **union catalog (union list)**.

university press   Of the various book publishers which identify themselves as university presses as well as publishers of women's studies books, the *Literary Market Place* lists: Duke University Press, Georgia State University, Indiana University Press, Northeastern University Press, Ohio University Press, Rice University Press, Syracuse University Press, University of Michigan Press, University of North Carolina Press, University of Oklahoma Press, University of Tennessee Press, University of Wisconsin Press, and Utah State University

Press. Several of these also self-identify as trade publishers (*see* **trade book**). *See* Chapter Three.

vanity press   A printer (**publisher**) of books whom the author pays to have her or his book "published." Compilations of information about persons who typically purchase a copy of the book are often generated by vanity presses. *See also* **subsidy (subsidy rights, subsidy publishing)**.

verso   The left-hand page of a book. The importance of this term relates mainly to the fact that the back of the title page is *the* verso, and displays the date of publication. *See also* **recto** and **title page**.

volume   Physically, a volume is a gathering of pages bound together in the form of a book. Numerically, a volume is a complete set of issues which comprises a serial volume bound together. Bibliographic citations use the term in the numerical sense.

Whorf-Sapir hypothesis   Benjamin Lee Whorf (1897–1941); Edward Sapir (1884–1939). Each language shapes the view of reality for its speakers, and therefore no two cultures show the same understanding of the world. This hypothesis, or theory, is in opposition to the conception of a universal grammar.

women faculty   Female academic staff members engaged in instruction, research, administration, or related educational activities.

women studies   *See* **women's studies**.

women's education   Education of females, not to be confused with women's studies.

women's studies   Curriculum or subject area encompassing the history and contemporary social, political, and cultural situation of women. [*Thesaurus of ERIC Descriptors*.] Feminists reason that this field of study is more accurately called women studies or feminist studies.

working title   An interim, descriptive title which the author uses to refer to a publication, usually a book, as it evolves. The working title sometimes appears on a book contract. The term is also used in connection with a **dissertation**.

writing for publication   Writings intended for acceptance by a publisher; outside of academe, writing for publication implies for payment as well.

General Reference Tools

In this and the sections that follow, an attempt has been made to list useful titles which are in print. The few titles no longer in print are available for use in most college and university and large public library collections.

Audio Video Market Place. New York: Bowker, annual. The AVMP's main section lists products, services, and companies. Consult the general Products and Services Index (pages A1–A12 of the 1988 edition), and be sure to read the How to Use AVMP (pages ix–xi) first. Related associations, periodicals, and reference books are identified in three useful sections. (Formerly *Audiovisual Market Place*.) See also *Literary Market Place*.

Bookman's Glossary, 6th edition. Revised and enlarged by Jean Peters. New York: Bowker, 1983. Terms used in production and distribution of books; includes foreign terms and proofreader's marks.

Books in Print. (Volumes by author, title, and a publishers' volume.) New York: Bowker, annual. The BIP is probably the most well known of the PTLA family. Most, but not all, United States publishers are included. It indexes *Publishers*

Trade List Annual. There are interim supplements as well as specialized Bowker Company spinoffs, e.g. *Children's Books in Print, Business Books in Print*, and *Paperbound Books in Print*. National "books-in-print" versions exist worldwide and can be found in *Guide to Reference Books;* they include *Canadian Books in Print* (University of Toronto Press) and *British Books in Print* (Whitaker). *See also Forthcoming Books in Print; Publishers Trade List Annual*.

Cassell's Directory of Publishing. Eastbourne, East Sussex, England: Cassell & The Publishers Association, c1986. The 1987 edition lists women's studies publishers. Comparable tools in university libraries' collections can be identified by searching under PUBLISHERS AND PUBLISHING—[NATION]—DIRECTORIES. See also *International Literary Market Place*.

Encyclopedia of Associations. Detroit, Michigan: Gale, annual. Available in print form and for on-line searching, this encyclopedic directory includes organizations which publish. Some, e.g. American Association of Univeristy Professors and the Older Women's League, are not listed in tools such as the *Literary Market Place*. Note that (1) the word "association" does not always appear in a group's title; (2) the index is a "keyword index"—worth learning; and (3) Volume 4 is devoted to international organizations. Gale also published in 1987 the first edition of *Association Periodicals*, which has an international volume.

Feminist Quotations: Voices of Rebels, Reformers, and Visionaries. Carol McPhee and Ann Fitzgerald. New York: Crowell, 1979. An excellent takeoff point for discussion and feminist theory. Contrast with Bartlett's *Familiar Quotations*, a bastion of masculine prose. See also *Quotable Woman*.

Forthcoming Books in Print. New York: Bowker. If there is criticism in your department when you list a contracted book which you have completed and dispatched to the publisher on your publications list or resume as "In press," delay until it is listed here! This bimonthly serial continues *Books in Print*, with the same author, subjects, and title approaches. See also *Books in Print*.

Gale Directory of Publications: An Annual Guide to Newspapers, Magazines, Journals, and Related Publications [Of America and Canada], *121st edition*. Detroit, Michigan: Gale, 1988. Two volumes formerly known as the *Ayer Directory of Publications*, this is a library standard, but not as relevant to journal article publishing as *Ulrich's*, for example. The category label "Women's Publications" is doubly misinformative in that it suggests publications, rather than just periodicals, *for* women.

Guide to Reference Books, 10th edition. Eugene Sheehy. Chicago, Illinois: American Library Association, 1986. The guide emphasizes sources related to scholarly research, although some popular titles are considered. Serials as well as books are included. Annotations enhance its utility. This is a basic which people in the know are aware of but with which they are rarely familiar!

International Directory of Little Magazines and Small Presses, 22nd edition, 1986–87. Edited by Len Fulton and Ellen Ferber. Paradise, California: Dustbooks, 1987. "Little magazines" and "small presses" can mean alternative, highly respected, counter-culture, etc. "Women's presses" are included. See also *Small Press Record of Books in Print*.

International Literary Market Place, 1988–89. New York: Bowker, 1988. Covers one hundred and sixty nations. Information and displays are similar to those in the *Literary Market Place* (both are published by Bowker), although there are no subject indexes. Most publishers' entries include for each a brief list of its subjects. United Kingdom entries encompass publishers which are familiar names in English-speaking nations. Information about copyright and lists of translation agencies, associations, and bookstores for each nation are useful provisions. Canadian publishers are included here as well as in LMP. An explanation of International Standard Book Numbering is provided. See also *Literary Market Place.*

Library of Congress Subject Headings, 11th edition. Washington, D.C.: Library of Congress, 1988. 3 volumes. With the 11th edition's format changes, the LCSH has moved away from its earlier main function as a cataloger's tool to one that enables the public's use too. The standard devices already in use in some other thesauri (e.g. ERIC) have been introduced: BT, for broader term, replaces xx; UF, for use for, replaces x; SA, for see also, replaces sa; USE replaces see; RT, for related term, has been introduced for terms associated in some manner other than hierarchical; NT, for narrower term, has been introduced. Scope notes abound. Forty percent of the subject-headings are accompanied by LC Classification classes. Whether a subject-heading can or cannot be subdivided geographically is indicated. *See also* Capek's *A Woman's Thesaurus;* and Dickstein, et al., *Women in LC's Terms.*

Literary Agents of North America Marketplace . . . , 1984–85. New York: Author Aid/Research Associates International, 1984. Annual, with geographic and subject indexes. Covers United States and Canada.

Literary and Library Prizes, 10th edition. Revised and edited by Olga Weber and Stephen J. Calvert. New York: Bowker, 1980. Covers the history and eligibility requirements of hundreds of mainly United States and Canadian awards.

Literary Market Place: The Directory of American Book Publishing. With Names & Numbers. New York: Bowker, annual. See discussion, Chapter 3.

Magazine Industry Market Place: The Directory of American Publishing. New York: Bowker. The MIMP is an annual compilation supportive of free-lance publishing in periodicals which are magazines. It does include some journals, but its main utility here is its section listing publishers of multiple periodicals. All or many of the journal titles published by each consortium, conglomerate, multiple publisher, university press, or other umbrella are listed.

National Trade and Professional Associations of the United States, 10th edition. Washington, D.C.: Columbia, 1985. Professional associations are sometimes major publishers. Subject sections include education, women, history, and sex. See also *Encyclopedia of Associations.*

Publishers, Distributors and Wholesalers of the United States, 8th edition. New York: Bowker, 1986. Annual. Lists major publishers, distributors, wholesalers, small presses, associations that act as publishers, and publishers of software.

Publishers Trade List Annual. New York: Bowker, annual. The PTLA's multi-volume set is arranged alphabetically by publishers, but look for the second, "small alphabet," as well as indexes including an index to publishers' series, inserted at the beginning of the first volume. Think of PTLA as the current catalogs, bound together, of most major United States publishers. *Books in Print* functions as an author index to PTLA.

Quotable Woman. Elaine Partnow. . . . *Eve to 1799.* New York: Facts on File, 1985. . . . *1800–1975.* Los Angeles, California: Corwin, 1978. . . . *1800–1981,* rev. ed. New York: Facts on File, 1983. These should be available in every college, university and public library. Thousands of quotations from throughout world history. Biographical and subject indexes. See also *Feminist Quotations.*

Small Press Record of Books in Print, 16th edition, 1987–88. Paradise, California: Dustbooks. Companion volume is *International Directory of Little Magazines and Small Presses.*

Studies on Women Abstracts, 1983–   . Abingdon, Oxfordshire, England: Carfax. An international — with British emphasis — service abstracting both books and jour-

nal articles, published quarterly. See also *Women Studies Abstracts.* Thesaurus of
ERIC Descriptors, 11th edition. Phoenix, Arizona: Oryx, 1987. See discussion,
Chapter 4. The ERIC clearinghouses are listed in the back of this volume. To
order ERIC documents, contact ERIC Document Reproduction Service, P.O. Box
190, Arlington, Virginia 22210; telephone (703)841-1212. Relevant ERIC descrip-
tors include FACULTY PUBLISHING, PROMOTION (OCCUPATIONAL),
PUBLICATIONS, PUBLISH OR PERISH ISSUE, and WRITING FOR PUB-
LICATION.

Ulrich's International Periodicals Directory, 26th edition, 1987-88. New York:
Bowker, 1987. *Irregular Serials and Annuals: An International Directory, 13th edition, 1987-88.* New York: Bowker, 1987. These two titles have been combined
into a three-volume set published in 1988 as the 27th edition. Volume 3 provides
vendors, cessations, international organizations, and ISSN and titles indexes. See
discussion of *Ulrich's* in Chapter 2.

Women Studies Abstracts, 1972- . Rush, New York: Rush. Useful indexing
headings include FEMINIST PERIODICALS, FEMINIST PUBLISHING,
FEMINIST SCHOLARSHIP, PUBLICATION RECORD, PUBLISHING, and
TENURE. See also *Studies on Women Abstracts.*

World of Learning, 38th edition. London, England: Europa, 1987. Annual. In addition to universities and colleges and affiliated institutions of most nations, brief
information about learned societies, research institutes, libraries, archives and
museums is provided.

English-Language Dictionaries and Wordbooks

Although published some time ago, Kenneth F. Kister's *Dictionary Buying
Guide: A Consumer Guide to General English-Language Wordbooks in Print* (New
York: Bowker, 1977) is a useful source for its information about standard titles and
for its comparative charts and the Special-Purpose Dictionaries and Wordbooks
section. Many titles are discussed under such categories as New Words, Etymology
and History of Words, Usage and Idioms, Style Manuals, Spelling and Syllabication,
Pronunciation, Abbreviations and Acronyms, and Foreign Words and Phrases Commonly Used in English. Elsie Stainton's "The Uses of Dictionaries" is often commended to scholars (*Scholarly Publishing* 11 [April 1980]: 229-41).

Here are some of the many basic English-language dictionaries and wordbooks
representing various writing and publishing needs. Editions, recent revisions,
prices, and publishers can be found in *Books in Print.*

The American Heritage Dictionary of the English Language is a popular abridged, or
"desk," dictionary despite having been banned because it is thought to contain
thirty-nine "dirty words." (Read "College Professors Urged to Fight Censorship
in Schools," *Chronicle of Higher Education* **27** [January 4, 1984]:8.) It is well-
illustrated and includes Proofreaders' Marks within the single alphabet.

Chambers Twentieth Century Dictionary: With Supplement. Revised edition by A.M.
Macdonald. First published in 1901. Cambridge University Press' new edition is
useful for new meanings of standard words and its British orientation and spelling.

A Dictionary of American English on Historical Principles by Sir William Craigie and
James R. Hulbert is modeled on its famous predecessor, *The Oxford English Dictionary.* Both give the history of words. "Craigie" covers significant developments
(new words and meanings) in the English language as used in the United States
and the American colonies.

A Dictionary of American-English Usage by Margaret Nicholson is based on *A Dictionary of Modern English Usage* (see below) but is simpler to use.

A Dictionary of Catch Phrases, British and American, from the Sixteenth Century to the Present Day and *A Dictionary of Slang and Unconventional English* are by Eric Partridge, who provides the approximate day of the first appearance of each word.

A Dictionary of Contemporary American Usage by Bergen and Cornelia Evans deals with words and phrases, idioms, grammar, style, and punctuation. It is a popular example of this type of word book; others can be located under the subject-heading AMERICANISMS in university libraries' catalogs. *Modern American Usage: A Guide* by Wilson Follett and edited by Jacques Barzun is another example of this type of title.

A Dictionary of Modern English Usage by Henry Watson Fowler, 2nd edition revised by Sir Ernest Gowers, is often referred to as "Fowler." It is a useful authority for problems of grammatical usage.

Oxford English Dictionary (originally, *The New English Dictionary on Historical Principles* by Sir James Murray) is a monumental, indispensable set which constitutes the most scholarly and authoritative dictionary of the English language, tracing the history of every word used in England from 1150 A.D. Consider, for example, ain't, bitch, fascinate, fornication, homely, mistress. Referred to variously as OED, NED, and *The Oxford Dictionary*. A "compact edition" is also available.

Random House College Dictionary and *Random House Dictionary of the English Language* (unabridged) italicize words of foreign origin which are still unassimilated. Its organization in "one alphabet"—mythological characters, proper nouns, places, and literary words included—is a useful feature for some authors and publishers.

Webster's New International Dictionary of the English Language, Second Edition and *Webster's Third New International Dictionary* are two different, unabridged dictionaries and concepts which should be understood. Both are found in most libraries' reference collections because they serve different purposes, needs, and users. The second edition is relied on as an authority in questions of good taste and because of its status-labeling of words. The third edition, on the other hand, is notable for its many new words and new meanings of old words, together with illustrative quotations often derived from popular sources. The user occasionally must make a decision, however. Dwight Macdonald's *New Yorker* article comparing them is worth reading. ("Books: Differences Between Webster's Second and Third Editions" **38** [March 10, 1962]: 130–34 +.) Definitions are provided in historical sequence in Webster dictionaries, i.e., the oldest meaning of a word is listed first, continuing to the current use, listed last.

Webster's Ninth New Collegiate Dictionary (1985) is used by some publications as authority for spelling, use of hyphens, and foreign words and phrases included in manuscripts that may be assumed to be familiar enough in English not to need italics.

Style and Usage Manuals—General

Some style manuals relate to preparation of journal articles in various disciplines, while others may provide for subject-specialized articles, books, and other formats. There are also many general style manuals, or guides, such as those included in the following group. Others in libraries' collections can be identified by use of the subject-heading AUTHORSHIP—STYLE MANUALS.

Baker, Sheridan Warner. *The Practical Stylist, 6th edition.* New York: Harper & Row, 1985. This is an example of the titles which function more as writing handbooks than as guides in style formatting. Other titles that may serve in this respect include Rudolph Flesch's *The Art of Readable Writing: With the Flesch Readability Formula, Revised* (New York: Harper & Row, 1974); Peter Elbow's *Writing with Power: Techniques for Mastering the Writing Process* (New York: Oxford University Press, 1981); Frederick T. Wood's *Current English Usage,* revised edition by R.H. and L.M. Flavell (New York: Macmillan, 1981); Sir Ernest Gowers' *The Complete Plain Words, 3rd edition revised* (HMSO, 1986); Robert Graves and Alan Hodge's *The Reader Over Your Shoulder: A Handbook for Writers of English Prose, 2nd edition revised* (New York: Random House, 1979); and John M. Kierzek and Walker Gibson's *The Macmillan Handbook of English, 6th edition* (New York: Macmillan, 1977). For *style,* see Nicholson.

Bernstein, Theodore Menline. *The Careful Writer: A Modern Guide to English Usage.* New York: Atheneum, 1965. Similar to Strunk and White's *Elements of Style,* but with more detail. Bernstein's *Do's, Don'ts & Maybes of English Usage* (New York: Quadrangle/Times, 1977) is also popular.

Campbell, William Giles, et al. *Form and Style: Theses, Reports, Term Papgers, 7th edition.* Boston, Massachusetts: Houghton Mifflin, 1986. Campbell includes information on abstracting. Although much used in the fields of education and psychology, his manuals are applicable generally.

The Chicago Manual of Style: For Authors, Editors, and Copywriters, 13th Edition Revised and Expanded. Chicago, Illinois: University of Chicago Press, 1982. *The* comprehensive, authoritative style manual. Useful section on Rights and Permissions.

Nicholson, Margaret. *A Practical Style Guide for Authors and Editors.* New York: Holt, Rinehart & Winston, 1967. Based on "Fowler" and aims to serve as a simplified adaptation to meet current American needs, retaining much of his tone.

Skillin, Marjorie E., and Robert M. Gay. *Words into Type, 3rd edition.* Englewood Cliffs, New Jersey: Prentice-Hall, 1974. Often used as the basis for decisions on capitalization, grammar, and usage changes in reviewers' copy.

Strunk, William, and E.B. White. *Elements of Style, 3rd edition.* New York: Macmillan, 1979. This classic provides "an approach to style" with a discussion of twenty-one "reminders." The entire small volume is basic reading or review, and consists of five parts: elementary rules of usage, elementary principles of composition, a few matters of form, words and expressions commonly used, and the approach to style.

Turabian, Kate L. *A Manual for Writers of Term Papers, Theses and Dissertations; Revised and Expanded by Bonnie Birtwistle Honigsblum, 5th edition.* Chicago, Illinois: University of Chicago Press, 1987. Usually referred to as "Turabian" (for many years, editor of official University of Chicago publications and dissertation secretary) and considered *the* guide for formal paper style, it is based on the *Chicago Manual of Style,* but preferred by many because it represents the move toward simplified scholarly documentation. Honigsblum's fifth edition includes several new features; one is a bibliography of style guides issued by various academic disciplines.

United States Government Printing Office Style Manual, Revised. Washington, D.C.: Government Printing Office, 1984. Provides the rules on which this office bases its copy preparation.

Style and Usage Manuals — Specialized

General style manuals often include lists of specialized style manuals. Honigsblum's revised fifth edition of Turabian's *A Manual for Writers of Term Papers, Theses and Dissertations* includes a bibliography of style guides issued by various academic disciplines. John Bruce Howell's *Style Manuals of the English Speaking World: A Guide* (Phoenix, Arizona: Oryx, 1983) includes university press guidelines for authors. AUTHORSHIP — STYLE MANUALS is a useful Library of Congress subject-heading for locating others.

Achtert, Walter S., and Joseph Gibaldi. *The MLA Style Manual.* New York: Modern Language Association of America, 1985. Used widely.

American Chemical Society. *The ACS Style Guide: A Manual for Authors and Editors.* Edited by Janet S. Dodd. Washington, D.C.: American Chemical Society, 1986. A relataively new style guide for authors and editors of scientific papers, which replaces the Society's author's handbook and is useful for Society papers as well as other publications.

American Institute of Physics. *Style Manual for Guidance in the Preparation of Papers for Journals Published by the American Institute of Physics and Its Member Societies, 3rd edition.* Prepared by David Hathwell and A.W. Kenneth Metzner. New York: American Institute of Physics, 1978. AIR Publication R-283. Offers guidance in technical writing as well as style.

American Mathematical Society. *A Manual for Authors of Mathematical Papers, 8th edition.* Providence, Rhode Island: American Mathematical Society, 1980.

American Medical Association. *Manual for Authors and Editors: Editorial Style and Manuscript Preparation, 7th edition.* Compiled for the AMA by William R. Barclay, M. Therese Southgate, and Robert W. Mayo. Los Angeles, California: Lange Medical Publications, 1981.

American National Standards Institute. *American National Standard for the Preparation of Scientific Papers for Written or Oral Presentation. . . .* New York: American National Standards Institute, 1979.

American Psychological Associaton. *Publication Manual of the American Psychological Association, 3rd edition.* Washington, D.C.: American Psychological Association, 1983. Includes "Guidelines for Nonsexist Language in APA Journals" (see pages 43–49, which include ethnic-related provision). Bibliography (pages 181–88).

American Society of Agronomy. *Handbook and Style Manual.* Madison, Wisconsin: American Society of Agronomy, 1976.

Council of Biology Editors. *Council of Biology Editors Style Manual: A Guide for Authors, Editors, and Publishers in the Biological Sciences, 5th edition, Revised and Expanded.* Bethesda, Maryland: Council of Biology Editors, 1983.

Fleischer, Eugene B. *A Style Manual for Citing Microform and Nonprint Media.* Chicago, Illinois: American Library Association, 1978. This is one of several examples; access others by querying the card or on-line catalog under AUDIOVISUAL MATERIALS — BIBLIOGRAPHY — METHODOLOGY.

Harvard Law Review Association. *A Uniform System of Citation, 14th edition.* Cambridge,Massachusetts: Harvard Law Review Association, 1986. Includes material on annotating as well as citing.

International Committee of Medical Journal Editors. "Uniform Requirements for Manuscripts Submitted to Biomedical Journals." *Annals of Internal Medicine* **96** (1982): 766–70.

Linguistic Society of America. *LSA Style Sheet for Publications of the Linguistic Society of America.* Usually included in the *LSA Bulletin* December issue.

Modern Humanities Research Association. *MHRS Style Book: Notes for Authors and Editors.* Edited by A.S. Maney and R.L. Smallwood. Leeds, England: Modern Humanities Research Association, 1971.

Modern Language Association of America. *MLA Handbook for Writers of Research Papers, Theses, and Dissertations, 1st edition.* By Joseph Gibaldi and Walter S. Achtert. New York: Modern Language Association of America, 1977. See pages 39–40 for specialized guides. See also Achtert and Gibaldi's *MLA Style Manual.*

New York Times Manual of Style and Usage, Rev. Edited by Lewis Jordan. New York: Quadrangle/Times, 1976.

United States Geological Survey. *Suggestions to Authors of the Reports of The United States Geological Survey, 6th edition.* Washington, D.C.: Government Printing Office, 1978.

Handbooks and Guides
to Writing and Publishing — General

Throughout, the emphasis is on available titles published or revised in the 1980s. Additional titles can usually be located by use of the AUTHORSHIP— HANDBOOKS, MANUALS, ETC. subject-heading.

Bernstein, Leonard S. *Getting Published: The Writer in the Combat Zone.* New York: Morrow, 1986. Most so-called writer's handbooks are directed to the author whose main interest is selling magazine articles and fiction. Some of these books are useful for writing and publishing in academe, and this one is a recent example.

Dorn, Fred J. *Publishing for Professional Development.* Muncie, Indiana: Accelerated Development, 1985.

Luey, Beth. *A Handbook for Academic Authors.* New York: Cambridge University Press, 1987. Includes consideration of multi-author books and anthologies and publication of college textbooks.

VanTil, William. *Writing for Professional Publication, 2nd edition.* Boston, Massachusetts: Allyn & Bacon, 1981.

Handbooks and Guides
to Writing and Publishing — Specialized

Alley, Brian, and Jennifer Cargill. *Librarian in Search of a Publisher: How to Get Published.* Phoenix, Arizona: Oryx, 1986. Inevitably Alley and Cargill's book has been compared with Sellen's *Librarian/Author,* published the year before by another publisher. See, for example, M. Cecilia Rothschild's review (*College & Research Libraries* 47 [November 1986]: 629–30). Alley and Cargill is more how-to, especially for the beginner; Sellen is a collection of essays along with the American Library Association "Guidelines for Authors, Editors and Publishers of Literature in the Library and Information Field."

Day, Robert. *How to Write and Publish a Scientific Paper, 3rd edition.* Phoenix, Arizona: Oryx, 1988.

DeBakey, Lois. *The Scientific Journal; Editorial Policies and Practices: Guidelines for*

Editors, Reviewers, and Authors. St. Louis, Missouri: Mosby, 1976. Includes writing and editing guidance as well as periodicals.

Huth, Edward Janavel, M.D. *How to Write and Publish Papers in the Medical Sciences.* Philadelphia, Pennsylvania: Institute for Scientific Information Press, 1982. Part of the ISI Press's *Professional Writing Series.*

Johnson, Richard Davis. *Writing the Journal Article and Getting It Published,* 2nd edition. Chicago, Illinois: Association of College and Research Libraries, 1983. *ACRL Continuing Education Program Series* CE 501.

Kurtz, David L., and A. Edward Spitz. *An Academic Writer's Guide to Publishing in Business and Economics Journals,* 2nd edition. Ypsilanti, Michigan: Eastern Michigan University, Bureau of Business Services and Research, 1974.

Levin, Joel. *Getting Published: The Educators' Resource Book.* New York: Arco, 1983.

Meiss, Harriet R., and Doris A. Jaeger. *Information to Authors, 1980–81: Editorial Guidelines Reprinted from 246 Medical Journals.* Baltimore, Maryland: Urban & Schwarzenberg, 1980.

Michaelson, Herbert B. *How to Write and Publish Engineering Papers and Reports.* Philadelphia, Pennsylvania: Institute for Scientific Information Press, 1982. Part of the ISI Press's *Professional Writing Series.*

Mirin, Susan K. *The Nurse's Guide to Writing for Publication.* Wakefield, Massachusetts: Nursing Resources, 1981.

Mitchell, John H. *Writing for Professional and Technical Journals.* New York: Wiley, 1968. Sometimes referred to as *Writing and Usage: Subject-Related Guides.*

Moulton, Janice M. *Guidebook for Publishing Philosophy,* 2nd edition. Newark, Delaware: American Philosophical Association, 1975.

National Cancer Institute. *A Compilation of Journal Instructions to Authors.* By Louis P. Greenberg. Bethesda, Maryland: U.S. Dept. of Health, Education, and Welfare, Public Health Service, National Institutes of Health, 1979. *NIH Publication Series* No. 80–1991.

O'Connor, Andrea B. *Writing for Nursing Publications.* Thorofare, New Jersey: Slack, 1981.

Sellen, Betty-Carol. *Librarian/Author: A Practical Guide on How to Get Published.* New York: Neal-Schuman, 1985. See Alley, Brian, and Jennifer Cargill, *Librarian in Search of a Publisher: How to Get Published.*

Sheen, Anita Peebles. *Breathing Life into Medical Writing: A Handbook.* St. Louis, Missouri: Mosby, 1982.

Silverman, Robert Jay. *Getting Published in Education Journals.* Springfield, Illinois: Thomas, 1982. Although directed to authors in the field of education who aspire to journal publication, this book is useful for social scientists in general and also in report writing. Refreshing recognition of gatekeeping in publishing.

Vargo, Richard J. *Author's Guide to Publishing in Business, Administration, and Management.* New York: Haworth, 1981.

Journal and Periodical Directories
Information for Various Disciplines

American Library Association Publishing Services. *How to Publish in ALA Periodicals.* Chicago, Illinois: American Library Association. Annual alphabetical list currently describing approximately fifty periodicals, published by the American Library Association, including newsletters and journals, which accept unsolicited submissions. Each entry includes a brief description of the periodical, materials accepted for consideration and editors' names and addresses. Gratis with SASE, 50 East Huron Street, Chicago, Illinois 60611.

Annotated Bibliographies of Serials: A Subject Approach. New York: Greenwood. This series is analyzed within this section.

Ardell, Donald B., and John Y. James, eds. .*Author's Guide to Journals in the Health Field.* New York: Haworth, 1980. In Haworth's *Authors' Guide to Journals* series.

Balachandran, Sarojini. *Directory of Publishing Sources: The Researcher's Guide to Journals in Engineering and Technology.* New York: Wiley-Interscience, 1982.

Barnett, Judith B. *Marine Science Journals and Serials: An Analytical Guide.* Westport, Connecticut: Greenwood, 1986.

Binger, Jane L., and Lydia M. Jensen. *Lippincott's Guide to Nursing Literature: A Handbook for Students, Writers, and Researchers.* Philadelphia, Pennsylvania: Lippincott, 1980.

Birkos, Alexander S., and Lewis A. Tambs. *Academic Writer's Guide to Periodicals* series. *Volume 1: Latin American Studies. Volume 2: East European and Slavic Studies. Volume 3: African and Black American Studies.* Kent, Ohio: Kent State University Press, 1971 (Volume 1) and 1973 (Volume 2). Littleton, Colorado: Libraries Unlimited, 1975 (Volume 3).

Bowman, Mary Ann. *Library and Information Science Journals and Serials: An Analytical Guide.* Westport, Connecticut: Greenwood, 1985.

Cabell, David W. *Cabell's Directory of Publishing Opportunities in Business and Economics, 3rd edition.* Beaumont, Texas: Cabell, 1985. Revised edition of *Cabell's Directory of Publishing Opportunities in Business, Administration, and Economics,* published in 1981.

_____. *Cabell's Directory of Publishing Opportunities in Education.* Beaumont, Texas: Cabell, 1984.

_____. *Directory of Publishing Opportunities in Business, Administration, and Economics, 2nd edition.* Beaumont, Texas: Cabell, 1981.

Clardy, Andrea Fleck. *Words to the Wise: A Writer's Guide to Feminist and Lesbian Periodicals and Publishers.* Ithaca, New York: Firebrand Books, 1986. Firebrand Books is at 141 The Commons, Ithaca, NY 14850.

Collins, Mary Ellen. *Education Journals and Serials: An Analytical Guide.* Westport, Connecticut: Greenwood, 1988.

Cornish, Graham P. *Religious Periodicals Directory.* Santa Barbara, California: ABC-Clio, 1986. Lists 1,763 religious periodicals worldwide. Each entry contains bibliographic information and coverage, scope, language used, indexes, and inclusion by abstracting and indexing services. Journals in the fields of history, anthropology, linguistics, sociology, archaeology, art, literature, and other fields are included where their contents contain significant relevant materials.

Fyfe, Janet. *History Journals and Serials: An Analytical Guide*: Westport, Connecticut: Greenwood, 1986.

Gerstenberger, Donna Lorine, and George Hendrick. *Fourth Directory of Periodicals Publishing Articles in English and American Literature and Language.* Chicago, Illinois: Swallow, 1974.

Hesslein, Shirley B. *Serials on Aging: An Analytical Guide.* Westport, Connecticut: Greenwood, 1986. Number 9 in *Annotated Bibliographies of Serials: A Subject Approach* series. Three hundred seventy-five serials are annotated, and periodical indexes in which each is indexed, abstracted, or cited, as well as any data bases in which it is included, are identified. Other useful information includes how articles are selected for publication, whether special issues are published, target audience and language of publication. Subject and geographical indexes.

Historical Periodicals Directory. Santa Barbara, California: ABC-Clio, 5 volumes, 1981–1985. *Volume 1: USA and Canada,* edited by Marie S. Ensign. *Volume 2: Europe: West, North, Central and South,* edited by Barbara H. Pope. *Volume 3: Europe: East and Southeast: USSR,* edited by Shirley A. Matullch. *Volume 4: Latin America and West Indies,* edited by Jessica S. Brown and Susan K. Kinnell. *Volume 5: Australia, New Zealand, and Cumulative Subject and Geographical Index to Volumes 1–5,* edited by Suzanne Ontiveros and Susan K. Kinnell. The editors interpret "history" in its broadest sense so that archaeology and many other related disciplines are included.

Huber, Bettina J. *Publishing Options: An Author's Guide to Journals.* Washington, D.C.: American Sociological Association, 1982. In the ASA Professional Information Series.

International Directory of Little Magazines and Small Presses, 22nd edition, 1986–87. Edited by Len Fulton and Ellen Ferber. Paradise, California: Dustbooks, 1987.

Jensen, Richard D., et al. *Agricultural and Animal Science Journals and Serials: An Analytical Guide.* Westport, Connecticut: Greenwood, 1986.

Lyle, Stanley P. "Authors' Guides to Scholarly Periodicals." *Scholarly Publishing* **10** (April 1979): 255–61 and **15** (April 1984): 273–79.

Manera, Elizabeth S., and Robert E. Wright. *Annotated Writer's Guide to Professional Education Journals.* Scottsdale, Arizona: Bobets, 1982.

Marquis Academic Media. *Directory of Publishing Opportunities in Journals and Periodicals, 5th* [and final] *edition.* Wilmette, Illinois: Marquis, 1981. Includes specialized journals and conference proceedings which accept submissions in English. For each journal, there is a brief description of contents or editorial purposes, the audience to whom it is addressed, specific subject areas covered (including any topical, geographic or chronological limitations), and manuscript requirements. Women's studies journals are listed on pages 493–496. Keep its age in mind.

Markle, Allan, and Roger C. Rinn, eds. *Author's Guide to Journals in Psychology, Psychiatry and Social Work.* New York: Haworth, 1977. *Author's Guide to Journals* series.

Mendelsohn, Henry. *Author's Guide to Social Work Journals, 2nd edition.* Washington, D.C.: National Association of Social Workers, 1986.

MLA Directory of Periodicals: A Guide to Journals and Series in Languages and Literatures, 1988–89 edition. Compiled by Eileen M. Mackesy and Dee Ella Spears. New York: Modern Language Association of America, 1988. The 1986–87 edition covered periodicals published in the United States and Canada and described 3,000 journals and series, but did not include information about the author-anonymous reviewing policy of each.

Parker, Barbara A. *Journal Instructions to Authors: A Compilation of Manuscript Guidelines from Education Periodicals.* Annapolis, Maryland: PSI, 1985.

Ruben, Douglas H. *Philosophy Journals and Serials: An Analytical Guide.* Westport, Connecticut: Greenwood, 1985.

Scull, Roberta A., comp. *Publishing Opportunities for Energy Research: A Descriptive Guide to Selective Serials in the Social and Technical Sciences.* Westport, Connecticut: Greenwood, 1986. Number 1 in the *Bibliographies and Indexes in Science and Technology* series.

Shore, David A. *Annotated Resource Guide to Periodicals in Human Sexuality.* Chicago, Illinois: Playboy Foundation [distributor], 1978. Journals and newsletters are listed, including foreign and "popular" titles.

Sichel, Beatrice, and Werner Sichel. *Economics Journals and Serials: An Analytical Guide.* Westport, Connecticut: Greenwood, 1986.

Steiner, Dale R. *Historical Journals: A Handbook for Writers and Reviewers.* Santa Barbara: ABC-Clio, 1981.

Sussman, Marvin B. *Author's Guide to Journals in Sociology and Related Fields.* New York: Haworth, 1987. *Author's Guide to Journals* series.

Tega, Vasile G. *Management and Economics Journals: A Guide to Information Sources.* Detroit, Michigan: Gale, 1977. *Management Information Guides* no. 33.

Tompkins, Margaret, and Norma Shirley. *Serials in Psychology and Allied Fields, 2nd edition.* Troy, New York: Whitson, 1976.

Warner, Steven D., and Kathryn D. Schweer. *Author's Guide to Journals in Nursing and Related Fields.* New York: Haworth, 1982.

Women's Institute for Freedom of the Press. *Directory of Women's Media, 1988 edition.* Edited by Martha Leslie Allen. Washington, D.C.: Women's Institute for Freedom of the Press, 1988. Hundreds of periodicals (newspapers, journals, magazines, newsletters) from throughout the world. Annotated. See pages 3–34. Cross-indexed geographically and by zip codes.

Woods, William F. *A Directory of Publishing Opportunities for Teachers of Writing.* Charlottesville, Virginia: Community Collaborators, 1979.

Miscellaneous Resources:
Abstracting, Proofreading, Indexing, Etc.

Alkire, Leland G., Jr., *Periodical Title Abbreviations, 6th edition.* Detroit, Michigan: Gale, 1988. Volume 1 by abbreviations, Volume 2 by titles. Wordwide journal titles.

American National Standards Institute. *American National Standard for Writing Abstracts, Revised edition.* New York: American National Standards Institute, 1979.

Association of American Publishers. *An Author's Primer to Word Processing.* New York: Association of American Publishers, 1983. *See also* Brock; Flugelman and Hewes; and Schillingsburg, all in this section.

Brock, Thomas D. "Generic Coding for Typesetting From Computer Files," pp. 246–62, and "Computers and Word Processors," pp. 137–57, in his *Successful Textbook Publishing: The Author's Guide.* Madison, Wisconsin: Science Tech, 1985.

Bunnin, Brad. *The Writer's Legal Companion: With a Chapter on the Author and the Business of Publishing by Peter Beren.* Reading, Massachusetts: Addison-Wesley, 1988.

Butcher, Judith. *Copy-Editing: The Cambridge Handbook, 2nd edition.* New York: Columbia University Press, 1981.

————. *Typescripts, Proofs, and Indexes.* New York: Cambridge University Press, 1980.

Chicago Guide to Preparing Electronic Manuscripts: For Authors and Publishers. Chicago, Illinois: University of Chicago Press, 1987. Comparable titles can be located under the subject-heading ELECTRONIC PUBLISHING—HANDBOOKS, MANUALS, ETC.

Chickering, Robert B., and Susan Hartman. *How to Register a Copyright and Protect Your Creative Work: A Basic Guide to the Copyright Law and How It Affects Anyone Who Wants to Protect Creative Work.* New York: Scribners, 1987. *See also* Bunnin; Elias; Johnston; Reed; Strong; Talab; and Weil, all in this section.

Cleveland, Donald B., and Ana D. Cleveland. *Introduction to Indexing and Abstracting.* Littleton, Colorado: Libraries Unlimited, 1983. A very *serious* book, but useful here for Chapter VII: Book Indexes; VIII: The Nature and Types of Abstracts; IX: Abstracting Methods and Procedures; and X: Indexing and Abstracting a Document.

Cremmins, Edward T. *The Art of Abstracting.* Philadelphia, Pennsylvania: ISI Press, 1982. In the *Professional Writing Series.*

Elias, Stephen. *Intellectual Property Law Dictionary.* Berkeley, California: Nolo, 1985. Attorney Elias uses simple language to define and explain copyrights, unfair competition, contracts, and other aspects of business and property.

Flugelman, Andrew, and Jeremy Hewes. *Writing in the Computer Age: Word Processing Skills and Style for Every Writer.* Garden City, New York: Anchor, 1983.

Harman, Eleanor. "Hints on Proofreading." A *Scholarly Publishing* 6 (January 1975): 150–57.

Johnston, Donald F. *Copyright Handbook, 2nd edition.* New York: Bowker, 1982. Includes forms.

Kister, Kenneth F. *Best Encyclopedias: A Guide to General and Specialized Encyclopedias.* Phoenix, Arizona: Oryx, 1986. Descriptive information about more than 500 general and specialized encyclopedic sources for North American readers. Kister is working on a comparable tool about dictionaries.

Kline, Mary-Jo. *A Guide to Documentary Editing.* Baltimore, Maryland: Johns Hopkins University Press, 1987. Kline considers what methods are most appropriate for editing historical and literary documents including diaries, financial records, letters, professional papers, and unpublished manuscripts.

Pearlman, Daniel D., and Paula R. Pearlman. *Guide to Rapid Revision, 3rd edition.* Indianapolis, Indiana: Bobbs-Merrill/Odyssey, 1982.

Reed, Mary Hutchings. *The Copyright Primer for Librarians and Educators.* Chicago, Illinois, and Washington, D.C.: American Library Association and National Education Association, 1987.

Schillingsburg, Peter L. *Scholarly Editing in the Computer Age: Theory and Practice.* Athens, Georgia: University of Georgia Press, 1986. Schillingsburg concentrates on editing that is "designed to make available for scholarly use works not ordinarily available or available only in corrupt or inadequate forms."

Strong, William S. *The Copyright Book: A Practical Guide.* Cambridge, Massachusetts: MIT Press, 1981.

Tufte, Edward R. *The Visual Display of Quantitative Information.* Cheshire, Connecticut: Graphics, 1983. For use in fields relying on statistics and graphs.

Weil, Ben, and Barbara Friedman Polansky. *Modern Copyright Fundamentals.* New York: Van Nostrand Reinhold, 1985.

Wheeler, Helen Rippier. *The Bibliographic Instruction-Course Handbook: A Skills and Concepts Approach to the Undergraduate, Research Methodology, Credit Course—For College and University Personnel.* Metuchen, New Jersey: Scarecrow, 1988. For administrators, librarians, planners, and teachers in the disciplines and interdisciplinary programs (e.g. ethnic and women's studies).

Gender Equity–Related Titles

Baron, Dennis. *Grammar and Gender.* New Haven, Connecticut: Yale University Press, 1986. Baron recognizes an antifeminist tradition that permeates both common linguistics and movements toward language reform, and he demonstrates that a heightened awareness of history may help steer language development away from perceived linguistic inequities. He shows "how attitudes toward men and women have become attitudes toward language" and describes reformers' efforts to eliminate sexual bias in English vocabulary and usage.

Berman, Sanford. *Prejudices and Antipathies: A Tract on the LC Subject Heads Concerning People.* Metuchen, New Jersey: Scarecrow, 1971. This little gem is out of print but is available in most university libraries. As usual, Berman provides suggestions and alternatives. See also Dickstein, this section.

Bosmajian, Haig A. *The Language of Oppression.* Washington, D.C.: Public Affairs, 1975. Bosmajian identifies the use of such words as "wop," "broad," and "nigger" as "the language of oppression" which affects our attitudes and behavior, which in turn affect our language, round and round. See also his "The Language of Sexism" in *ETC.: A Review of General Semantics* 29 (1972): 305–313, which has been reprinted widely.

Briere, John, and Cheryl Lanktree. "Sex-Role Related Effects of Sex Bias in Languages." *Sex Roles* 9 (May 1983): 625–32. Cautious description of a study with a useful methodology.

Burr, Elizabeth, et al. "Women and the Language of Inequality." *Social Education* 36 (1972): 841–45. This is an example of an early contemporary women's movement article. The following year Burr, Susan Dunn and Norma Farquhar made available, through the [Los Angeles] Westside Women's Committee, guidelines for equal treatment of the sexes in social studies textbooks.

Campbell, Patricia B. "Racism And Sexism In Research." pp. 1515–1520 in *Encyclopedia of Educational Research, 5th edition.* New York: Macmillan, 1982.

_____, and Susan Kelin. "Equity Issues in Education" pp. 581–87 in *Encyclopedia of Educational Research, 5th edition.* New York: Macmillan, 1982.

Canadian Corrections Service. *On Equal Terms: How to Eliminate Sexism in Communications.* Ottawa: Canadian Corrections Service, 1984. This government document is in French and English languages.

Canadian Library Association. "CLA Guidelines on Non-Sexist Language." *Canadian Library Journal* 33 (August 1976): 369–71. The 1970s produced several professional associations' and publishers' guidelines related to sexist language. There appears to be no ALA counterpart. *See also* Publishers, this section.

Capek. Mary Ellen S., ed. *A Women's Thesaurus: An Index of Language Used to Describe and Locate Information By and About Women.* New York: Harper & Row, 1987. At one point this National Council for Research on Women document was referred to as *The Women's Index.* More than 4,000 terms relate to research projects and public policies affecting females' lives. SUBJECT HEADINGS— WOMEN is a subject heading which may lead to comparable publications: *see also* Berman; Dickstein; and Marshall, all in this section.

Cherry, Kittredge. *Womansword: What Japanese Words Say About Women.* Tokyo and New York: Kodansha International, 1987. Such an approach should be taken to publications about women, feminism, and sexism in relation to other nations and their languages.

Council on Interracial Books for Children. *Guidelines for Selecting Bias-Free Textbooks and Storybooks.* New York: Council on Interracial Books for Children, (1841 Broadway, New York, New York 10023), 1980.

Dickstein, Ruth, et al. *Women in LC's Terms: A Thesaurus of Library of Congress Subject Headings Relating to Women.* Phoenix, Arizona: Oryx, 1988. Library of Congress classification classes, as well as LC subject-headings, which relate to females are provided.

Dumond, Val. *Sheit: A No-Nonsense Guidebook to Writing and Using Nonsexist Language.* Tacoma, Washington: Val Dumond (P.O. Box 97124, Tacoma, Washington 98497) 1984.

Engle, June L., and Elizabeth Futas. "Sexism in Adult Encyclopedias." *Reference and Information Services,* pp. 130–44. Metuchen, New Jersey: Scarecrow, 1986. Reprinted from RQ's fall 1983 issue, this includes a bibliography and charts.

Frieze, Irene, et al. "Guidelines For Nonsexist Language in APA Journals," section 2:12. *Publication Manual of the American Psychological Association, 3rd edition.* Washington, D.C.: American Psychological Association, 1983. Pages 43–49 include guidelines for nonsexist language; a bibliography is provided on pages 181–88. These guidelines were published in the *American Psychologist* and relate to language and to research.

Gray Panthers of San Francisco. *Media Guidelines for Sexuality and Ageing.* San Francisco, California: Media Watch Committee of the Gray Panthers of San Francisco (50 Fell Street, San Francisco, CA 94102), 1979. Caroljean Wisnieski, Susan Leigh Star and Christiane Herman initiated this two-page document.

Hill, Alette Olin. *Mother Tongue, Father Time: A Decade of Linguistic Revolt.* Bloomington, Indiana: Indiana University Press, 1986. Hill examines the debate over such questions as whether a "women's language" exists.

Kett, Merriellyn, and Virginia Underwood. *How to Avoid Sexism: A Guide to Authors, Editors and Publishers.* Chicago, Illinois: Lawrence Ragan Communications (407 South Dearborn Street, Chicago, Illinois 60605), 1978.

Klann-Delius, Gisela. "Can Women's Language Cause Changes?" *Journal of Pragmatics* 4 (December 1980): 537–42. The possible need for developing a "women's language" for equitable communication *and* for political action to overcome inequality is considered.

Kramerae, Cheris. *Women and Men Speaking: Frameworks for Analyses.* Rowley, Massachusetts: Newbury House, 1981.

————, and Paula Treichler. *A Feminist Dictionary.* New York: Pandora Press, 1985. Kramerae and Treichler, with assistance from Ann Russo, have compiled feminist terms and concepts as used by feminists. They notably consider *gatekeeping* and *ageism.* Reviewers (e.g. Barbara Smith, *New Statesman*) sometimes find it necessary to point out that some of the entries are "humorous" and "eccentric." But it is serious, a lengthy tool with definitions and quotations, and an extensive bibliography. Many references are made in academe today to feminist theory; consult *A Feminist Dictionary* if you need help in understanding or applying it.

Lakoff, Robin. *Language and Woman's Place.* New York: Harper & Row, 1975. An early (in the contemporary women's movement) exploration of the relationship between sexist language and women's historical social and psychological oppression.

Lee, Rhonda. *Guide to Nonsexist Language and Visuals.* Madison, Wisconsin: University of Wisconsin, Madison Extension, 1985. Available from the Extension Bookstore, 432 North Lake Street, Madison, Wisconsin 53706.

Lloyd, Susan M., ed. *Roget's Thesaurus, New Edition.* Harlow, Essex, England: Longham House, 1982. Available in the United States from Caroline House, Inc., 5 South 250 Frontenac Road, Naperville, Illinois 60540. Lloyd received the Pandora Award from the British organization Women in Publishing for editing out sexist language from *Roget's Thesaurus.*

McConnell-Ginet, Sally, et al. *Women and Language in Literature and Society.* New York: Praeger, 1980. A collection of essays by anthropologists, linguists, and literary critics exploring the effects of sexist language.

Madsen, Jane M. "Racism and Sexism in Children's Literature." pp. 1507–15 in *En-cyclopedia of Educational Research, 5th edition.* New York: Macmillan, 1982.

Maggio, Rosalie. *The Nonsexist Word Finder: A Dictionary of Gender-Free Usage.* Phoenix, Arizona: Oryx, 1987. With Writing Guidelines.

Marshall, Joan K. *On Equal Terms: A Thesaurus for Nonsexist Indexing and Catalog-ing.* New York: Neal-Schuman, 1977. Marshall provides everyone with more than a thesaurus for nonsexist indexing and cataloging. Check out the introductory essay, "Sexism in Language." In its attempt to remove sexual biases from the in-fluential Libary of Congress' *Subject Headings,* it automatically contributes to elimination of sexual and other social and political biases, including ageism.

Miller, Casey, and Kate Swift. *The Handbook of Nonsexist Writing, 2nd edition.* New York: Harper & Row, 1988. Expanding the book published in 1980, this edition helps writers who are themselves committed to gender equality *and* clarity in their use of language.

National Center on Educational Media and Materials for the Handicapped. *Guidelines for the Presentation of Exceptional Persons in Educational Materials.* Columbus, Ohio: National Center on Educational Media and Materials for the Handicapped, 1977.

National Council of Teachers of English. *Guidelines for Nonsexist Use of Language in NCTE Publications.* Urbana, Illinois: National Council of Teachers of English, November 1975. This eleven-page document is an example of professional association concern. The Council's Committee on the Role and Image of Women in the Council and the Profession was influential in its creation. It is available as ERIC ED 113758. The Council is at 1111 Kenyon Rd., Urbana, Illinois 61801.

National Organization for Women, South and West St. Louis County. *Practical Guide to Non-Sexist Language.* St. Louis, Missouri: South & West St. Louis County NOW (1025 Barry Court, St. Louis, Missouri 63122), 1986. Brochure of examples, alternatives, and solutions to sexist language.

National Retired Teachers Association/American Association of Retired Persons. *Truth About Aging: Guidelines for Accurate Communications.* Washington, D.C.: 1984.

Orr, Elaine L., and Marie B. Rosenberg-Dishman. *The Right Word: Guidelines for Avoiding Sex-Biased Language.* McLean, Virginia: Section for Women in Public Administration of the American Society for Public Administration, 1985. This eleven-page brochure is available from P.O. Box 6165, McLean, Virginia 22106. (The Section's address is 1120 G. Street, N.W. #500, Washington, D.C. 20005.)

Philips, Susan U., et al. *Language, Gender and Sex in Comparative Perspective.* New York: Cambridge University Press, 1987. This anthropology and education work considers how women and men in several cultures use language differently. Unlike some of the others, it includes discussion of children's language and physiological aspects including brain research.

Pickens, Judy E., et al. *Without Bias: A Guidebook for Nondiscriminatory Com-munication.* San Francisco, California: International Association of Business Communicators, (870 Market Street, #940, San Francisco, California 94102), 1977.

Project on the Status and Education of Women. *Guide to Nonsexist Language.* Washington, D.C.: Association of American Colleges (1818 R Street, N.W., Washington, D.C. 20009), 1986.

Publishers. The 1970s produced several publishers' and professional associations' guidelines related to sexist language. While a telephone call to a publisher may produce denial or lack of knowledge of their existence, the influence of the work of feminist employee groups in some cases survives. Examples include:

- Ginn & Co. *Treatment of Minority Groups and Women.*
- Houghton Mifflin. *Avoiding Stereotypes.*
- McGraw-Hill. *Guidelines for Equal Treatment of the Sexes in McGraw-Hill Book Company Publications.* 1972. (Reprinted in *Elementary English* **52** [May 1975]: 725–733.) *Guidelines for Bias-Free Publishing* appears "courtesy of the McGraw-Hill Book Company" appended in Thomas D. Brock's *Successful Textbook Publishing: The Author's Guide* (Madison, Wisconsin: Science Tech, 1985).
- Macmillan. *Guidelines for Creating Positive Sexual and Racial Images in Educational Materials.* 1975.
- Random House. *Random House Guidelines for Multi-ethnic Nonsexist Survey.* 1976.
- Scott, Foresman. *Guidelines for Improving the Image of Women in Textbooks.* 1972.

Sale, Marilyn M. "Some Opinions on Sexist Language." *Scholarly Publishing* **10** (October 1978): 84–89. While views on sexist language may have varied from publishing house to publishing house, a small sampling of commercial and university publishers by Sale (who was apparently at Cornell University Press) uncovered no set policies on the "question" in 1978.

Sapir, Edward. "The Status of Linguistics as a Science." *Language* **5** (1929); reprinted in his *Selected Writings* edited by David G. Mandelbaum (1963). "The fact of the matter is that the 'real world' is to a large extent unconsciously built up on the language habits of the group. . . . We see and hear and otherwise experience very largely as we do because the language habits of our community predispose certain choices of interpretation." See also Whorf, this section.

Spender, Dale. *Man Made Language, 2nd edition.* London, England, and Boston, Massachusetts: Routledge & Kegan Paul, 1985. ". . . fascinating and comprehensive analysis of the ways in which our language is 'man-made,' of all the subtle and not so subtle ways in which the masculine is asserted as the norm, while feminine experience is muted and pushed to the margins of life and languages." (Margaret Walters, *New Society.*) Includes ten-page bibliography.

Thorne, Barrie, and Nancy Henley. *Language and Sex, Difference and Dominance.* Rowley, Massachusetts: Newbury House, 1975. Georgetown University and Center for Applied Linguistics. Publisher's series in sociolinguistics.

Tuttle, Lisa. *Encyclopedia of Feminism.* New York: Facts on File, 1986. Includes *gatekeepers, gatekeeping theory,* and *publishing* entries among definitions for major figures, events, organizations, books, and ideas of the women's movement.

U.S. Department of Labor, Manpower Administration (since renamed Education and Training administration). *Job Title Revisions to Eliminate Sex and Age Referent Language from* The Dictionary of Occupational Titles, 3rd edition. Washington, D.C.: Government Printing Office, 1975.

Vetterling-Braggin, Mary. *Sexist Language: Modern Philosophical Analysis.* Totowa, New Jersey: Rowman and Littlefield, 1981. Essays representing "pro" and "con" analyses by contemporary philosophers of the feminist view that much of language is sexist and that the use of such language should be discontinued or supplanted by use of nonsexist language. Racism in language is considered by feminists as well as sexism and truth in language.

Wandor, Michelene. *On Gender and Writing.* New York: Pandora, 1983. Essays on feminism and literature and sex role in literature.

Whorf, Benjamin Lee. "Science and Linguistics." *Technology Review* **42** (April 1940); reprinted in his *Language, Thought, and Reality,* edited by John B. Carroll

(1956). Whorf, a linguist, writing in 1940, answers "yes" to the question, must the language change if the norm is to change?

Women and Language, 1975– . 244 Lincoln Hall, 702 South Wright Street, University of Illinois, Urbana, Illinois 61801. *"Women and Language* is an interdisciplinary research newsletter which reports books, journals, articles and research in progress; identifies courses, conferences, and other events relevant to the study of language and gender, and publishes short articles. We include scholarship from anthropology, communication, linguistics, literature...."

Some Useful Library of Congress Subject-Headings

The following subject-headings are derived mainly from the tenth and eleventh editions of the Library of Congress *Subject Headings* thesaurus, published in 1986 and 1988. Between editions, interim supplements are issued, and the whole is available in cumulated microform. A discussion of their use in locating research and publication-related information and documents is included in Chapter 4. Dickstein (see "Gender Equity-Related Titles," preceding this section) elaborates on application of subdivisions. In the list that follows, the subject-headings are alphabetized as they would be in a library catalog, word-by-word (not letter-by-letter); that is, shorter words are filed before longer words beginning with the same letters.

This Way	*Not This Way*
New Bern	Newark
New England	New Bern
New York	Newborough
New Zealand	New England
Newark	Newmarket
Newborough	Newport
Newmarket	New York
Newport	New Zealand

In this same sense, shorter subject-headings such as WOMEN (a one-word subject-heading) precede longer ones beginning with the same word, e.g. WOMEN AUTHORS. However, note that all of the subject-headings which can be created by addition, following the dash, of separate subdivisions added to WOMEN dash (WOMEN–) are consolidated in that location and precede WOMEN AUTHORS.

ABSTRACTING
ABSTRACTING AND INDEXING SERVICES
ABSTRACTS–STANDARDS
ADVERTISING–BOOKS–HANDBOOKS, MANUALS, ETC.
AGED–PERIODICALS
AGED–RESEARCH
AGING–RESEARCH–U.S.–DIRECTORIES
AMERICAN PERIODICALS
AMERICAN PERIODICALS–DIRECTORIES
AMERICANISMS
AUDIO-VISUAL MATERIALS–BIBLIOGRAPHY–METHODOLOGY
AUDIO-VISUAL MATERIALS–DIRECTORIES
AUTHORS–LEGAL STATUTES, LAWS, ETC.–U.S.

```
                        —WOMEN
TECHNICAL WRITING
                        —STANDARDS
TEXT-BOOK BIAS
                —U.S.
TEXT-BOOKS
                —AUTHORSHIP
                —PUBLICATION AND DISTRIBUTION
                —U.S.
UNDERDEVELOPED AREAS—EDUCATIONAL PUBLISHING
UNDERGROUND PRESS—BIBLIOGRAPHY
                        —DIRECTORIES
U.S. FREEDOM OF INFORMATION ACT OF 1966.
VOCABULARY
WOMEN
        —BIBLIOGRAPHY
        —JAPAN [etc.]—LANGUAGE
        —RESEARCH—METHODOLOGY
        —U.S.—SCHOLARSHIPS, FELLOWSHIPS, ETC.—DIRECTORIES
                —SOCIAL CONDITIONS
WOMEN AND LITERATURE
WOMEN AUTHORS
WOMEN AUTHORS, AMERICAN
                        —20th CENTURY
WOMEN AUTHORS, BLACK
WOMEN AUTHORS, SCANDINAVIAN [etc.]
WOMEN IN THE PRESS
                —GREAT BRITAIN
                —U.S.
WOMEN PUBLISHERS
WOMEN'S ENCYCLOPEDIAS AND DICTIONARIES
WOMEN'S PERIODICALS, AMERICAN
WOMEN'S PERIODICALS, ENGLISH
WOMEN'S STUDIES
                —BIBLIOGRAPHY
                —LIBRARY RESOURCES
WORD PROCESSING
WRITING
```

Some Related ERIC Descriptors

See also Chapter Four.

ACADEMIC RANK
  (PROFESSIONAL)
ACADEMIC STANDARDS
ACCOUNTABILITY
ACTION RESEARCH
ADMINISTRATION
  EVALUATION
AFFIRMATIVE ACTION

AGING IN ACADEMIA
ANDROGYNY
ANTHOLOGIES
ASSESSMENT CENTERS
  (PERSONNEL)
AUTHORS
BIBLIOGRAPHIES
BOOK REVIEWS

BOOKS
CAREER LADDERS
COEDUCATION
CONTINUING EDUCATION
CONTRACTS
DOCTORAL DISSERTATIONS
EDITORS
EMPLOYED WOMEN
EMPLOYMENT PRACTICES
EMPLOYMENT
    QUALIFICATIONS
EQUAL OPPORTUNITIES (JOBS)
FACULTY DEVELOPMENT
FACULTY EVALUATION
FACULTY PROMOTION
FACULTY PUBLISHING
FEMALES
FEMINISM
GUIDES
INDIVIDUAL DEVELOPMENT
INSERVICE EDUCATION
INSTRUCTIONAL MATERIALS
LEADERSHIP TRAINING
LITERATURE
LITERATURE REVIEWS
MENTORS
NETWORKS
NONPRINT MEDIA
NONTENURED FACULTY
PEER EVALUATION
PERIODICALS
PROBATIONARY PERIOD
PRODUCTIVITY
PROFESSIONAL CONTINUING
    EDUCATION
PROFESSIONAL
    DEVELOPMENT
PROFESSIONAL TRAINING
PROMOTION (OCCUPATIONAL)

PUBLICATIONS
PUBLISH OR PERISH ISSUE
PUBLISHING INDUSTRY
RESEARCH
RESEARCH METHODOLOGY
SABBATICAL LEAVES
SCHOLARLY JOURNALS
SCHOLARSHIP
SCHOOL PUBLICATIONS
SENIORITY
SERIALS
SOCIOLINGUISTICS
SPOUSES
STAFF DEVELOPMENT
STATE OF THE ART REVIEWS
TEACHER EMPLOYMENT
    BENEFITS
TEACHER EVALUATION
TEACHER IMPROVEMENT
TEACHER PROMOTION
TEACHER RIGHTS
TENURE
TENURED FACULTY
TEXTBOOK BIAS
TEXTBOOK CONTENT
TEXTBOOK EVALUATION
TEXTBOOK PREPARATION
TEXTBOOK PUBLICATION
TEXTBOOK RESEARCH
TEXTBOOK SELECTION
TEXTBOOK STANDARDS
TEXTBOOKS
THESES
WOMEN FACULTY
WOMENS ATHLETICS
WOMENS EDUCATION
WOMENS STUDIES
WRITING FOR PUBLICATION

Index